CRITICAL THINKING
A Campus Life Casebook

SECOND EDITION

Madeleine Picciotto
University of California–San Diego

PEARSON

Prentice
Hall

Upper Saddle River, New Jersey
Columbus, Ohio

Library of Congress Cataloging in Publication Data

Picciotto, Madeleine.
    Critical thinking : a campus life casebook / Madeleine Picciotto.—2nd ed.
      p. cm.
    ISBN 0-13-111519-7 (pbk.)
    1. Critical thinking—Study and teaching (Higher)—United States—Case studies. 2.
College student orientation—United States—Case studies. I. Title.

LB2395.35.P53 2004
370.15'2—dc21

2004044461

Vice President and Executive Publisher: Jeffery W. Johnston
Senior Acquisitions Editor: Sande Johnson
Assistant Editor: Cecilia Johnson
Editorial Assistant: Erin Anderson
Production Coordination: Carlisle Publishers Services
Design Coordinator: Diane C. Lorenzo
Cover Designer: Jeff Vanik
Cover art: Corbis
Production Manager: Pamela D. Bennett
Director of Marketing: Ann Castel Davis
Marketing Manager: Christina Quadhamer

This book was set in New Aster by Carlisle Communications, Ltd. It was printed and bound by
R.R. Donnelley & Sons Company. The cover was printed by The Lehigh Press, Inc.

Note: The characters, location, and episodes depicted in the following cases are entirely fictitious. Any relationship to actual people, places, or events is completely coincidental.

Pearson Education Ltd.
Pearson Education Singapore Pte. Ltd.
Pearson Education Canada, Ltd.
Pearson Education—Japan

Pearson Education Australia Pty. Limited
Pearson Education North Asia Ltd.
Pearson Educación de Mexico, S.A. de C.V.
Pearson Education Malaysia Pte. Ltd.

10 9 8 7 6 5 4 3 2 1
ISBN: 0-13-111519-7

Contents

Note to Readers

The fifteen fully developed cases and ten mini-cases that constitute *Critical Thinking: A Campus Life Casebook* depict the goings-on during a single semester at Cromwell College, a fictitious institution of higher learning. Cromwell is a small, selective liberal arts college somewhere in the United States, but the events that occur there are not unlike those that occur at many real-life colleges and universities across the country. Although many of the cases focus on Cromwell's first-year students, most of whom are the traditional college age of eighteen, many of the dilemmas confronted and the issues raised—including racism, rape, cheating, childbearing, cults, and computer fraud—should be of interest to students of any age at any college.

Cromwell may or may not resemble your own educational institution. It is, after all, a fictional construct; the setting and the cases themselves are partially drawn from existing realities, but they are not real. Cromwell is a particular type of college that may be very different from the one you are attending, and it attracts a student population that may be very different from the students you see on your own campus. You may wish to think about the similarities and differences between your own realities as a college student and the "realities" faced by the unique group of individuals at Cromwell.

To assist you in investigating the cases and the issues they raise, an introductory chapter ("Thinking Critically") presents basic techniques for taking an active approach to the text. More important than remembering the name of every logical fallacy, however, is acquiring the general habit of inspecting every situation you enounter closely, carefully, and critically.

As you read through the cases, imagine yourself in the situations presented and try to figure out how you would deal with the ethical, political, social, and spiritual dilemmas that Cromwell's students encounter. Each of the fully developed cases includes "Some Questions to Consider" that invite you to explore your own thoughts as you analyze the cases. Try to articulate for yourself *why* you think the way you do. There is no right answer to these questions; what is more important than any individual response is the ability to provide a thoughtful and convincing justification of your point of view.

A consistent set of additional questions and suggestions follows each case. "Thinking Critically" exercises encourage you to apply the critical thinking strategies discussed in the introductory chapter. "Reading Closely" questions call for a careful focus on issues of language and presentation. A "What If" section raises alternative options for further consideration.

"Connecting the Cases" questions invite you to investigate the ways in which the various cases might relate to one another. Exploring the connections and examining the similarities and differences in the ways that particular issues are presented will help you to synthesize the various perspectives offered and come to some larger conclusions of your own. "Bringing It Home" questions encourage you to make a further connection—to your own institution.

"Suggestions for Writing" enable you to use various written formats, from informal journal entries to business memos to research-based academic essays, to express your thoughts. The "Out Loud" suggestion at the end of each case provides an opportunity to use presentations, role-plays, or debates for further development of your ideas.

It is the author's hope that this text will provide an engaging vehicle for the thoughtful exploration of significant issues, and that by further pursuing this exploration orally and in writing, you will learn to present your views clearly, coherently, and convincingly.

NEW TO THE SECOND EDITION

The second edition of *Critical Thinking: A Campus Life Casebook* includes new mini-cases and extended examples which raise several issues relevant to current campus life: Internet-based plagiarism, special academic assistance for athletes, college logo apparel manufactured under questionable labor conditions, and problems faced by students who must deal with competing demands and expectations.

Development of critical thinking skills is enhanced by more extensive explanations and more opportunities for practice in the introductory "Thinking Critically" chapter. In addition, two new sections ("Reading Closely" and "What If") have been added to the end of each case, in order to stimulate students' analytical abilities. New writing topics provide further practice in articulating ideas on paper.

Throughout the text, care has been taken to maintain a contemporary, student-friendly approach.

ACKNOWLEDGMENTS

My students at Oglethorpe University, Spelman College, Miramar College, and the University of California at San Diego, who have over the years explored with me the many facets of Cromwell College, have provided numerous suggestions and comments on the text as it has evolved. I am especially grateful to students and colleagues who have contributed concepts, titles, characters, or plot elements for individual cases or mini-cases: Kendra Carlisle, Jeneen Cook, Diamond Dubose, Jameelah Grant, Naiyana Gravely, Akiba Harper, and Charla Trotman.

The editorial staff at Prentice Hall—especially Sande Johnson and Cecilia Johnson—have been unfailingly helpful and enthusiastic, and the reviewers who commented on both the first and second editions provided many excellent recommendations for improvement. I would particularly like to thank Christy Cheney, Valencia Community College; Adrian Cloete, DeVry Institute of Technology–Dallas; Karan Hancock Grier, University of Alaska–Anchorage; Nancy Thompson, University of Georgia; and Jeane Treese, University of Chicago, for their comments on the first edition. For their helpful suggestions regarding proposed changes to the second edition, I would like to thank Norma Jeanne Campbell, Fayetteville State University; Charles R. Frederick, Jr., Indiana University–Bloomington; Joseph D. King, Colorado Christian University; Sanne McCarthy, Colorado Christian University; and Jon M. Young, Fayetteville State University.

Most of all, I would like to thank my husband Donald Rutherford, my most careful reader and constant supporter, for his encouragement and assistance at every stage of the project.

Introduction
Thinking Critically

The alarm clock goes off. Tanya, a first-year student at Cromwell College, is immediately confronted with the need to make a decision. Possibilities abound: Should she turn off the alarm and go back to sleep, missing her 8:00 A.M. class? Should she let the alarm buzz for awhile, thereby ensuring that she is fully awake but perhaps, in the meantime, awakening her roommate who was up late studying and who has no reason to rise for another hour? Should she vent her frustration at her continual lack of sleep by hurling the clock against the wall? Should she turn the alarm off immediately and, by sheer strength of will, bound out of bed?

This is just the first of many decision-making moments Tanya will face in her day. Indeed, at every minute she will encounter the need to make decisions: some trivial (whether to wear the black socks or the brown ones) and some significant (whether to cheat on her chemistry exam). What does she need to do to make conscious, well-reasoned decisions? What kind of questions should she ask as she assesses the situations facing her?

Tanya needs to be a critical thinker. She needs to evaluate the situations she encounters carefully and thoughtfully. She needs to become familiar with a set of techniques and approaches that will enable her to examine critically not only the texts she reads in her classes, but the everyday events of college life.

I'M ENTITLED TO MY OPINION

Let's say that Tanya runs into her friend Kevin at the library. He seems upset about something, and Tanya is concerned. When she asks what's troubling him, Kevin blurts out, "I think it's ridiculous the way some professors here take attendance, and count it as part of the course grade. It shouldn't be allowed!"

"Why not?" Tanya asks.

"What do you mean, 'why not'?" replies Kevin. "It's just what I believe. After all, it's a matter of opinion, and I'm entitled to my opinion. Isn't my opinion as good as anyone else's? Besides, I feel really strongly about this."

Whether or not class attendance should be considered in the grading process is indeed a matter of opinion. And although there may be no "right" opinion, some opinions on this issue—and on any issue—can be more convincing than others. Kevin's opinion may be strongly felt, but in order for Tanya to decide whether she should agree with him, she needs to discover whether his opinion is well-supported. An opinion that cannot be supported rationally is simply not as credible, or believable, as one that can.

Tanya therefore needs to encourage Kevin to go beyond a mere expression of his feelings about the issue at hand, inviting him to explore why he feels the way he does. If he can provide a well-reasoned justification for his position, Tanya will be much more likely to go along.

After Tanya insists that Kevin explain his viewpoint in greater detail, he launches into the following statement:

#1

My persnickety sociology professor takes attendance every day, and if you miss a certain number of class meetings, then he takes points off your grade. He's always whining about how ditching classes shows a careless attitude, and he claims that you can't do well if you don't show up. He seems to want to control student behavior like professors decades ago who required college students to attend chapel services. But we're living in a different age now, and the faculty can't exert that kind of control anymore. And anyway, I don't think he's taking a just approach to grading, because he isn't dealing with us fairly. In my opinion, as long as you do the work, showing up for class should be irrelevant.

The point is, why should attendance have any impact on our grades? Students like us know we should be able to choose for ourselves whether or not to go to class. We're smart; we know what we're doing. We're in college now, and we're mature enough to be responsible. Sure, if attendance didn't count then a few people might skip too many classes and end up not learning the material, but that would just be a small minority. And if we don't get the opportunity to make mistakes, how will we ever learn to stand on our own two feet? Professors need to either leave the choice of attending classes to us or admit that they don't want to treat us like adults.

You know, some people may not need to come to class every day—they may be familiar with the subject matter already, or they may be able to learn it just by doing the reading or talking to their classmates. If they can get the papers done, pass the tests, and so on, I don't see why attendance should have anything to do with their grades. After all, three students missed the review session our sociology professor held in the class meeting before our last exam, and these three students all got A's on the exam. It looks like missing class can actually help your course performance!

I've done pretty well on all the written course work so far, too, even though I've been unable to attend at least seven classes. Maybe the professor resents that—I guess it makes him look bad if students can do okay without actually having to be in the same room with him all the time. I have a hunch that's why he's threatening to drastically lower my grade. He's just being malicious and trying to get back at me. It's no surprise that he has such low teaching evaluations. My friend Susan, who's a senior sociology major, says she heard he's really insecure. That makes sense to me, because if he was secure in himself, he wouldn't be so concerned about us showing up.

Actually, lots of Cromwell faculty members agree with me about the attendance issue. Of the four courses I'm taking this semester, the professor takes attendance in only one of them; three out of four just don't see the point of doing it. My roommate Quentin, who's an education major, just did a study for a term paper that shows that most professors in the Education Department don't take attendance either and that there isn't any significant difference in grade distributions between the professors who count attendance and the ones who don't. My sociology professor is just out of step.

Using attendance as a factor in grading is like judging people's artistic talent by how much time they spend in the studio. It's narrow and neurotic. Next thing you know, they'll start asking how long it takes us to do the assigned reading and give higher grades to people who take longer!

Kevin has certainly moved beyond his initial remark that "it's a matter of opinion, and I'm entitled to my opinion." Now Tanya needs to approach Kevin's explanation of his position closely and critically in order to determine whether it is well-reasoned and well-supported.

WHAT'S THE POINT?

One of the first questions Tanya needs to ask as she examines Kevin's statement is, "What's the point?" In other words, what is the central issue under discussion? Once she figures this out, she can then investigate the **thesis** being offered concerning the issue at hand. The thesis is the message being conveyed or the position being taken; it is what an author or speaker is trying to prove.

Tanya should be able to identify the issue at stake here: Should class attendance in itself have an impact on a student's course grade? Kevin, after all, makes it fairly easy for her to locate the main issue by highlighting it at the beginning of the second paragraph with the key phrase "The point is. . ."

Tanya should also be able to <u>identify Kevin's thesis</u> concerning the issue: <u>Showing up for class</u>—or not showing up for class—should in itself have <u>no bearing on the grading process</u> ("as long as you do the work, showing up for class should be irrelevant"). In some cases, a thesis may not be apparent until the conclusion of a discussion, but Kevin provides Tanya with a strong sense of direction by stating his thesis at a relatively early point in his presentation. He again gives her a tip-off phrase ("In my opinion. . .") that serves as a handy signpost to indicate that he is about to identify his position on the issue. Even without such indicators, however, Tanya—if she is to approach Kevin's presentation critically—must be able to locate his thesis before she can proceed to evaluate the reasoning he uses to support it.

SO WHAT?

Before she invests too much time in discussing the issue with Kevin, however, Tanya needs to ask another set of questions: <u>Is this a **signifi-cant** issue?</u> Is the matter at hand really <u>meaningful to her?</u> Is it <u>worth her time and energy?</u> Is it just Kevin's pet peeve, or does it have larger importance? Could engaging in this discussion bring her to any new realizations? Could she learn something?

All right, Kevin's sociology professor takes attendance into account when assigning course grades—so what? Why should Tanya care? If she can't think of any reason why she *should* care, then maybe she needs to change the subject. If, upon reflection, she decides that the issue does have some importance for her, then she should continue to examine Kevin's statement.

After listening to Kevin's initial presentation of his views, Tanya may reflect upon her own classroom experiences and the ways in which counting attendance might be having an impact on her behavior—or her grades. She may perceive <u>a problem of inconsistency</u>, with <u>some professors valuing attendance and others not</u>, leading to inequities in expectations and student responsibilities. She may wonder whether it is fair to have no difference in grades between the student who shows up for every class and the one who relies on her roommate's lecture notes to get her through the course. Any of these considerations could be enough to convince her that the issue Kevin has raised is indeed a significant one.

IS THAT A FACT?

Kevin's conclusion is <u>supported by a set of **reasons**</u> that explain *why* he believes in his thesis. For instance, one of Kevin's reasons for discounting attendance is that some students may not need to attend class meetings because "they may be familiar with the subject matter already, or they may be able to learn it just by doing the reading or talking to their classmates." The thesis and all the reasons supporting it work together to constitute Kevin's **argument.**

Throughout his argument, Kevin makes a number of **claims** or assertions about the way things are or the way they ought to be. A claim that is intended to describe the way things actually are is a **descriptive** claim. Kevin makes a descriptive claim when he maintains that "we're living in a different age now"—he is saying something about what he perceives to be the current reality. A **prescriptive** claim, however, goes further; it offers a suggestion for the way things ought to be, as when Kevin says, "we should be able to choose for ourselves whether or not to go to class."

Descriptive claims can often seem like statements of fact, but Tanya needs to assess whether Kevin's claims are indeed factually based. For example, Kevin says that one reason why class attendance should be irrelevant in grading is because "we're mature enough to be responsible." Kevin may believe that he is describing reality when he makes this assertion. But is it actually a fact? A **fact** is something that is known to be true, something that has been verified. A **tentative truth** is something that *may* be true, but that still awaits verification. An **opinion** is something that may be *believed* to be true, but that is questionable or debatable. Where, among these possibilities, does Kevin's claim fall? Has it been solidly verified that college students are generally mature and responsible? If not, what kinds of tests or studies would need to be conducted to establish the truth of this claim? Is such a claim even verifiable?

Tanya needs to determine the extent to which Kevin is going beyond logical, factually based reasoning and using strategies simply to affect her feelings. For instance, Tanya, like Kevin, is a college student; he may be trying to use their shared position ("we're in college now") in order to engage her support for his cause. She needs to remain critically aware of such techniques in Kevin's argument.

PROVE IT!

Tanya can gain a clearer sense of the effectiveness of Kevin's argument by assessing the **evidence** he provides in support of his claims. If Kevin wants one of his assertions to be convincing, he needs to prove it by backing it up with credible evidence. What kind of evidence does he provide to ground his claims, and how credible is it?

In fact, Kevin offers various types of evidence, including personal experience and individual example, intuition, appeal to authority, and a research study. Tanya must evaluate *all* forms of evidence in Kevin's argument to determine its credibility.

To begin with, Kevin provides his own **personal experience** to support his case: he has "done pretty well" in his course work even though he has missed a number of classes. Tanya needs to consider whether Kevin's view of his own experience is really an objective one—*he* may think he has "done pretty well," but would his professor agree? Would Tanya herself agree? What exactly constitutes "doing well" for Kevin—getting A's, getting B's, or getting passing grades?

Tanya also must think about whether Kevin's experience is necessarily representative or typical of the experience of all students. Kevin may have been able to do well without attending class because his roommate is also taking the class and has been generously sharing his notes with Kevin—but would that necessarily be the case for every student? Whenever someone offers a specific **example** or **case study** of a *fair?* single individual's experience (whether it is their own experience or the experience of another), the question of whether or not the experience is representative must be addressed.

After Kevin asserts that he does not need to attend all of his classes in order to complete the course work successfully, he goes on to claim, "Maybe the professor resents that—I guess it makes him look bad if students can do okay without actually having to be in the same room with him all the time." Expressions such as "maybe," "I guess," and "I have a hunch" that appear in Kevin's statement suggest that he does not know *for a fact* that the professor feels this way; he merely infers it based on his **intuition.** Intuition may help us to identify points that could benefit from further development and support, but intuition can never be a substitute for concrete evidence.

Kevin appeals to external **authority** when he cites the information provided by his friend Susan, a senior sociology major: "she heard he's really insecure." But is Susan a credible authority on this issue? *credible?* Although her presence in the sociology department may give Susan some acquaintance with its faculty members, does it really endow her with enough **expertise** (special knowledge about the subject) to determine that Kevin's professor is insecure? In fact, Kevin himself notes that this is just something that Susan has "heard"—a point which may do even more to call her credibility into question. If Kevin were to somehow come across the notes taken by his professor's psychotherapist detailing the professor's long-standing struggle with feelings of inadequacy, he would have a much stronger authority for his claim. The psychotherapist would of course have much more extensive knowledge of the professor and his problems than Susan would, and the psychotherapist's skills, experience, and education would make him a much more credible expert on the issue of insecurity than Susan is at the moment.

Kevin appeals to another sort of authority when he brings up his roommate Quentin's term paper, a **research study** that he offers as evidence to corroborate his reasoning. Tanya should examine a number of factors in reference to this study. First of all, she may wonder about *accurate?*

the qualifications and expertise of the researcher, as well as his neutrality. Is a college senior necessarily the most authoritative source on this subject? Does he have sufficient training and experience to develop and carry out a complex research project? Is it possible that Quentin's own position as a student has affected his **perspective**—perhaps even determining the approach he is taking, the questions he is asking, and the interpretations he is drawing from the data collected? Would he have a different perspective on the professors he is studying if he were a fellow professor rather than a student?

Tanya also may question the credibility of a single, rather limited research study. Is the **sample** (the selection of people studied) large, broad, and representative enough? What percentage of the total Education Department faculty did Quentin survey, and how many individual professors were involved? If there are only four professors in the department and Quentin surveyed three of them, he may have ended up covering three-quarters of the department, but three professors is simply too small of a sample to be statistically significant.

In addition, Tanya should consider whether Quentin's **focus** on the Education Department might make it difficult to appropriately apply his findings to consideration of attendance and grading in other departments, such as sociology. Might there be factors relating to education courses in particular (for example, small class size) that could make the taking of attendance unnecessary?

When assessing the legitimacy of any research study, it is important to investigate whether the study has been **replicated** by other researchers. If Quentin is the only person to have ever explored the possible correlation between taking attendance and grade distributions, the results of his study could appear to be idiosyncratic. However, if other researchers have conducted similar studies—and especially if their studies have demonstrated the same findings as Quentin's—then the credibility of Quentin's research would be enhanced.

Of course Tanya must not forget to assess the **relevance** of this study to the matter at hand. Quentin's study apparently determined that "there isn't any significant difference in grade distributions between the professors who count attendance and the ones who don't." Assuming that Quentin's conclusion is correct, this could be an interesting finding, as it suggests that students in general end up with similar grades whether or not attendance is taken into account. But what bearing does this have on the issue of whether or not attendance *should* play a part in course grading? Tanya must be careful not to allow a descriptive claim (Quentin's conclusion that counting attendance has no significant impact on grading patterns) to distract her from Kevin's prescriptive claim about what he believes *ought* to be happening regarding attendance and grading.

CHECK THE NUMBERS!

Tanya also needs to take a closer look at the **statistics** Kevin offers in *misused?*
support of his argument; specifically, the statistical evidence ("three
out of four professors") in the fifth paragraph of his statement. Is this
figure a convincing component of Kevin's reasoning? There's something about numbers that often seems to give them an aura of truth.
Tanya can't really argue with the fact that Kevin is taking courses with
four different professors, and that three of them do not take attendance. However, she needs to consider whether Kevin's sample (the
four professors he happens to have this semester) is too limited to be
persuasive. Would Kevin's argument be more convincing if he supported his claim with a survey of *all* the college's professors, indicating
that 75 percent of them do not take attendance? What about a survey
of thousands of college professors nationwide?

Does it even matter how many professors do or do not take attendance? If what Tanya is trying to evaluate is whether or not attendance
should be a component in professors' grading criteria, is it really relevant to assess to what extent it *is* a component? Once again, we may
have a confusion between the descriptive and the prescriptive. The statistical evidence in this case may help to establish a descriptive claim
about what professors *do*, but it does not really address Kevin's prescriptive claim about what professors *should* do—unless Kevin can
also succeed in convincing Tanya that all professors should simply do
what the majority of their colleagues do.

WHO SAYS?

No matter how much evidence Kevin provides, Tanya needs to make sure
that the sources of his evidence are reliable. We have already seen that
there may be questions about the credibility of Susan and Quentin as authoritative, dependable sources. We've noted, for example, that Quentin's
position as a student may lead to a particular **bias** or slant in his approach
to his research study—whether or not he himself is aware of this.

In fact, Kevin's own credibility could be called into question as
well. He admits, in the fourth paragraph of his statement, that his
sociology professor is threatening to lower Kevin's grade because of
repeated absences. Is it possible that this threat has affected Kevin's
perspective on the issue of attendance as a component of grading?
Is it possible that Kevin's sudden attention to the issue of attendance
and grading has been directly caused by this threat, and that his argument grows out of his own **vested interest** in the matter? Does ✓
his argument constitute a rational, disinterested exploration of the
issue, or is it merely a vehicle for him to complain about his own
personal situation? Tanya needs to consider the extent to which
Kevin's personal involvement may undermine the credibility of his
presentation.

WHERE ARE YOU COMING FROM?

Kevin's approach to the subject may be governed by his unspoken thoughts concerning higher education in general. In order to determine where Kevin is coming from, Tanya needs to explore what Kevin does *not* explicitly express: the **assumptions** he takes for granted about how the world is or should be. Once she can uncover these unspoken assumptions, she will be able to determine whether or not she believes these assumptions to be legitimate. If she does not, then she will have a hard time agreeing with the claims that are built upon the foundations of Kevin's assumptions.

For example, Kevin asserts that "as long as you do the work, showing up for class should be irrelevant." There are a number of unspoken assumptions underlying this claim. One of the most significant is that "the work" of a course is what is done outside of regular class meetings—papers, exams, problem sets, lab reports, and other out-of-class assignments. Kevin's reasoning can proceed only by conceiving of "course work" as something that is not undertaken in class. If Tanya were to consider participation in class discussion or taking notes on a lecture as part of the work of a course, then it would be more difficult to agree with Kevin's conclusion that "showing up for class should be irrelevant." Kevin's **descriptive assumption** concerning what course work *is* governs his entire argument.

Kevin also makes a number of **prescriptive** or **value assumptions** about how things *ought* to be, and these, too, govern his argument. For instance, Kevin asks this question: "And if we don't get the opportunity to make mistakes, how will we ever learn to stand on our own two feet?" Here he presupposes that learning "to stand on our own two feet" is a valuable component of a college education. If Tanya does not agree that this is part of what college students *should* be learning, then she will be unconvinced by Kevin's reasoning.

SAY WHAT?

Because of the assumptions he makes and the biases he brings to the issue at hand, Kevin's language may not always be as neutral or precise as it could be. Tanya would be well advised to look closely at Kevin's choice of specific words and phrases.

Some of the words Kevin uses are obviously **slanted.** For instance, he refers at the beginning of his argument to his "persnickety" professor's "whining," and he uses the word "neurotic" in a pejorative or negative sense at the very end of his statement. At other points, the slanting of terminology is a bit more subtle. For example, Kevin says that his professor "claims that you can't do well if you don't show up." By using a word such as "claims" (rather than, say, "states"), Kevin conveys a sense of questionability, suggesting that what the professor says is opinion rather than fact and is therefore open to doubt.

In some cases, Kevin's use of loaded language can be characterized as **euphemism** or **dysphemism.** A euphemism is a gentle or positive-sounding word or phrase that may be used to soften a harsh or negative meaning. For example, when speaking of the sociology classes he has missed, Kevin refers to them as classes he has "been unable to attend." Stating the case in this way enables Kevin to deflect blame from himself, subtly suggesting that he would have eagerly attended all the classes had he not been unavoidably detained. Dysphemism—the opposite of euphemism, and so the use of harsh or negative language—can be seen when Kevin reports on his professor's attitude toward students "ditching" classes. The accusatory tone of the word "ditching"—implying that students are simply tossing their educations overboard—contributes to Kevin's characterization of his sociology professor as cranky and out of touch.

In all cases, whether the loaded language is subtle or overt, Tanya must think critically about the effects of Kevin's specific terminology, looking beyond the mere **denotation** of a word (its explicit meaning or definition) and taking into account its potential **connotations** (the meanings associated with or suggested by it). For instance, when Kevin speaks of "the opportunity to make mistakes," he uses the word "opportunity" to connote a beneficial, favorable chance for self-improvement. Making mistakes is thus presented in a positive light.

Tanya should also be aware that many of the words Kevin uses are **ambiguous**—they may have multiple meanings, or they may simply be vague and undefined. For example, in his second paragraph he characterizes college students as "mature enough to be responsible." What exactly do words such as "mature" and "responsible" mean here? Could they have different meanings for different people? Could they have different meanings in different contexts? How mature is "mature enough"? Can levels of maturity be measured? How can responsible behavior be defined or assessed? What about words like "just" and "fairly," which Kevin uses in the first paragraph of his statement? What might it mean to act in a just or fair manner? Tanya may want to insist that Kevin define his terms more clearly and precisely.

RUN THAT BY ME AGAIN!

So far Tanya has come across a number of areas in which Kevin's argument could bear further examination. As she investigates possible weaknesses in his reasoning, she may want to run through a checklist of common logical **fallacies**—flaws in reasoning that can seriously undermine the credibility of an argument.

1. Emotive language: As we have already seen, Kevin has a tendency to depend on emotional appeals and emotion-laden language. Specific logical fallacies that fall under the category of emotive language include appeals to fear, pity, flattery, and peer pressure. For example, Kevin uses flattery when he says, "We're smart; we know what we're doing." He appeals to the vanity of his student audience in order to draw them into his argument.

2. False dilemma: Sometimes called the "either-or" fallacy, this describes the strategy of presenting only two extreme alternatives and excluding any middle ground. Kevin does this when he says, "Professors need to either leave the choice of attending classes to us or admit that they don't want to treat us like adults." Are those really the only available options?

3. Slippery slope: Often presented in the form of an "if-then" or "the next thing you know" statement, this fallacy suggests that if one thing happens, something else will necessarily follow. This may also be familiar as the "domino theory" or "ripple effect." We can see Kevin making use of this approach at the end of his argument: "Next thing you know, they'll start asking how long it takes us to do the assigned reading and give higher grades to people who take longer!" The problem is that we have no logical reason to believe that the first thing (using attendance to determine grades) will necessarily lead to the second (using length of reading time).

4. Circular reasoning: Sometimes described as a form of "begging the question" (that is, avoiding the issue), circular reasoning moves—as you might guess—in a circle. In other words, the justification of a claim is simply a restatement of the claim itself in a slightly altered form. When Kevin says, "I don't think he's taking a just approach to grading, because he isn't dealing with us fairly," his explanation simply proceeds by the use of near-synonyms: the approach isn't just because it isn't fair. Has he really explained anything?

5. Ad hominem: From the Latin phrase meaning "to the person," this fallacy uses a personal attack on an individual as a substitute for a reasoned critique of the individual's position. When Kevin refers to his sociology professor as "persnickety" and "insecure," and when he says, "He's just being malicious and trying to get back at me," he is engaging in ad hominem attacks.

6. Ad populum: From the Latin phrase meaning "to the people," this fallacy makes an appeal to the shared values or beliefs of the audience, playing on people's natural desire to be part of a group. Kevin uses this strategy in the second paragraph of his statement when he refers to what "students like us know."

7. Common practice: Here the appeal is not to popular beliefs, but to popular behavior—an "everyone is doing it" or "bandwagon" approach. When Kevin argues that three of his four professors do not take attendance and that, according to Quentin's study, most education professors do not take attendance either, he seems to suggest that the majority behavior is the norm, and that his sociology professor's policy is an aberration which should be rectified.

8. Red herring: This fallacy involves distraction—using an un-related point to distract the audience's attention from the real issue at hand. Its name derives from the old practice of using a dead fish to dis-tract dogs from the scent of their prey. One "dead fish" in Kevin's ar-gument can be found when he refers, in his fourth paragraph, to his sociology professor's "low teaching evaluations." What does this point have to do with the issue of using attendance as a factor in grading?

9. Straw man: When the arguments of the opposition are exag-gerated or distorted and then attacked, we end up with a "straw man" that is easily knocked down. In his opening paragraph, Kevin says that his sociology professor "seems to want to control student behavior like professors decades ago who required college students to attend chapel services." He then continues, "But we're living in a different age now, and the faculty can't exert that kind of control anymore." Is Kevin nec-essarily giving an accurate portrayal of his professor's position when he talks about what his professor "seems to want"? When he makes the point that "we're living in a different age now," is he rebutting his pro-fessor's actual position, or merely an imaginary position that Kevin himself has created?

10. Generalizations: Frequently signaled by such words as "all," "every," "always," "never," and "none," **broad generalizations** or **overstatements** are unqualified statements about all members of a cat-egory or group. Stereotyping is one form of overstatement. A conclusion based on a limited or unrepresentative sample is a **hasty generaliza-tion.** We see Kevin falling into this fallacy when he provides the "three out of four professors" statistic and draws the conclusion that "lots of Cromwell faculty members agree with me about the attendance issue." Based on his sample of only four professors, can he legitimately draw a conclusion about the views of "lots of Cromwell faculty members"?

11. False analogy: An **analogy** is a comparison that highlights the resemblance or similarity between two different things. When eval-uating the soundness of an analogy, we need to examine how similar the two things being compared actually are and how significant the similar-ities may be. False analogies are sometimes referred to as "comparing apples to oranges." In the final paragraph of his statement Kevin says, "Using attendance as a factor in grading is like judging people's artistic talent by how much time they spend in the studio." Is grading a student in a particular course really comparable to judging artistic ability? Is at-tending class really comparable to spending time in an art studio?

12. Post hoc: Sometimes referred to as "false cause" reasoning, this fallacy takes its name from the Latin phrase *post hoc ergo propter hoc,* meaning "after this, therefore because of this." The suggestion is that there is a cause-effect relationship between two events simply be-cause one came first. We can see this reasoning in Kevin's third para-graph: "After all, three students missed the review session our sociology professor held in the class meeting before our last exam, and these three students all got A's on the exam. So it looks like missing class can actually help your course performance!" The implication is that the students got A's on the exam *because* they missed the prior review session—but of course the two events could be entirely unrelated.

13. Non sequitur: In Latin, this means "it does not follow." It can refer to any portion of an argument in which the reasoning simply does not connect or make sense; for example, when Kevin says that if his sociology professor "was secure in himself, he wouldn't be so concerned about us showing up." What exactly is the link between the professor's possible insecurity and his grading policy? It may make sense to Kevin, but the connection may not be clear to anyone else.

WHAT'S MISSING?

Tanya needs to consider not only whether the argument Kevin presents is flawed or slanted, but whether he is leaving out any important factors. Altogether, Kevin may be presenting a rather limited view of the issue. Are there **alternative interpretations** of the information he has offered? For example, Kevin notes that three of his professors this semester do not take attendance, and leads us to the conclusion that they do not do so because they do not think it is a legitimate component of grading. But could it instead be because their courses are so hugely enrolled that attendance-taking would be difficult—or because their classes are so small that officially taking attendance would not be necessary in order to determine who is present? Could it be due to the nature of their courses, their goals and methods as teachers, or even their laziness?

Tanya also needs to consider whether there may be any **negative consequences** to Kevin's view that he neglects to mention. Kevin himself admits that "if attendance didn't count then a few people might skip too many classes and end up not learning the material," but he claims that this would involve only "a small minority" of students. Even if it were only a small minority, an impact might still be felt on class participation, the professor's ability to connect with students, and the morale of those students who do attend class regularly—not to mention the possibility that faculty members might find their office hours taken up by students who have missed class and require a further explanation of course materials.

There are many more weaknesses in Kevin's argument than we have so far explored. Tanya would do well to undertake further examination of his presentation, attempting to uncover additional examples of problems with his reasoning. Once Tanya has fully evaluated Kevin's argument, she will be ready to reply with an argument of her own. She will be able to use her evaluation of Kevin's argument to build her case, for an awareness of the flaws in his reasoning will enable her to avoid such flaws herself.

PLAY IT AGAIN

Just to make sure that she has fully absorbed a critical-thinking approach, Tanya might want to examine another argument. She had an excellent opportunity to do so the day after her conversation with Kevin about class attendance and grading. As she settled into her favorite seat near the back of her English composition classroom a few minutes before her class was scheduled to begin, she overheard two of her classmates, Elise and Dalton, engage in the following discussion:

#2

"Don't you think that T-shirt you're wearing is tacky?" asked Elise.

"Why should I think it's tacky? I'm showing my school spirit! Don't you support the Cromwell Chiefs?" Dalton replied.

"I have nothing against our athletes," Elise explained, "but I do have a problem with the school's mascot, especially the way he's portrayed on your T-shirt—feathers, war paint, and tomahawk in hand. I've taken a couple of courses here at Cromwell about Native American literature and culture, and I know that the image on your T-shirt doesn't reflect reality. It's a representation of every possible mindless cliché that's been perpetuated since white folks first came into contact with indigenous peoples. Just calling the athletic teams 'the Chiefs' is bad enough; the name alone gives a limited, stereotypical view of Native Americans. And when you associate that name with the cartoonish figure on your T-shirt, it's even worse. It makes Cromwell look like we're out of step and behind the times—honestly, I'm totally humiliated whenever my friends at other schools see a Cromwell T-shirt."

"Oh, come on, Elise. First of all, it's just a picture. Why make such a big deal over it? And what's wrong with calling our teams 'the Chiefs'? It's a positive image, after all—noble, courageous, in charge. It helps us here at Cromwell feel proud of our school and our athletes. Besides, it's a name that's been associated with our athletic program for generations, ever since Cromwell was founded. You can't change that kind of long-standing tradition—the alumni would never go for it. I ought to know—my father is an alumnus, and I can guarantee you he'd be furious if they changed the team name. Anyway, all you need to do to get a clue about alumni opinion is to read the letters to the editor in Cromwell's alumni magazine; it seems like three-fourths of them point out all the ways the college is changing for the worse. What would you want to change the name to, anyway? Something nice and sweet like 'the Cromwell Chrysanthemums'? A team name is supposed to connote strength, victory, and power. A word like 'Chiefs' does that perfectly."

"But it's not the only powerful choice," Elise pointed out. "We could be 'the Cromwell Cougars,' for example, which at least wouldn't be offensive. I've never heard of anyone on any campus objecting to a name like that."

"How do you know? Probably some animal rights fanatics out there would have a problem with it," Dalton said. "Wasn't there a big blow-up at Reston College when they named their newspaper *The Reston Roadkill*? I remember my roommate telling me something about that . . . ".

"Now you're just being dumb. I don't know why I listen to anything a jerk like you has to say about serious issues."

At that point the professor entered the classroom. The conversation ceased, but Tanya continued to think about what she had overheard. She knew there were a number of points she needed to consider as she pondered Elise and Dalton's interchange.

Evaluating a Truth Claim (assertion, argument)

- **What's the issue at hand** and **what is the thesis being presented?** What exactly is the point of the discussion: the alleged tackiness of Dalton's T-shirt or the larger issue of associating a college team with a specific cultural image or artifact? Although Elise begins by focusing on the T-shirt, her subsequent statement ("I do have a problem with the school's mascot") begins to clarify the issue as well as Elise's position on the issue.

- **Is it significant?** Does Tanya care enough about this issue to spend any more time thinking about Elise and Dalton's exploration of it? As a Cromwell student, Tanya may indeed want to consider potential problems with the images the college uses to represent itself.

- **Is there a factual basis** for the claims being made? For example, when Dalton asserts that Cromwell alumni "would never go for" a change in the team name, is he stating a fact? Has his assertion been verified? What procedures would be necessary to establish verification of such an assertion?

- **What kind of evidence is being provided in support of the claims?** When Elise notes that she has "never heard of anyone on any campus objecting" to animal names being used for athletic teams, is she providing adequate concrete support to back up her assertions? Just because she herself hasn't heard of objections, does that mean that they do not exist?

- **Is the use of statistics or other numerical evidence credible?** What should Tanya make of Dalton's point about three-fourths of the letters to the editor in the alumni magazine pointing out "all the ways the college is changing for the worse"? Is this a legitimate use of statistical evidence? Might the phrase "it seems like" introducing this evidence raise questions about the accuracy of Dalton's "three-fourths" figure? Are letters to the editor necessarily a representative sample of alumni opinion? Is it possible that people are more likely to make the effort to write a letter when they feel the urge to complain?

- **How credible are the speaker and the sources cited?** Are Elise and Dalton presenting themselves, and the other sources they cite, as credible? For instance, when Elise points out that she's taken a couple of college courses dealing with Native American culture, is this enough to establish her as an authoritative figure? When Dalton asserts that he "ought to know" about alumni opinion because his father is an alumnus, has he provided sufficient support for his presentation of himself as an authority? Does Dalton give Elise any reason to believe that his roommate is a credible source for information about events at Reston College?

- **What assumptions underlie the claims being made?** What do Elise and Dalton take for granted? What perceptions or attitudes govern the ways in which they view the issue at hand? For example, what do they each seem to assume about the function of a college team mascot? Elise's embarrassment when her friends at other colleges see the Cromwell mascot may suggest that she views the mascot as a vehicle for representing Cromwell to the outside world; Dalton's focus on the positive emotions that the name "Chiefs" can generate among Cromwell students and alumni may suggest that he views the mascot as a source of internal collegiate pride. Might these differing assumptions lead to differing perceptions of the image on Dalton's T-shirt?

- **Is the language that is being used loaded or slanted in any way?** Do any ambiguous words or phrases appear in the discussion? How does Elise's use of a phrase such as "mindless cliché" or an adjective such as "cartoonish" affect the message she is conveying? What is the connotation of Dalton's reference to the "long-standing tradition" of the Cromwell team name? What exactly is meant by the expression "school spirit"? Could it mean different things to different people?

- **Are there any logical fallacies in the argument?** Examples can be found throughout the discussion of such fallacies as emotive language ("Don't you support the Cromwell Chiefs?"), false dilemma ("What would you want to change the name to, anyway? Something nice and sweet like 'the Cromwell Chrysanthemums'?") ad hominem attacks ("I don't know why I listen to anything a jerk like you has to say about serious issues"), or false analogy ("Wasn't there a big blow-up at Reston College when they named their newspaper *The Reston Roadkill*?")? Can you spot any other logical fallacies?

- **Is anything important being left out of the presentation?** Are Elise and Dalton neglecting to consider alternative interpretations or negative consequences? For example, is it possible that changing the team name and mascot could result in a reduction of alumni donations to the college? Is it possible that keeping the name and mascot could stimulate protests and generate negative publicity for the college?

After exploring each of these issues in some depth, Tanya will have a much fuller understanding of the arguments that Elise and Dalton are presenting. As she did with Kevin's argument, she will be able to evaluate the positions being presented to her and at the same time construct a position of her own that is clear, coherent, and convincing. Tanya will be able to do this effectively because she has learned to think critically.

ONE MORE TIME

See if you, like Tanya, can think critically about college life by examining the following argument presented by Tanya's friend Hope.

3   I know a lot of people who whine and complain about the children of alumni having an easier time getting into Cromwell than other applicants. I've heard from a friend of mine who does work-study in the admissions office that the average applicant to Cromwell has a one in ten chance of being admitted, but alumni children—they call them "legacies"—have a four in ten chance. Some people think that's an unfair advantage, but I don't agree. I think legacies *do* deserve extra attention from the admissions office. My dad is a Cromwell alumnus, so I know about this firsthand.

Legacy applicants are more likely to do well when they get to Cromwell, because they understand what the college is all about. They know the old traditions and have a stronger feeling of school pride. They feel committed to Cromwell because of their family connection to it, so they won't want to do anything to jeopardize their success here. They probably have higher retention rates, because legacies won't ever want to transfer to another school. Besides, if your parents graduated from Cromwell, that means they must have been smart—which means that you're smart, too, so you deserve a greater chance of admission to the college. The students I know who happen to be children of Cromwell alumni are all pretty intelligent. I'm afraid I can't say the same for Cromwell students in general.

And we shouldn't forget that legacies aren't the only ones who get favorable treatment in the admissions process. Cromwell gives special consideration to other groups, too: athletes, underrepresented minorities, students with special artistic or musical talents, and so on. Why not add alumni children to the list?

The real clincher, though, is that alumni children, when they become alumni themselves, are going to be major donors to the college. The more of a family tradition you have of being connected to the school, the more likely you are to make major financial contributions. In Cromwell's alumni magazine, I read about a research study that showed that in their first two years after graduation, 78 percent of legacies donated a total of $100 or more to Cromwell. Only 36 percent of non-legacy graduates donated $100 or more in their first two years out. Like most colleges, Cromwell depends on alumni support to raise funds. If we cut down our number of legacy admissions, what would happen to the college budget? We might not even be able to keep things running! I guess that's why most private colleges across the country admit alumni children at higher rates—Cromwell is just doing what all the other colleges do.

I think the people who complain about legacy admissions are jealous and mean-spirited. They need to calm down and take a longer view of things. After all, their children will be able to benefit from the legacy admission advantage as well.

- **What's the issue at hand, and what is the thesis being presented?** Can you identify the topic under discussion, as well as Hope's position on the topic? Is there a particular sentence in Hope's statement that encapsulates her thesis?

- **Is it significant?** Do you care about this issue? If so, why? If not, why not?

- **Is there a factual basis for the claims being made?** You might want to focus on the several claims that Hope makes in the second paragraph of her statement. Are these assertions facts, tentative truths, or opinions?

- **What kind of evidence is being provided in support of the claims?** Does Hope make effective use of personal experience, research studies, and other forms of evidence?

- **Is the use of statistics or other numerical evidence credible?** What do you make of the numerical data that Hope introduces in the first paragraph, or the statistical overview of legacy and non-legacy donations that she cites in the second-to-last paragraph?

- **How credible is the speaker as well as the sources cited?** Does Hope's position as the daughter of an alumnus enhance her authority, or does it undermine her credibility? Is her friend who has a work-study job in the admissions office an authoritative source?

- **What assumptions underlie the claims being made?** For example, try to identify the assumptions about intelligence that Hope seems to be making in the following statement: "Besides, if your parents graduated from Cromwell, that means they must have been smart—which means that you're smart, too, so you deserve a greater chance of admission to the college."

- **Is the language that is being used loaded or slanted in any way? Do any ambiguous words or phrases appear in the discussion?** What kind of message is being conveyed in the phrase "whine and complain" that appears in the very first sentence of Hope's statement? What about "school pride," which she uses in her second paragraph—could it be open to a variety of interpretations?

- **Are there any logical fallacies in the argument?** Can you find any instances of false analogies, ad hominem attacks, slippery slope reasoning, appeals to common practice, or any other fallacies in Hope's statement?

- **Is anything important being left out of the presentation?** Can you think of any alternative interpretations of the information Hope provides—for example, the study of legacy and non-legacy donations? Can you think of any negative consequences of favoring alumni children in college admissions?

Sometimes it's easier to criticize someone else's flawed presentation than to think of ways to convey a position effectively, but you may be able to develop your critical thinking powers more fully by considering the ways in which Hope could have strengthened her case. How could she have presented her case more convincingly? What could she have done to create a more logically reasoned and solidly supported argument?

ON YOUR OWN

Here are two statements recently presented by Cromwell students in an open forum on campus issues. How would you approach these statements now that you are learning to think critically?

1. Athletic Support: Fellow students, we have some serious problems with fairness and equity here at Cromwell. We're all here to get an education, to fulfill our academic potential—or at least that's why we're supposed to be here—and one thing I just can't tolerate is a college system that seems to give special privileges to people based on anything but their academic achievement. I can see the value of giving extra attention to students who are highly talented in music or art, because those are areas that contribute to the educational mission of the college. But I'm fed up with the special consideration that athletes seem to get here, especially in the matter of tutorial support. It's unfair to everyone else and inappropriate in an institution of higher learning.

From the very beginning, we have unfairness in the admissions policies, which give favorable consideration to star athletes. Sure, the folks in the admissions office say that no one gets accepted to Cromwell unless they meet the college's academic criteria, but don't we all know students who would definitely never have gotten in here if not for their athletic abilities? Face it, even though they sometimes call them "scholar-athletes," the sports stars who get admitted to Cromwell aren't exactly intellectual giants.

And then when they get here, they get all sorts of academic perks that the rest of us regular students don't have access to. Never mind all the rumors about gifts and favors and wining and dining. Let's talk about tutoring! I would never even have known about the special academic tutoring services that athletes have if not for the fact that my roommate is on the soccer team.

I want to tell you about one of my personal experiences to illustrate the problem. My roommate, the soccer player, and I are both taking the same anthropology class this semester, and if you've taken Anthro. 317 you know it's not an easy course. Well, I've done my best to get through it, working like crazy to do all the reading and pass the exams and finish the impossible papers that we have to write. About halfway through the term I was really struggling with one of the writing assignments, and even after going to talk to the professor I was still totally lost. I went to the Academic Assistance Center to see if I could get one of the tutors there to help me figure out how to approach writing the paper. Well, anthropology is not such a popular field, so there was only one tutor who could help, and she was fully booked until days after the assignment was due! I did my best on my own and ended up getting a C+ on the paper.

That would have been the end of the story if I hadn't witnessed the totally different experience with this assignment that my roommate had. You may know that there's an office here at Cromwell called Athletic Support Services. My roommate has a counselor there who helps him with all his academic and personal problems. I wish I had someone like that! Anyway, on the day before the paper was due he went and told his counselor about the difficulty he was having with the anthro. assignment. She called around and quickly found a senior anthro. major who spent four hours with him that afternoon explaining the assignment and helping him get his ideas together for writing the paper. With assistance like that, he was able to get an A- on the paper!

This isn't just a fluke occurrence, either. I went with my roommate to soccer practice one day and asked around among his teammates. It turns out that of the nine players I talked to, seven had gotten last-minute tutoring assistance through Athletic Support Services this semester alone. This is simply unfair, since non-athletes don't have this option.

I know I'm not the only one who feels this way. I've heard lots of students complaining about how hard it is sometimes to get to see a tutor at the Academic Assistance Center, and at least one professor has raised concerns about athletes' access to special tutoring services. Remember Prof. Mitchell's letter to the editor in last week's *Cromwell Clarion*? Now I'm asking the rest of you to make your voices heard against this injustice. Either we all need to have access to the kind of academic assistance that the athletes get, or they can suffer through their courses like the rest of us!

2. Sweatshirts from Sweatshops: Friends, I know that many of you saw the article in yesterday's *Cromwell Clarion*, revealing the fact that our Cromwell College sweatshirts and T-shirts are manufactured by underpaid and overworked sweatshop laborers. For those of you who might not have heard, let me explain that our campus newspaper conducted an investigation into the sources of Cromwell's officially licensed college apparel. According to Cromwell's director of auxiliary services, more than 90 percent of the logo merchandise is produced by Transterra Textiles, a garment company which supplies clothing to a number of American colleges and universities. The vast majority of Transterra's college apparel is manufactured in a factory in Honduras which employs primarily women and children who operate under horrific working conditions.

Here are some details about Transterra Textiles' operations. According to a recent report by the WorldWeave Foundation, a nonprofit organization funded by American garment workers' unions, Transterra owns five factories in Third World countries. Its four smaller factories focus on the production of baby and children's wear, although they do produce some college merchandise. Transterra's largest factory, in Honduras, concentrates on college logo apparel and employs 720 workers, of whom approximately 300 are under the age of eighteen. Almost 70 percent of the Honduran workers are female. In a recent tour of Transterra's Honduran factory, WorldWeave observers noticed some children who appeared to be as young as eleven or twelve working with dangerous fabric-cutting machines—in spite of local laws that prohibit anyone under the age of fourteen from doing factory work. All the factory employees, no matter how young, work ten-hour shifts at physically exhausting and mentally deadening jobs, and they are often forced to work overtime. Temperatures in some portions of the factory exceed 100 degrees, air circulation is limited, and there is no safe drinking water available to employees. For this dangerous and degrading work, laborers are paid an average of only 68 cents per hour!

Think about it: a little girl the age of an average fifth grader, working hour after hour without a break amid the deafening roar of machinery, trying to keep up with the rapid pace of production without getting her fingers sliced off, trying not to collapse from heat and exhaustion, earning a pittance for her labor—just so we can buy Cromwell sweatshirts to show off to our friends and families. It's obscene, and it has to stop!

There are two things we can do to put an end to this exploitation. We can demand that Cromwell obtain its logo merchandise only from garment companies with socially responsible labor practices, and we can refuse to wear or purchase any Cromwell clothing until the college switches to an acceptable apparel supplier.

Knowing what we now know, if we continue to wear and buy Cromwell logo apparel we become accomplices in the abusive employment practices of Transterra Textiles. We have a choice: to do what we can in support of global economic justice, or to become the oppressor. I therefore call upon you to join me in a campaign of letters, e-mails, and phone calls to convince Cromwell's director of auxiliary services to investigate the employment practices of other garment suppliers and to explore possible alternatives. And I call upon you to boycott all Cromwell apparel—not to wear any sweatshirts or T-shirts you may already have, and not to purchase any more—until we see a positive change.

Welcome to Cromwell College!

The admissions recruiters for Cromwell College (CC) are proud to note that the school "looks like a college is supposed to look." Indeed, the well-manicured Academic Quad and neo-Gothic classroom buildings do make excellent subjects for the glossy full-color photographs in the admissions office's brochures. CC offers an oasis of green along a commercial strip on the fringes of a major American city.

Many of the school's 2,000 full-time students come from the surrounding area, but every year more and more of these promising young men and women come from out of state and abroad. This year, forty-two states and seventeen foreign countries are represented in the Cromwell student body. In addition to geographic variety, recent recruitment initiatives have led to increased percentages of African-American, Asian-American, Latino, and Native American students in the CC population. A dozen different religious organizations have been formed on campus, and the Cromwell Chapel provides meeting and worship space for the organized religious groups. In addition, several new student organizations (such as the Gay and Lesbian Alliance, the Association of the Physically Challenged, and the International Students' Federation) have been formed. Altogether, the Cromwell of today presents a very different picture from the Cromwell of twenty or thirty years ago. Whether they commute from their parents' homes, live in nearby apartments, or reside in campus residence halls, CC's students are acutely aware that they are part of an institution that is becoming more cosmopolitan and diverse.

Cromwell's national reputation as a selective liberal arts college has been steadily growing over the past ten years. The school's increased visibility is largely thanks to the efforts of its current president, who is recognized in the academic community for her extraordinary abilities in fund-raising and public relations and who is determined to tell the world about Cromwell's academic excellence. Many of CC's faculty members have earned Ph.D.'s from the nation's most prestigious universities, and the caliber of the student body—as measured by such indicators as standardized test scores—rivals that of many better-known colleges.

This year's entering class continues Cromwell's trend of selectivity in its student body. With average test scores well above the national norms and an uncounted number of student council presidents, high school newspaper editors, and accomplished athletes, CC's first-year students have distinguished themselves both in and out of the classroom. In their first few days at college they've also proven that they know how to have fun—as has been demonstrated by a couple of already-legendary orientation parties in the Lower Quad.

Almost all the members of this high-achieving, fun-loving, and somewhat innocent first-year class are looking toward the coming year at CC with eager anticipation—and a little bit of anxiety. College life promises new experiences, new freedom, new friends—but it also presents challenges and obstacles to be met and overcome. Cromwell's pleasant, homey atmosphere, however, soon sets the entering students at ease. Everyone seems to know everyone else, and although a certain cliquishness can be detected in, for example, the dining hall seating arrangements, CC appears to be a fairly close-knit community. This sense of openness and inclusiveness is emblemized by the college's Latin motto, *Veritas et communitas* (Truth and community).

There are, of course, a few cynics who see the dark side of life at a school like Cromwell College. All may not be as cozy as it seems, they suggest. The size of the student body can encourage a sense of community, but it can also lead to social claustrophobia and a quest for conformity. Close faculty-student contact can generate meaningful intellectual exchanges, but it can also stifle individual independence and creativity. Moreover, when everyone knows everyone else, the cynics say, it becomes impossible to avoid discovering things you'd rather not find out. Unpleasant confrontations and disturbing encounters simply cannot be side-stepped.

The cynics may, in part, be right. When something happens at CC, when unforeseen circumstances ruffle the school's ordinarily placid existence, students cannot help but be drawn into the situation. They are inevitably involved and inevitably must take a stand. They may find themselves in sharp disagreement with roommates, classmates, professors, and friends—and these disagreements can sometimes escalate into all-out battles.

So this year's entering students will discover in the unusually turbulent semester ahead. In the narratives that follow, we will explore the reactions of the Cromwell community to a series of events that will trigger anger, anguish, resentment, and recriminations—and that perhaps, in the end, will lead to a new level of awareness and understanding throughout the college.

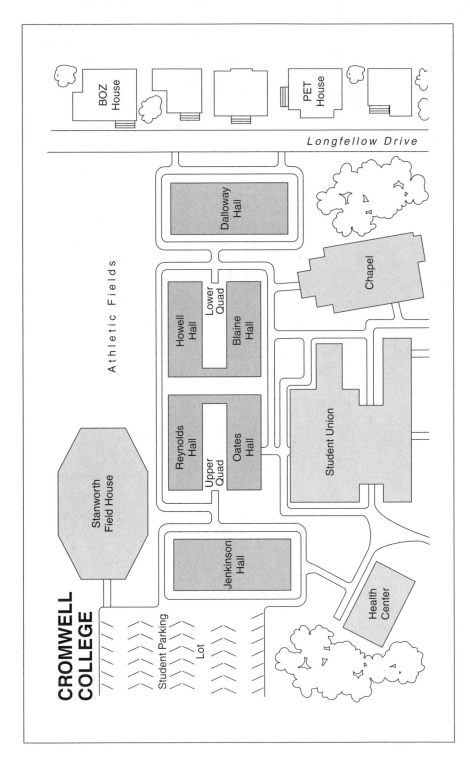

CROMWELL COLLEGE

BOZ House

PET House

Longfellow Drive

Dalloway Hall

Chapel

Athletic Fields

Howell Hall

Lower Quad

Blaine Hall

Reynolds Hall

Upper Quad

Oates Hall

Student Union

Stanworth Field House

Jenkinson Hall

Health Center

Student Parking Lot

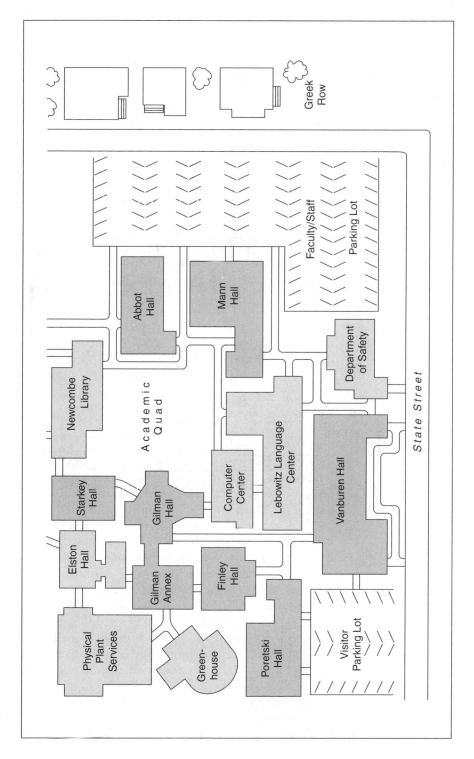

Greek Row

Faculty/Staff Parking Lot

Abbot Hall

Mann Hall

Department of Safety

Newcombe Library

Academic Quad

Starkey Hall

Gilman Hall

Computer Center

Lebowitz Language Center

Vanburen Hall

Elston Hall

Gilman Annex

Finley Hall

Physical Plant Services

Green-house

Poretski Hall

Visitor Parking Lot

State Street

CASE 1

Getting to Know You
Disability and Discriminatory Harassment

As part of its attempt to increase the diversity of the student body, the administration of Cromwell College has recently begun to pay greater attention to the plight of disabled students, and a number of campus initiatives have been undertaken to make CC a more welcoming environment for those who are wheelchair-users, visually impaired, hearing impaired, or otherwise physically challenged. As the community outside the walls of Cromwell has learned of the attempts the college is making to create a more accessible campus, applications from disabled students have increased dramatically. This has resulted in the inclusion of a number of physically challenged students in this year's entering class.

Among this group is Gregory Cervenko, a young man who was seriously injured in a car accident three years ago and who subsequently had to have one of his legs amputated above the knee. Greg required multiple operations, several intermittent hospital stays, and many long hours of physical therapy to physically adjust to an artificial leg. In the process, he lost much of his sophomore year of high school, but since he was already one grade ahead of his age group and was a gifted student, catching up academically was not a problem.

Social adjustment, however, posed many difficulties. Even before the accident, Greg had never been a popular student. Although his short, slight frame made him physically nonthreatening, his biting and sarcastic comments had brought many classmates to the breaking point. He was cynical and pessimistic about the world and reserved a particular bitterness for his peers, whom he believed to be generally shallow and stupid.

After his amputation, Greg's view of the world was even more bleak and his behavior toward others became more nasty every day. The nurses who cared for Greg during his several hospital stays tried their best to remain cheerful and professional with him, but their habitual calm was sometimes shattered by Greg's brutal remarks as he criticized everything from their physical appearance to their medical ability. When Greg returned to his high school classes using a cane to help him walk, his classmates soon began to fear his frequent outbursts of rage and resentment.

As much as possible, Greg's parents and teachers tried to excuse his verbal abusiveness, arguing that losing a limb would, of course, be a tragic and traumatic event in anyone's life, especially that of a sensitive fifteen-year-old. Greg's peers tried to be sympathetic, but they remembered that he had always been a nasty character and saw his current behavior as just a slightly more extreme version of the Greg they had known and loathed. No one, however, wanted to criticize him openly—they were all afraid that they would be perceived as being insensitive to Greg's situation as a physically challenged individual. Instead, they silently suffered his presence until graduation, and then breathed a collective sigh of relief after learning that he'd be leaving town to attend Cromwell College.

Upon being left by his parents at his room in Blaine Hall, one of Greg's first actions was to wander down the hallway in search of fellow students. This was not due to any newfound sociability on his part; Greg's negative attitude toward his peers had not abated. He was, however, feeling abandoned and insecure, and the only way that he knew to release such feelings was through verbal invective. What he was looking for was someone to insult. It didn't take him long to find a target—just two rooms away, an open door gave him a full view of a young man sprawled on the floor, awkwardly attempting to hook up his desktop computer system. Greg stuck his head in the doorway and sneered at the struggling student, thumping his cane on the floor to get his hallmate's attention.

"Yes?" said the young man, sitting up and looking at Greg while trying to untangle a knot of wires. "Can I help you?"

"What makes you think I need help?" demanded Greg. "Just because I'm a cripple? Looks to me like *you're* the one who needs help. I can't believe you can't figure out how to hook that thing up. What would you do if you had a *real* computer, not just a rinky-dink setup like that one? Where'd you get it, Bubba? Comp-Mart? Or did you order it from the back of a cereal box?"

"Hey!" interjected the young man. "My name isn't Bubba, it's Frank McFarland. And this may not be the fanciest computer in the world, but it's all I could afford and it works pretty well. I was having problems getting it hooked up, but I think I've just about got it now. Anyway, I certainly didn't mean to make you feel like you need help, because of your condition or anything else. I was just wondering what you were doing standing in my doorway."

"Do you have a problem with someone in my 'condition,' as you put it, standing in your doorway?" asked Greg.

"No," Frank replied, "I have a problem with anyone I don't know standing there and staring down at me."

"Okay, my name is Greg. I live down the hall from you. I have an artificial leg. Now you know me. You still have a problem with me standing here?"

"Well, it would probably be more comfortable if you would come in and sit down," offered Frank.

"Look, just because I use a cane doesn't mean I need to sit down all the time. I don't like being patronized, especially by an incompetent klutz like you."

"Sorry. I didn't mean to sound patronizing," Frank apologized, as he stood up and walked over to Greg. "I just thought we could talk more easily if we were in the room together, at more or less the same eye level."

"What makes you think I want to talk to you?" Greg asked. "Given your inability to figure out a ridiculously simple wiring scheme, you couldn't have enough intelligence to contribute a whole lot to a conversation. How did you get into Cromwell, anyway?"

Frank shrugged. "Same way you did, I guess—grades, test scores, recommendations, extracurricular activities, the usual stuff. Fortunately for me, the application didn't include any tests of mechanical aptitude."

While Frank was speaking, Greg busied himself by looking around the room. After a moment or two of silence, he pointed at a framed photo on Frank's desk. "Who's that sorry-looking creature? Can't she afford to get a decent haircut? And someone really should tell her about the wonders of electrolysis."

Frank held his breath and counted to ten before he responded, "She's my twin sister. Her name is Florence."

"Florence? That's a *name*? Don't your parents know that it's a city in Italy? I mean, that would be like naming your kid Miami or Chicago or Detroit! No wonder she looks so pathetic in the picture."

"Look," exploded Frank, "I don't mind you putting me down because I can't figure out my computer hookup, but you can't talk about my sister like that."

"Oh? I can't? What are you going to do about it—hit a cripple?"

"Get out of my room!" Frank demanded. "Take your cane, take your artificial leg, and limp on down the hall! Just leave me alone, okay?"

"Hey, wait a minute! I'm not going to let you get away with saying something like that," Greg exclaimed. "It's clearly stated in the Cromwell College discriminatory harassment policy: anyone who uses language that demeans someone else on the basis of race, religious belief, gender, age, sexual orientation, or *disability* is subject to disciplinary action. I made sure before I came here that CC had such a policy, since I knew that I was going to face discrimination because of being disabled. And I was right—I haven't even been here for an hour, and already I'm being abused. I'm going to report you to the dean of students immediately."

"Hang on," said Frank. "I didn't mean to offend you. I just got ticked off because you were being so nasty about my sister. I'm sorry about what I said. I really don't think this is a case of harassment."

"It doesn't matter what you think, or what you meant, or whether you're sorry or not. That's not the point. The point is how you've made me feel—and you've made me feel pretty bad," Greg stated.

"How do you think you've made *me* feel?" Frank asked, but by then, Greg had turned his back on Frank, walked to his own room, and called the office of Sylvia Stevens, Cromwell's dean of students, to report a violation of the campus discriminatory harassment policy.

Some Questions to Consider

Has Frank violated Cromwell's discriminatory harassment policy? (See the appendix for a full statement of the policy.) Does Greg's previous behavior toward Frank in any way justify Frank's response to him? Was Greg in some sense "asking for it," and does that affect the way you view Frank's remark? How do you think the dean of students should deal with this case? What do you think about the very existence of a discriminatory harassment policy at Cromwell? Is it appropriate to limit student speech and behavior in this way?

Thinking Critically

One of the most significant moments in this case is Frank's exhortation to Greg: "Take your cane, take your artificial leg, and limp on down the hall!" In order to determine whether the remark is, as Greg insists, a form of discriminatory harassment, we must look carefully at the underlying significance of Frank's word choice. What, for example, might be the emotional impact of such a verb as "limp"? Would the remark have been interpreted differently had Frank instead chosen the verb "go"? Examine the denotations and connotations of Frank's remark, and explore the ways in which bias may or may not be reflected through his use of specific wording.

Reading Closely

Reread the second paragraph of Cromwell's discriminatory harassment policy. Paying special attention to the phrases "because of" and "the purpose or reasonably foreseeable effect" which appear in the first sentence of the paragraph, assess whether Frank's remark does in fact fit the definition of discriminatory harassment that is provided here.

What If

What if, instead of the "Take your cane, take your artificial leg, and limp on down the hall!" remark, Frank had called Greg a string of un-printable names—vile and vicious names, but without any reference to his disability—and insisted that Greg never enter his room again. Would this constitute a case of discriminatory harassment?

Bringing It Home

Investigate your own college's accommodations for disabled students. Do you think your campus is making an appropriate effort to support the disabled? Why or why not?

Suggestions for Writing

1. Imagine that you are Frank's next-door neighbor, and that you witnessed everything that occurred during his encounter with Greg. Write a note to your resident adviser that conveys your own perception of the events and your opinion about what should be done at this point.

2. Assess the ways in which Cromwell's discriminatory harassment policy does or does not apply to this case. Write a memo to the dean of students with concrete suggestions about the application of the policy to the encounter between Frank and Greg.

3. Are discriminatory harassment policies like Cromwell's a legitimate means to ensure tolerant and civil behavior, or are they an infringement of the right to freedom of speech? Write an essay that argues for or against the presence of such policies on college campuses.

Out Loud

The dean of students has called both Frank and Greg into her office to present their views concerning the conflict between them and to reach a resolution together. Act out this encounter with a group of three students: one playing the part of the dean, one playing the part of Frank, and one playing the part of Greg.

CASE 2

Flag Day
Race, Rights, and Roommates

PART ONE

When Sondra Johnson decided to attend Cromwell College, her parents were crestfallen, especially her mother. Sondra's mother was an alumna of Hudson University, and she had her heart set on her daughter following in her footsteps and attending her alma mater. Sondra, however, was determined to strike out on her own. As a straight-A student with high standardized test scores, she had numerous college options available to her. After investigating various possibilities, she decided on CC. She felt that it would provide an excellent academic environment, and at the same time, offer a more diverse social milieu than Hudson. The attractive scholarship package CC offered made the college even more appealing. Her mother shook her head every time the subject came up, predicting trouble for Sondra at Cromwell. But both parents knew that their daughter was a strong-willed, sensible, and mature young woman, and so they finally accepted Sondra's choice.

When Sondra moved into her room in the residence hall the evening before orientation, she was dismayed by its size. A one-room double is never an attractive living environment, and when the inhabitants are forced into a space less than 12 ft. × 12 ft., that makes matters even worse. Two roommates would have to be fairly congenial to make this setup work, but Sondra, who thought of herself as being very easy-going, was sure she could get along with just about anyone. She had arrived before her roommate, but was careful not to spread her belongings throughout the empty room. She hadn't brought much with her—just her clothes,

some books, and a few keepsakes from home—so she didn't have a difficult time confining her possessions to her closet and a small bookcase.
After unpacking, she headed to a reception at the student union.

When Sondra returned to her room in Howell Hall a couple of
hours later, it was apparent that her roommate had arrived. The gi-
gantic Confederate flag hanging on the wall caught her attention immediately, as did the elaborately framed photograph on one of the
desks depicting a blonde-haired, blue-eyed young woman in full *Gone
With the Wind* regalia. The only information Sondra knew about her
roommate was her name: Corinne Stanworth. Could the belle in the
photograph be Corinne? Sondra looked down at her own grubby
T-shirt, tattered jeans, and well-worn running shoes. She wasn't exactly
a Scarlett O'Hara look-alike, in more ways than one. Could she stand
to share a tiny cubicle with someone who apparently presented herself
as a flower of southern femininity?

As Sondra's anxiety mounted, she heard footsteps and voices outside the door. The delicate tones and pronounced southern drawl of one
of the speakers led her to believe that it was Corinne; two other voices,
also displaying southern accents, she took to belong to her father and
mother. Indeed, as the door to the room opened, Sondra saw that her sur-
mise was correct. There stood the young woman in the photograph, now
wearing linen shorts instead of the plantation ball gown. She was flanked
by two people who looked so much like her that they had to be her parents. The three newcomers were obviously surprised to see Sondra. They
looked at her speechlessly for several moments before Mr. Stanworth
curtly demanded, "Exactly what do you think you're doing in this room?"

Sondra, a little taken aback herself, responded, "Well, um, I live
here."

"Don't be ridiculous," exclaimed Mr. Stanworth. "You can come
up with a better story than that. If you were thinking of walking off
with my daughter's laptop computer, you should know that its serial
number is on record with the local police department."

Now Sondra was beginning to get angry. "Look," she retorted, "my
parents paid good money for this room, so I'd appreciate it if you
wouldn't treat me like some kind of criminal."

Mr. Stanworth turned on his heels and headed toward the door, announcing his intention of summoning campus security to remove Sondra
from the premises. As he was about to disappear into the hallway, his
daughter caught his arm. "Daddy," she murmured, "do you think it
might be possible that this . . . person . . . is actually my roommate?"

"Of course I'm your roommate," said Sondra testily, turning to face
Corinne directly. "My name is Sondra Johnson, and you must be
Corinne Stanworth."

"Oh, my goodness!" exclaimed Corinne. "She *is* my roommate!"

"Yes, I am," reiterated Sondra, "and I guess we'll both have to make
the best of it."

"I'm sorry if I seem a little surprised," said Corinne, "but I some-how never expected I'd have a roommate who was . . . well, you know, who was . . . ."

"Black?" said Sondra, supplying the unspoken word.

"Well, yes," Corinne admitted.

"There *are* a number of us here at Cromwell, you know," Sondra remarked.

"Yes, I know," said Corinne.

"If I could have foreseen this situation, I wouldn't have been so willing to let you live in a double room," snapped Mr. Stanworth. "I know first-year students aren't supposed to be granted singles, but I'm sure we could have arranged something. I'd be willing to pay twice the usual charge to keep you from having such an unsuitable roommate."

"Oh, Daddy, please don't cause a scene," Corinne pleaded. "I think having a black roommate will be just fine. After all, Ruby has taken care of me since I was a little baby, and I get along wonderfully with her. I'm sure Sondra and I will be able to work things out."

"Well, Corinne," her mother interjected, "if you'd like to spend the night in our room back at the hotel, we certainly wouldn't object."

"No, Mother, I'm better off staying here, so that I can be sure to be on time for orientation tomorrow," insisted Corinne.

After wishing a fond farewell to their daughter, the Stanworth parents reluctantly left. As he walked out the door, Mr. Stanworth turned to give Sondra a few parting words: "You may not know this, girl, but I myself am a Cromwell alumnus. I have many important friends on this campus. And Corinne's older brothers Marshall and Ted are both students here, living right nearby in Blaine Hall. If there's any trouble, they'll know how to handle it." Sondra, stunned at the implied threat and the antiquated attitude, simply stared at Mr. Stanworth.

As soon as the adults were gone, Sondra turned to Corinne and said, "I can already tell that you and I come from very different worlds, but that's no reason why we can't get along as roommates. As long as we're sensitive to each others' feelings, we shouldn't have any serious trouble."

"Oh, yes, I completely agree," Corinne responded. "And you know, I really do like that hip-hop music."

"That's too bad," said Sondra, "because I can't stand it."

"Oh," Corinne murmured. "Well, I hope we can at least agree on the decorating scheme for the room. Do you like the flowered curtains I put up? How about the posters? I have an extra bedspread that matches mine and I'd be happy to lend it to you. I'm sure you've noticed that the lilac color of the spread picks up the lilac in the curtains."

"The curtains and posters are just fine," Sondra responded, "but I don't really need to borrow a bedspread. My great-aunt is almost fin-ished with a blanket she's knitting for me and I'd like to put that on my bed when she's done. Now that you've brought up the decorating, though, there were a couple of things I wanted to ask you. First of all, don't you think the Confederate flag sort of clashes with the purple flowers in the curtains?"

Corinne laughed. "Well, I guess it does. But I'm a Southerner, and I'm proud of it. I just want to let everyone know how I feel about my heritage. You know, my family has been in the South since colonial times."

"Yeah," muttered Sondra, "so has mine—but in a slightly different capacity."

"Well, there's one thing we do have in common: our southern background! So I think the Stars and Bars is something we can both relate to," Corinne happily concluded.

"Think again," said Sondra. "Frankly, I find the Confederate flag offensive and insulting. To me it represents an Old South characterized by plantation slavery, a society in which *your* ancestors were able to get rich and stay that way on the backs of *mine*. To glorify the Confederacy is to validate a vile system of oppression that African-Americans are just beginning to overcome today."

After a few moments of silence, Corinne responded, "Well, I don't quite know what to say. I mean, of course I think slavery was terrible, and if I had been one of those slaveowners I surely would have given my slaves their freedom right away. But there were a lot of good values in the Old South; people knew how to behave like ladies and gentlemen, and there was a lot of chivalry and all that. To me, it's those wonderful traditional values that the Confederate flag represents."

Sondra shook her head in frustration. "Don't you understand? Those genteel manners were only made possible by the use of slave labor to provide leisure and material comforts for the plantation owners. Every time I look at that flag, it reminds me of all my ancestors who died—or, even worse, wished they were dead—just so that some pampered white girl could wear sixteen petticoats. And there's no way I can avoid looking at it—it's too big an object in this small room for me to just ignore. It almost seems like a form of harassment! Don't you see how it could be offensive to me?"

"Not really," said Corinne. "It's a flag, like any other country's flag. You might not like all the customs of France, for example, but would you find a Frenchman's display of the French flag to be insulting? Forgive me, but I think you're just being too quick to take offense. My brother Marshall warned me that I might come across attitudes like yours, and I guess he's right. His fraternity, Beta Omicron Zeta, sometimes flies the Confederate flag in front of their house, and he says a lot of your kind here at CC complain about it. I honestly don't understand why. I mean, you seem to think everything is an expression of racism. Just because some folks—like me, for instance—think that there were some positive values in the Old South doesn't mean that we believe in slavery, and just because we admire the Confederacy and what it stood for doesn't mean we're racists."

"Oh, come on, what do you think the Confederacy stood for, if not racism? Wake up and smell the coffee," Sondra snapped. "Exactly what planet are you living on?"

"I'm not used to being spoken to in such a manner," said Corinne icily. "I thought you were the one who was talking about the necessity of being sensitive to your roommate's feelings just a few minutes ago."

"Yeah, well, I guess I was so overwhelmed by *your* sensitivity toward *my* feelings that I just kind of lost my senses," Sondra retorted.

"That's where you're wrong," Corinne pointed out. "I was not being insensitive in the least. You're just being too thin-skinned and defensive. It's like you've got some kind of chip on your shoulder. Pretty convenient, isn't it: anytime someone does something you don't like, you can just say it's racism. And anytime you can't make it on your own, you can just claim it's because of prejudice or discrimination. It's not like we don't cut you people a lot of breaks, either. I'll bet you only got into Cromwell because of affirmative action. So if I were you, I would just keep quiet and be thankful instead of complaining."

"Excuse me, but I got into CC on my own merits—which is probably more than you can say, since I'll bet your daddy's fat wallet and his being an alumnus didn't exactly hurt your chances. Besides, even if affirmative action had played a role in my case, it would only be fair. Haven't you ever heard of compensatory justice? The idea is that groups of people who have been discriminated against for generations deserve a little extra help to compensate for past wrongs and to get them to a level of equality with the rest of society. In case you hadn't noticed, blacks and whites still aren't playing on a level field, so affirmative action is perfectly appropriate. But that's neither here nor there. It's a waste of my time to try to discuss social policy with a throwback to the 1950s—or 1850s—like you."

At that point, Corinne turned her back and walked out the door. She used the pay phone in the hallway to call her mother and father. They hadn't made it back to the hotel yet, but she left a message with the front desk, imploring her parents to immediately return to Cromwell and pick her up. Right after hanging up the telephone, she went to the lounge on the ground floor to await her rescue.

Some Questions to Consider

Is Sondra justified in her attitude toward the display of the Confederate flag? She comments that it "almost seems like a form of harassment"; could display of the flag be legitimately viewed as a violation of Cromwell's discriminatory harassment policy? (See the appendix for a full statement of the policy.) Does Corinne have the right to express herself through whatever items she chooses to exhibit in her room? Are Corinne's arguments in support of the flag's display convincing? Are any logical fallacies present in her argument? Is Corinne's attitude toward race any different from her father's? How do you feel about each student's behavior during their altercation? How do you feel about Corinne's decision to ask her parents to come pick her up and take her back to the hotel?

PART TWO

Like many other colleges, Cromwell gives its students a range of housing choices: residence halls that are completely coed with men and women assigned to rooms on the same corridor; halls that are coed by floor; and single-sex halls with strict visitation rules. Arthur Larson decided to go with the first option, and he was thus assigned to Howell Hall.

It was the evening before orientation, and people were still moving in, busily organizing their rooms. Art hadn't had much of a chance to meet the other students in the hall yet, aside from a brief hello to Sondra, the woman next door. The walls were thin, though, and Art was already getting to know a lot about his neighbors. On one side were a couple of guys who apparently were very good friends, since they could understand one another simply by communicating in a series of grunts. Lucky for them, since not much more than that could have been heard over the music they were playing on their state-of-the-art sound system.

On the other side was Sondra, who seemed pretty quiet. After she left, Art heard Sondra's roommate Corinne move in with her parents' help. Art came out of his room to introduce himself to Corinne and her family. They greeted him politely, but seemed too busy with interior decorating to chat. Then Corinne and her parents left for dinner and, a while later, Sondra came back to the room. When Corinne and her family returned, Art was able to hear every word of their conversation with Sondra, and when the loud argument erupted between Corinne and Sondra, he was a reluctant earwitness.

"Oh, well," Art murmured to himself, "it's none of my business." When Corinne went downstairs to wait for her parents, he was thankful for the peace and quiet. But by the next morning, the situation apparently had become Art's business. He was awakened at eight o'clock when Victor Barrera, the resident assistant assigned to that section of the residence hall, knocked insistently on his door.

"We need your help," Victor informed Art. "The director of residence life is considering a roommate transfer for your next-door neighbors, and he's asked me to give him some input. We were wondering if you might have seen or heard anything that could help us."

"Gee . . . I don't know . . . I mean . . . I don't think . . . that is . . . ," Art mumbled.

"Look," said Victor, "just get showered and dressed and come down to the lounge as soon as you can. That'll give you some time to clear your head a little, and then we can find a quiet corner to chat. Hear me out, and afterwards, if you don't feel like telling me anything, you don't have to. Okay?"

Art nodded and proceeded to follow his R.A.'s advice. Fifteen minutes later he found himself seated in one of the armchairs in the deserted lounge, while Victor explained the situation.

"There's some complicated stuff going on," he began, "and if you have any information to offer us, we'd really appreciate it. I'll be frank with you, so that you understand why this is such a serious case. Of course, I expect you not to say a word about this to anyone else."

Art wasn't really sure that he wanted to hear what was coming, but he figured that Victor was going to tell him whether he wanted him to or not, so he went ahead and assured him that he would keep his mouth shut.

"Here's the story," Victor began. "About an hour ago Sylvia Stevens, Cromwell's dean of students, got a phone call at her home from Peter Stanworth, a Cromwell alumnus and a major donor to the college. Have you heard of the Stanworth Field House here on campus? Yeah, *that* Stanworth. It's no secret that the Stanworth family millions helped foot the bill for the residence hall renovations that were done this summer, so Dean Stevens was obviously anxious to find out why Mr. Stanworth was calling her so bright and early.

"Well," continued Victor, "Stanworth is apparently very worried about his daughter Corinne, who had been assigned a roommate he describes as 'vicious and vindictive.' Stanworth says his daughter called his hotel in tears last night after being insulted by her roommate, and she's refusing to return to the residence hall until a room transfer can be put into effect.

"Of course, the dean spoke to Sondra Johnson, Corinne's roommate, immediately after getting Stanworth's call. Sondra claims that Stanworth and his daughter are out-and-out racists, and that they want a room transfer just because they can't stand the thought of integrated residence halls. She doesn't think this is a legitimate reason for a roommate change.

"Dean Stevens then handed the case over to the director of residence life. His position is that of course we can't change room assignments based on racial discomfort. However, we do try to be flexible in cases of personality clashes or obvious incompatibility—and I guess we can't discount the perspective of someone as influential as Mr. Stanworth. So we were hoping that, as their next-door neighbor, you might have overheard some of the interchange between Sondra and Corinne last night and could shed some light on the situation."

"Well, I really don't know what to tell you," Art began.

"Oops," Victor interjected, as a sharp beeping sound emitted from his jeans' pocket. "That's my beeper, letting me know that they want me in the residence life office. I have to run now, but you can catch me there anytime this morning. Come by and talk to me after you've had a chance to get some breakfast." With a quick good-bye nod, Victor got up and left the lounge.

Some Questions to Consider

What should Art say to Victor? Is the issue one of racism or simple incompatibility? Does what Art overheard the previous night provide him with enough evidence to reach any conclusions about the situation? Should the financial influence of the Stanworth family have any bearing on how this case is decided? Should the director of residence life approve a room transfer for Corinne? If so, what sort of student should be assigned as her roommate? What sort of student should be assigned as Sondra's roommate?

PART THREE

After a quick breakfast, Art decided that he needed to talk directly to Sondra before going to see Victor in the residence life office. He returned to his hall and knocked on his neighbor's door. Sondra opened her door a crack and asked, "Who's there?"

"It's me—Art—your next-door neighbor. We met yesterday."

"Oh, of course," said Sondra, throwing the door wide open. "Come on in. How are you doing? Did you get all your stuff moved in okay?"

"Yeah, no problem. How about you? I hear you've been having some roommate trouble."

"Actually, it's the southern belle rooming with me that's having trouble. She apparently doesn't want to live with someone of my complexion. She spent last night in her parents' hotel room, and now she's asked for a room transfer. Part of me agrees that given her attitude, it would be a mistake for us to live together, but the rest of me doesn't want to give in to what I see as a willingness to keep the residence halls segregated if some rich dinosaur of an alumnus wants it that way."

"It's the principle of the thing," Sondra went on to explain. "If it makes Corinne uncomfortable to have a black roommate, that's too bad—maybe a little discomfort would teach her a thing or two. So I'm refusing to change rooms, and I don't think Corinne should be allowed to transfer. She and her family need to face up to the fact that this is the twenty-first century, and black and white students are going to sometimes end up sharing rooms at Cromwell."

"Maybe," said Art, "but it sure doesn't sound like things will be easy for either of you."

"Hey," Sondra replied, "isn't college supposed to be a challenge?"

Art nodded, smiled, and told Sondra he'd see her later. Then he walked over to the student union, where the residence life office was housed. He was unsure of what he would say to Victor, and as he entered the building still considering the issue, he noticed Corinne sitting on a sofa in the student union lobby.

"Hi," said Art as he approached her. "Remember me? I'm Art, your next-door neighbor."

"Oh, hello," said Corinne. "I do remember you. But I'm not sure we're going to be neighbors after all. I've requested a room transfer."

"Really? How come? I thought your room looked okay—certainly no worse than any of the others."

Corinne sighed. "It's not the room that's the problem, it's my roommate, Sondra. Have you met her? I honestly did my best to be friendly to her—I even offered to let her use my extra bedspread—but she just turned on me and lashed out. I don't think we'll ever be able to get along, so I've told the director of residence life that because of our incompatibility, I need another room assignment. He's thinking about it, and said he'd let me know sometime later this morning. That's why I'm waiting here."

"Well, good luck," said Art. Then he crossed the lobby and headed for the residence life office. As he walked through the door, he saw Victor sitting on one of the administrative assistant's desks, while a somewhat irritated young woman urged him to get out of her way and stop bothering her.

"Okay," said Victor, "I'll go. Anyway, here's the person I've been waiting for." He asked Art to come with him to a little alcove around the corner where they could talk comfortably.

"I don't know how useful I can be to you," said Art to Victor, "but I do have a few thoughts on the situation. Given what I heard last night, it does seem to me that race may be a factor. Sondra and Corinne do appear to be incompatible, but it's possible that the incompatibility is based on Corinne's reaction to Sondra's being black. Corinne's father is about as racist as they come; his daughter certainly isn't as blatant about it as he is, but I don't think she's used to dealing with blacks as peers and she may perceive Sondra's strong character as threatening.

"I don't think Sondra likes Corinne any more than Corinne likes Sondra," Art continued, "but Sondra thinks there's a principle at stake. She doesn't want to make it easy for Corinne by going along with a room transfer, and I guess she's willing to put up with a lot of unpleasantness for the sake of racial progress." Art then proceeded to support his interpretation of the situation by providing Victor with a synopsis of relevant statements made by Sondra and Corinne the previous night and that morning.

After listening to Art's account, Victor sighed and said, "It's sort of a no-win situation: give in to Corinne's request for a room transfer and you look like you're supporting racism, not to mention playing favorites based on her father's position as a major donor to the college; force the two to room together, and you're setting Sondra up for a lot of abuse. But the bottom line is that transfers have been allowed in cases of incompatible personalities—and as you've said, we certainly seem to have serious incompatibility here, whatever the underlying reasons may be. I don't know what the director of residence life is going to do, but I'm sure he'll appreciate hearing your perspective. I'll try to pass it on to him as clearly as I can."

After Art left the student union, he headed for the orientation activities that were scheduled to begin shortly. After the first round of activities and a half-hour spent checking out the location of various classroom buildings, he decided to make a brief stop back at his room before going to lunch. As he was crossing the Lower Quad, he ran into his R.A. "What finally happened with my next-door neighbors?" inquired Art. "Did the director of residence life reach a decision?"

Victor nodded. "It was a tough call," he replied, "but he finally came to the conclusion that Sondra and Corinne were never going to be able to live together amicably. He's moved Corinne to a room in Reynolds, the all-female residence hall, with a roommate from Brooklyn. Corinne will probably hate living with a Yankee, but I guess she'll appreciate the fact that at least she's white. Sondra is staying in her assigned room, with a new roommate, an international student from Martinique. Odette, Sondra's new roommate, has already moved most of her stuff into the room."

"Is Sondra satisfied with this solution?" Art asked.

Victor shook his head as he replied, "Not entirely. I just spoke to her a few minutes ago. She likes Odette, but she claims that by moving Corinne into a room with another white student and assigning a black student to be Sondra's new roommate, we're—as she put it—'ghettoizing' the residence halls. She says we're supporting the Stanworth family's racist attitudes and that we're doing so just because of the Stanworth money.

"I know the director of residence life was worried that Sondra might have this reaction, but he felt that such an arrangement would be in Sondra's best interest, protecting her from the possibility of racial abuse or insensitivity. I explained this to Sondra and she replied that it was patronizing to think that she needed to be protected. I don't think her anger will last too long, though. In the long run I think she'll simply resign herself to the situation and make the best of it—she seems to be a pretty upbeat and flexible person in general."

Upon hearing this news, Art decided to go back to the hall and try to make his neighbors feel welcome. As he climbed up the stairs, he heard screams. When he reached the second floor, he was confronted by a disturbing scene. Sondra was shouting, and another black woman, who turned out to be her new roommate, was sobbing. The word "NIGGER" had been spray-painted in red below a poster of Harriet Tubman that Sondra had tacked up on the front of her door earlier that morning. Red paint dripped down to the floor and the poster itself had been ripped down the middle.

One of the other hall residents filled Art in on what had happened. Sondra had been helping Odette unpack when she heard some noise at their door. She opened the door just in time to see a young man carrying a can of spray paint dart around the hallway corner and down the stairwell. When she realized that an act of vandalism had been committed, she tried to chase him, but he had disappeared. She hadn't been able to get a good look at him, and no one else had seen him. All she could remember was that he was tall and thin, had curly blond hair—hair that she said looked remarkably like Corinne's short curly locks—and was wearing a blue T-shirt emblazoned with Greek letters. She wasn't sure she would recognize him if she saw him again under different circumstances, but Sondra was furious and felt the need to take some action.

After a few minutes of venting her anger in the hallway, Sondra marched off to Dean Stevens' office to demand that disciplinary proceedings be initiated. She reasoned that her situation, which included written abuse and the destruction of property, constituted a clear and serious violation of Cromwell's policy concerning discriminatory harassment.

In the meantime, Art felt that he needed some lunch, so he went to the dining hall. About twenty minutes after he sat down to eat his grilled cheese sandwich and fries, he heard Sondra talking to some other students at a nearby table. He got up and walked over to them to find out what was going on.

"Well," one of the students at the table was saying, "after all, Sondra, it's only a word. It doesn't have to bother you if you don't let it."

"You don't get it!" said Sondra. "It's not the word itself that's the issue; it's the intention behind it. This act of vandalism was clearly meant to intimidate and harass Odette and me. I'm sure it must have been one of Corinne's brothers who did it—after all, Mr. Stanworth threatened that they'd intervene if his precious daughter didn't get the kid-glove treatment he thought she deserved. The guy I caught a glimpse of did kind of look like Corinne, and he had a fraternity T-shirt on—you know one of Corinne's brothers is a frat member. But Dean Stevens doesn't think that's enough evidence to convict anyone. She assured me that the door would be repainted by this afternoon, but I don't see how that's going to resolve anything."

"You'll just have to try to forget it and go on the best you can," one of the other students suggested. "Whoever it was has probably gotten it out of his system. CC really isn't a racist campus, and I don't think you'll have any more problems."

"How can you say CC isn't racist after what's just happened?" someone else angrily interjected.

"Racist or not," Sondra concluded, "I'm not sure there's much more I can do about it. I've talked to the dean, but I don't see any other options. I guess I'll simply have to stick it out, and prove to those jerks that they can't scare me away. I made the decision to come to Cromwell, and here I stay."

The discussion continued, but Art suddenly realized he was late for a crucial placement test to find out whether or not he'd be exempted from Cromwell's mathematics requirement. As he dashed to Gilman Hall, he realized that math was just about the last thing on his mind.

Some Questions to Consider

Do you agree with Art's assessment of the situation between Sondra and Corinne? Has he provided Victor with an objective analysis? How do you feel about the decision to transfer Corinne to another residence hall, and to move Odette in with Sondra? What do you think about Sondra's dissatisfaction with this solution, and her initial insistence that she and Corinne should remain as roommates? Can you think of any alternative solutions? What should be done about the vandalism to Sondra and Odette's door, given the fact that no one can precisely identify the perpetrator? Is there anything further that anyone could or should do to follow up on the situation?

Thinking Critically

In her lunchtime discussion with her friends, Sondra expresses the belief that one of Corinne's brothers is guilty of the vandalism to her door. What evidence does she offer to support this conclusion? Is her evidence convincing? She is the only one who saw the perpetrator, albeit fleetingly; is she a credible eyewitness or might her personal involvement in the case affect her perceptions? Assess the credibility of Sondra's arguments for the identity of the perpetrator.

Reading Closely

One of Sondra's friends, in urging her not to become too upset about the vandalism incident, remarks that "it's only a word. It doesn't have to bother you if you don't let it." Is the epithet "nigger" really "only a word"? What are its connotations, historically and today? Does its meaning vary depending on who says it, to whom, and in what context? Is there a difference between speaking it and writing it? Does it matter whether it is uttered in private conversation, or written in a public and visible location? Would it be a violation of Cromwell's discriminatory harassment policy to use this word in *any* situation?

What If

What if Sondra, upon entering her room and seeing the Confederate flag hanging there, had removed the flag from the wall, folded it neatly, and placed it on Corinne's bed? Would that have been a violation of Corinne's rights? What if Corinne, instead of hanging a large, visually unavoidable Confederate flag on the wall, had instead affixed a small Confederate flag sticker to a notebook that she placed on top of her desk? Would it be legitimate for Sondra to object to this?

Connecting the Cases

How does Cromwell's discriminatory harassment policy apply to any aspect of this case—for example, to Corinne's display of the Confederate flag, or to the vandalism of Sondra and Odette's door? Is there any difference between the ways in which the policy might be applied here and the ways in which it might be applied to case 1? If there are distinctions, what are they, and on what basis do they rest?

Bringing It Home

Does your own campus have a discriminatory harassment policy? If so, how does it compare to Cromwell's? How would you apply your own campus's policy to a case such as this one?

Suggestions for Writing

1. Write a memo to the director of residence life, evaluating his decision regarding Sondra and Corinne's rooming situation and explaining whether you think he should take any further action in the case.

2. Imagine that you are a student journalist working for the Cromwell campus newspaper. Write a news article that objectively reports on the incidents presented in this case.

3. Is Corinne's display of the Confederate flag a legitimate exercise of free expression? Is the spray-painting of Sondra and Odette's door a legitimate exercise of free expression? Write an essay that analyzes the similarities and differences between these two actions.

Out Loud

The dean of students decides to charge Corinne's brother, Marshall Stanworth, with the vandalism to Sondra and Odette's door. You are serving *either* as Marshall's student advocate *or* as Sondra's during a campus disciplinary hearing. Make an opening statement that presents your point of view.

CASE 3

Cult Following
Religious Freedom on Campus

Dorothy Vogel stared out the window at the heavy downpour that had turned Cromwell's Lower Quad into a sea of mud. It had been raining off and on for the past couple of days, and the weather seemed to match Dorothy's mood on this Saturday morning: gray, gloomy, and full of foreboding.

Her first weeks at college had been difficult—much more difficult than she had expected. Dorothy was a slight, shy, and sensitive seventeen-year-old, not particularly confident of her ability to succeed in social situations and embarrassed by her sense that, as her irritating thirteen-year-old brother put it, she "had the looks and personality of a toothpick." But in her small rural high school, surrounded by people she had known since kindergarten, she had managed to overcome her natural hesitancy and reticence. She was thoughtful and intelligent, and so she went on to graduate second in her class with a respectable roster of extracurricular activities.

Dorothy had known that encountering the complexities and challenges of Cromwell College would require her to adapt and grow, but she had felt confident that her academic strengths and her solid sense of priorities would see her through the experience. Her parents, although they were rather lackadaisical in their commitment to organized religion, had instilled in her a strong value system that stressed discipline, self-control, and long-range planning.

Dorothy was set adrift, however, by the uncontrolled, unpredictable environment of a contemporary college campus. In the middle of her first night in Howell Hall, she was awakened by the sound of her roommate, Tama Gould, throwing up all over the floor after having drunk too much beer at a "Welcome to the Ivory Tower" party on CC's Greek Row. What was more disturbing than the late-night vomiting was the fact that the next morning, although she had a splitting headache and a queasy stomach, Tama displayed no signs of remorse. "You don't get as sick if you drink hard liquor. Next time I'll stay away from the beer and go for the vodka," she remarked to Dorothy with a weak grin.

The Cromwell social scene in general seemed to Dorothy to be bewildering at best, terrifying at worst. She attended an orientation party with Tama out of a sense of duty, feeling she shouldn't miss out on any aspect of the college experience, but the tendency of her peers to drink to excess unsettled her, as did the apparent ease with which they explored their sexuality in ways they had not dared to do in their home settings.

Despite these disturbing experiences, Dorothy felt sure she would be on solid ground once classes began. However, she was totally disoriented by her very first class meeting: Introduction to Philosophy, taught by the popular and dynamic Professor Hal Banner. She had enrolled in the class because she was looking forward to expanding her thoughts beyond the limits that had been set for her at Lincoln High School. But Prof. Banner proved to be a bit *too* mind-broadening for Dorothy. In the first fifteen minutes of his opening lecture, he managed to touch on everything from Plato's allegory of the cave to the ethics of human genome research.

Dorothy understood that Prof. Banner was trying to give the class a broad overview of philosophical issues and problems, but by the end of class, her mind was reeling. She remarked to Tama, who was also taking the course, that she didn't know how she would get through the rest of the semester with Prof. Banner.

"Come on, it wasn't that bad," replied Tama.

Dorothy sighed, "Oh, not for you, maybe. But every time I started thinking about one of the points he was making—like that thing about cannibalism and moral relativism—my thoughts would spiral down and then suddenly I would hear his voice coming through to me with some other mind-boggling concept."

Tama laughed. "That's your problem, Dorothy. You're actually thinking about the stuff he says. Big mistake. You'll never get through college, let alone a semester of Intro. Philosophy, unless you learn to turn off your brain."

Dorothy was shocked. "What do you mean, 'turn off your brain'?" she demanded. "Aren't we here to develop our brains further, to explore new areas of interest, to try to solve some of the problems plaguing our world, to . . . ."

"To boldly go where no one has gone before?" interrupted Tama with a giggle. "You don't really believe all that, do you? People come to a college like Cromwell to get away from home, to meet some interesting and attractive people, to have fun, and to get a degree that will provide some kind of credential for employment. For that last item, you need to go through the motions—do some of the required reading, take notes on the lectures, be able to give the teachers what they want on the final exam. But *thinking?* You must be kidding."

Dorothy was puzzled. "Why are you taking a class like Introduction to Philosophy, then?" she asked.

Tama smiled. "Because it satisfies the humanities requirement, it fits into my course schedule, and Prof. Banner is easy on the eyes."

Dorothy found this interchange with Tama to be profoundly depressing; not only did Tama not share Dorothy's idealistic notions about the life of the mind, but she seemed to mock any expression of intellectual curiosity. Even if she had wanted to, Dorothy simply couldn't follow Tama's advice to turn off her brain. She kept thinking about the issues that Prof. Banner raised in his lectures, and these thoughts led to others—about God, life, love, and death. Shy to begin with, she found herself withdrawing more and more into her private speculations.

When Tama brought friends over to their room, Dorothy always found some excuse to go to the library, the student union, or the computer center. She found it increasingly difficult to tolerate their brash and carefree attitude. Dorothy shared her thoughts with no one, convinced that everyone at Cromwell was bent on leading a totally superficial existence.

That is, until she met Lizette West. Lizette had a sort of otherworldly look about her that struck Dorothy the first time she saw her in the Howell Hall laundry room. Lizette had a book open on her lap, but she wasn't looking at it; instead, her eyes were fixed on the mass of purple and red clothing that swirled behind the glass door of the ancient dryer. Lizette's lips moved slowly, and Dorothy could hear an almost imperceptible whisper—something that sounded like a chant or a prayer. Dorothy quickly gathered up her own laundry, sitting clean and wrinkled in a dryer across the room, but afterwards watched for Lizette around campus, intrigued by the perpetual look of tranquillity and transcendence on her face.

It was Lizette who made the first direct contact. She walked up to Dorothy, who was sitting under a tree in the Academic Quad and frowning as she leafed through her Introduction to Philosophy notes in preparation for a test Prof. Banner would be giving later that morning. As Lizette approached, Dorothy glanced up quickly, startled when she saw that she was the object of Lizette's interest.

"Hello, my name is Lizette. I've seen you around campus a lot lately. Is this your first year at Cromwell?"

Dorothy nodded.

"Me too," continued Lizette. "How do you like it here so far?"

Dorothy responded with a shrug—but then suddenly, a torrent of words spilled out about her confusion, her dismay, her horror at the triviality of college life, her sense that no one around her cared about the deep issues, the age-old questions, and the search for truth and meaning that had become increasingly important to her in the last few weeks.

Lizette listened. She didn't laugh at Dorothy; she didn't mock her, or dismiss her, or belittle her the way Tama would have. On the contrary, she gave Dorothy the sense that her concerns were significant and that what she had to say was important. For the first time since her arrival at Cromwell, Dorothy felt appreciated.

Dorothy began to spend more and more time with Lizette, who really seemed to understand her. She discovered that Lizette, in her short time at Cromwell, had already developed a solid network of friends: a group of quiet, ethereal-looking students who generally dressed in red or purple and who greeted one another "in the Spirit of the Cosmos." Lizette's friends readily accepted Dorothy, and together they spent many hours in late-night conversations about chaos, conflict, coherence, the Creator—God, life, love, and death.

Although she was happy at last to have found a group of fellow students who, like her, hungered for a life beyond superficialities, Dorothy wondered about some aspects of the group: the clothes, the ritualized greetings, and so on. Lizette explained that these were just elements that helped to bind them together, sort of like a club, and she suggested that Dorothy might feel more connected to the group if she, too, adopted their mode of dress and other conventions. She was hesitant at first to do this, but in the end she went along. She had always liked red and purple anyway, and had many items in her wardrobe that were the appropriate colors; as for the greetings and other customs, they seemed innocuous enough.

Dorothy had become increasingly distant from Tama, and although they were still roommates, they rarely spoke to one another. One evening, however, Tama came back to the room uncharacteristically early and confronted Dorothy.

"What's going on with you lately?" she demanded. "You spend all your time hanging out with Lizette and her crew, and you've even started wearing the red and purple clothes. You'd better watch your step. Do you know what you're getting yourself into? Have you already officially joined the 'Cosmos Cult'? Do you go to their meetings in the woods behind the health center? Have they done that initiation thing with you, with the crystals and the feathers and the blood?"

"What on earth are you talking about?" asked an incredulous Dorothy.

"Don't tell me you don't know—everyone on campus knows! They're a cult, Dorothy. It all got going three years ago when a couple of the group members who are seniors now had just arrived at Cromwell and thought they had some kind of extraterrestrial encounter in the woods late one Saturday night. They think the 'Creative Force of the Cosmos' is in control of all our lives, and that soon, like next week or something, this Creative Force is going to come to earth in a spaceship and gather up all the believers and carry them to another life on the other side of the universe.

"That's why they wear the red and purple clothes, so they'll stand out in a crowd and the Creative Force will recognize them. Doesn't give you much confidence, does it, if the Creative Force can't recognize the believers unless they're wearing the right outfits! What if he comes when they're in the shower?" Tama mocked.

"Come off it, Tama," Dorothy interjected. "Lizette and her friends aren't a cult. People on this campus just don't understand them because they don't spend all their time partying—they actually think about things."

"They don't think. They follow the party line."

"That's not true," objected Dorothy. "I've heard them have lots of conversations exploring all sorts of possibilities about life and death and stuff. Anyway, they've never pressured me to agree with them, or follow their line, or anything like that. Funny *you* should be concerned about freedom of thought, though—aren't you the same person who told me I should learn to turn off my brain? Lizette and her friends have never said anything like that. Besides, cults are always organized around one dominant leader who controls everyone else. There's no leader here, no authoritarian tyrant."

"Haven't you ever heard of tyranny of the group?" asked Tama. "There doesn't have to be a single all-powerful leader to create a cult. You can have the same effect of total conformity when you have a bunch of lunatics getting together for a sort of communal thought-control."

"Lizette and her friends aren't lunatics, and they don't do thought-control, and they aren't big on conformity—they're probably the greatest nonconformists on this campus."

"So why are you wearing the purple and red clothes?" asked Tama.

"Well, Lizette thought it might make me more part of the group," Dorothy responded.

"Mmhmm. Not big on conformity, huh? Sounds like a cult to me."

"More like a club," replied Dorothy. "You know how the fraternities and sororities all have their matching jackets. This is the same sort of thing."

"You're fooling yourself, Dorothy," said Tama. "You've gotten involved with them because they make you feel accepted, but you're in over your head. You don't really know everything they're up to, and if you'll take my advice, you won't stick around to find out."

"What do you know?" snorted Dorothy. "They may be a little unusual in their dress and their beliefs might sound unorthodox, but that doesn't make them a cult. I admit I've heard them talk about the Creative Force of the Cosmos and the Great Mothership of Life, but is that really so different from people who believe in Jesus Christ and who are waiting for the Second Coming? What makes one set of beliefs a religion, and another set of beliefs a cult?

"There are a lot of groups on this campus, religious ones and otherwise, that have all sorts of customs, rituals, rites of passage, bonding experiences, whatever: everything from the Greek societies to the Gospel Warriors to the Sons of Africa to that group of drama students that wears the weird hats—what do they call themselves?—Theater in the Streets. Do you think all these groups are cults?

"And anyway, whatever Lizette and her friends believe, at least they aren't wasting their lives by getting drunk every other night and having indiscriminate sex. They abstain from drugs and alcohol, they're celibate, they actually study for their classes, and they spend their leisure time in conversation about important subjects. There's nothing cultish about that. It's a much healthier lifestyle than yours—so who are you to put them down?"

Tama shook her head. "It's not just me. Your precious friends have quite a reputation all over this campus. Apparently they meet every Saturday at midnight in the back woods, mumbling their chants to the Creative Force and doing some kind of trance-like dance that's supposed to send vibrations into the heavens. Pretty harmless, I guess, but weird.

"What's not so harmless is that whenever they find someone needy and naive enough to listen to their cosmic nonsense—like you—they latch on to the poor soul and swallow her up into their little 'club,' demanding more and more conformity to their customs and beliefs. When they're sure they've got you hooked, they do this bizarre initiation thing where they cover you in feathers and make you spill some of your own blood—cutting yourself with a knife, for goodness' sake—while they wave crystals over you or something.

"And once you've been initiated, you're stuck; you're always with the other group members, you don't have an existence of your own, and if you change your mind and want to leave the group they make your life miserable," said Tama.

"Sounds like most of the cliques around campus," Dorothy remarked.

"No, Dorothy, this Cosmos stuff is different, more dangerous," Tama insisted. "Haven't you heard about the guy who transferred out of Cromwell last year because after he quit the Cosmos group they tormented him with late-night phone calls, threatening notes, and things like that? There was even a story about it on the local TV news.

"You may not want to listen to me, but I've heard enough stuff about this crowd to really make me worry. I feel like I need to let you know, that it's my responsibility as your roommate and sort-of friend to at least clue you in. Then if you still want to go ahead and mess up your life, I guess that's your prerogative," Tama concluded with a shrug.

"I don't believe a word you're saying," retorted Dorothy. "It's all just a bunch of silly, exaggerated rumors concocted by people who are threatened by the spirituality of Lizette and her friends."

With that, Dorothy stormed out of the room and set off for a long walk across the athletic fields. She didn't return to her room until after midnight. Tama was gone, probably out partying. Dorothy went straight to bed and slept fitfully.

The next day dawned gray and drizzly—the beginning of an extended spell of bad weather. Dorothy got up and dressed quietly, so as not to wake the snoring Tama who lay sprawled, fully clothed, halfway off her bed. Dorothy had instinctively thrown on a red sweatsuit, and just as she started to walk out the door, she wondered if she should change to something else—maybe something blue or green or brown or yellow. But she quickly banished the fleeting thought and trudged across the damp grass to the student union for breakfast, arriving there just as the dining hall doors opened. As she sat down at a table and began to eat her bran flakes with skim milk, she saw Lizette come in.

"I'm glad you're here early," Lizette said as she approached Dorothy's table. "I need to talk to you alone about something important."

Dorothy was surprised to find herself feeling apprehensive. Lizette's presence had never made her nervous before, but after her conversation with Tama about the so-called Cosmos Cult, she found it difficult to maintain her composure. "Sure, have a seat," she said, but avoided making eye contact.

Lizette did not seem to notice Dorothy's discomfort. She leaned across the table and lowered her voice. "I really feel like you've become a part of our group now, Dorothy. You bring so many interesting ideas to our discussions, and you add so much to the group experience. I think it's time to formalize your relationship with us, your connection to the whole. We have a little ceremony we go through whenever someone new joins the group, and I'd like to invite you to celebrate your union with us. We meet in the woods behind the health center every Saturday night—we were hoping you could make this Saturday's gathering a really special one by letting us initiate you as a full Sister of the Cosmos."

Dorothy didn't know what to say. "Um, I'm flattered," she stammered, "but I'm not sure I'm ready for a step like that."

Lizette smiled. "Of course you are," she said softly, putting her hand on Dorothy's arm protectively. "I believe in you. We all believe in you. You're one of us."

"What is the initiation like?" Dorothy asked.

"Well, our meetings always start off with some singing and chanting and with some mystical dances that we find put us into a deeply spiritual state," Lizette explained. "We call on the Creative Force of the

Cosmos to dwell in us and make us pure. Then, when we're doing an initiation, we shower the new sister or brother with feathers to symbolize lightness of heart and spirit, we use crystals to invoke the power of light and clarity, and we ask the initiate to demonstrate a willingness to join with the group."

"How? By doing what?" Dorothy asked.

"Oh, it will come to you. I'm sure you'll think of something to show your dedication and commitment. If not, we'll give you some suggestions," replied Lizette. "We'll expect to see you in the woods at midnight on Saturday." With that, she got up from the table and went to get her breakfast.

Dorothy, too confused and uncomfortable for any further conversation with Lizette, took the opportunity to leave the dining hall. She stumbled back to her room in a daze. Tama was gone, but she had left a note on Dorothy's desk, with the following message:

> I'll be out of town for the next couple of days, visiting my friend Ray. Don't do anything stupid while I'm gone, okay? I mean it, Dorothy. This Cosmos Cult is dangerous! The psychological abuse they dish out is bad enough, but the harm isn't just psychological—it's physical, too. It's fine to be all open-minded about spiritual expression, but when it comes to bodily harm, isn't that a line that shouldn't be crossed? Everyone says that the Cosmos folks make you do some kind of injury to yourself at their initiation, and I think that makes it pretty clear that these are people you need to avoid like the plague. How could you go along with anyone who asks you to hurt yourself? Have some self-respect!

After reading Tama's note, Dorothy collapsed on her bed. It was now Thursday morning—she had just three days before she would be expected to appear at the Saturday night meeting in the woods. Should she go? She thought about what Tama had said, about the possibility that she was being seduced into joining a potentially dangerous cult. Then she thought about how vague Lizette had been when Dorothy had asked her to describe the "dedication and commitment" part of the initiation. She also thought about how happy she had been when Lizette first befriended her, how understood and appreciated she had felt, how deep and meaningful the group's discussions had been, and how wonderful it was to be a part of something. Would this give her the support system she needed to survive at Cromwell? Should she solidify her standing with Lizette and her friends, become a Sister of the Cosmos, and forge a new identity for herself?

Dorothy proceeded to do something very out of character: she skipped all her classes for the next two days. Aside from occasional breaks to grab some food from the dining hall—never lingering for more than a few minutes in order to avoid any encounters with Lizette and her friends—she stayed in her room, staring out the window at the rain, trying to figure out who she was, who she could be, and what she should do.

Some Questions to Consider

Has Dorothy's exposure to, and frustration with, students like Tama somehow driven her to associate with Lizette's group? Do you agree with Tama's perception that Lizette and her friends constitute a cult? Is Tama a trustworthy source regarding the "Cosmos Cult"? Why or why not? What do you think about Dorothy's comparisons between Lizette's group and other campus groups? How do you draw the line between club and cult? According to Cromwell's hazing policy, could the Cosmos initiation procedure be viewed as a form of hazing? (See the appendix for a full statement of the policy.) Given the rumors circulating about the "Cosmos Cult," should there be any administrative intervention into the activities of Lizette and her friends, or should they be left free to pursue their own form of spirituality? At what point does the need to protect students outweigh their freedom of religious or spiritual expression?

Thinking Critically

In determining whether or not Lizette and her friends actually constitute a cult, one of the most problematic issues is the definition of the word "cult" itself. To what extent is this word ambiguous? To what extent are our definitions of the word instrumental in our assessment of the group? Given what Tama and Dorothy each say about their perceptions of the Cosmos group, how do you think each of them would define the word "cult"? What role might prior assumptions play in their understanding of the word "cult" and consequently in their approach to Lizette and her friends?

Reading Closely

In her brief note to Dorothy, Tama does not have the time to present a fully supported argument; her reasoning is somewhat sketchy and underdeveloped. It is clear, however, that she is particularly disturbed by the possibility of self-inflicted injury in the Cosmos initiation process. Why do you think Tama finds this to be such a crucial point? Does she give us any hints or suggestions in her note that could help us to understand her position more fully?

What If

What if, instead of a belief in extraterrestrial salvation, Lizette and her friends espoused some form of a better-known, organized religion: Christianity, Judaism, Islam, Hinduism, Buddhism, Taoism, or any other well-established faith? What if, instead of greeting one another "in the spirit of the Cosmos," they wished one another "a blessed day"; what if, instead of wearing red and purple, they were enjoined to dress modestly and traditionally; what if, instead of an initiation involving crystals, feathers, and blood, they were asked to fast for twenty-four hours to express their commitment to their faith? Would you view this case any differently?

Connecting the Cases

When two very different people come into contact, their existing differences can become exacerbated; they may exaggerate their own positions or take more extreme attitudes in response to one another. Has this occurred in the encounters between Greg and Frank, between Sondra and Corinne, or between Tama and Dorothy? What effect has each individual had on the other? How has the presence of one person shaped or affected the behavior of the other? To what extent is each individual responsible for the responses of the other?

Bringing It Home

Think of an organization on your own campus that includes rituals, uniforms, or other elements stressing group identification. Could this group be considered a cult? Why or why not?

Suggestions for Writing

1. One of your friends from home has asked you whether Cromwell is really "crawling with weirdos." Write a letter responding to this question, given what has been presented in this case concerning the "Cosmos Cult."

2. You have been randomly selected to serve on a committee investigating so-called cults at Cromwell College. Your task is to create a policy that clearly defines what constitutes a cult and that outlines what actions should be taken on the part of the college administration should it be discovered that a cult has formed on the campus. You are also expected to provide a rationale for the proposed policy, explaining why you feel it is appropriate.

3. Dorothy argues that the beliefs of the Cosmos group are not very different from those of "people who believe in Jesus Christ and who are waiting for the Second Coming," and she goes on to ask, "What makes one set of beliefs a religion, and another set of beliefs a cult?" Write an essay in response to Dorothy's question.

Out Loud

Organize a debate with several of your classmates. Designate one group to argue that Lizette and her friends do indeed constitute a cult; designate another group to argue that they are not a cult. Have each group work together to present a well-argued position, and then allow the class as a whole to evaluate the opposing arguments.

CASE 4

BOZ Will Be BOZ
Acquaintance Rape and Responsibility

PART ONE

As they settled into life at Cromwell, many first-year students found themselves focusing on the same concerns that have occupied college students for generations: how to get a date for Saturday night, how to party till you drop and still pass all your classes, and how to dress so that you don't look like a geek. Especially for those students whose schoolwork had not yet become oppressive, social questions often seemed to outstrip academic ones in importance. Many of the young men and women who felt they needed a group identity, as well as those who just thought it was "the thing to do;" focused on Cromwell's Greek societies as the key to success. With the arrival of Rush Week, it seemed like half the campus was talking about "going Greek," or at least planning to attend as many fraternity and sorority parties as possible.

Years ago, Rush Week at Cromwell had been a time of nonstop drunken revelry. Residents of Longfellow Drive, the road adjacent to campus where five of CC's six fraternities and all four of its sororities are housed, had almost become accustomed to finding their mailboxes upended, their trash cans overturned, and their sidewalks strewn with garbage during Rush. They had frequently complained about the vandalism to the fraternity and sorority officers as well as to the college administration but to no avail.

The CC administration had done little to discipline those responsible, even though it arguably had some jurisdiction since the fraternities and sororities rented their houses from the college and thus were located on Cromwell-owned property. For many years, the inability to identify specific perpetrators had resulted in lax enforcement of the rules governing student behavior on college property.

Things began to change, however, when a Cromwell student who was hoping to join CC's chapter of the national fraternity Zeta Omicron Omicron (ZOO) slipped into an alcohol-induced coma as a result of excessive drinking during a Rush function. Friends of this young man claimed that he had been pressured by ZOO brothers to drink more than he wanted to, pressure he succumbed to in his eagerness to be accepted. Although the student eventually returned to consciousness and regained his health (he went on to found Cromwell's Sobriety Society), the incident led to a number of meetings between the college's senior administrators and the officers of the Cromwell Greek Council (CGC), an umbrella organization representing CC's fraternities and sororities.

The upshot of these discussions was an agreement on the part of the CGC to change the nature of Rush in order to reduce the incidence of irresponsible drinking. First of all, a "dry" Rush would be instituted: no alcohol would be served at any official Rush events. Moreover, Rush, which traditionally had occurred during the first week of classes, would be postponed until later in the semester, after incoming students had a chance to get their bearings and become perhaps a bit less impressionable. These modifications were a great comfort to the administration and to the Sobriety Society, as well as to the Cromwell Women's Caucus (CWC), an organization of CC students who had come together to fight harassment of and discrimination against female students, faculty, and staff, including the abuses that sometimes result from alcohol-induced rowdiness.

The dry Rush plan did not prevent the fraternities and sororities from serving alcohol at late-night parties which, although they occurred during Rush Week, were not officially on the Rush schedule—a practice that all of CC's Greek societies engaged in to some extent, thus obeying the letter but not the spirit of the agreement. "After all," one fraternity officer commented when he thought no one of consequence was listening, "all that stuff about brotherhood and leadership is a smokescreen. The main reason guys join frats is the chance to party—you know, get drunk and act like goons. If we didn't offer alcohol-based events during Rush Week, we'd never get any members." Not all fraternity and sorority members agreed with him, but the drinking continued.

This year's Rush had been, in this respect, no different from those of the recent past. After three days of Rush, untold numbers of drunken young men and women had passed out in various locations around campus. Aside from potential pledges, the fraternities had been eagerly welcoming females into their house parties, some of whom planned to join sororities, some of whom planned to become fraternity "Little Sisters," and some of whom were just out for a good time. Angelica Caputo fell into this last category.

Angelica was not the kind of young woman whom you would expect to "go Greek." She cultivated a "bad girl" image that was at odds with the perception most people had of CC's sorority sisters. Although only a first-year student and thus a newcomer to the Cromwell campus, the leather miniskirts, skimpy tops, and stiletto-heeled shoes that were her usual attire had already made her a celebrity. She conveyed the impression of having "been around": eavesdropping on her lunch table chats, a listener would get the idea that she had visited every major European capital; had known (in every possible sense of the word) dozens of famous artists, writers, and musicians; and had danced at half the after-hours clubs in the country.

Angelica had a flair for the dramatic that led her to exaggerate the natural elements of her character to an extent that was sometimes amusing, sometimes maddening, but always attention-getting. It was the sort of pose you either loved or hated. Fifteen minutes after meeting her, most CC students either found her witty, attractive, and engaging, or else thought she was a self-centered slut.

The big surprise came in the classroom, where Angelica kept her flamboyance in check. She'd already turned out to be one of the intellectual stars of this year's entering class, performing particularly well in class discussions and writing assignments. Her standardized test scores confirmed her apparent academic talents: her test results were among the highest of CC's entering students. Her provocative style of dress notwithstanding, Angelica's professors were thrilled that she had chosen to attend Cromwell.

Of course, given Angelica's attire and demeanor and given the proclivities of many male students, the Cromwell men seemed to be more aware of her body than her brains. When she showed up at an "unofficial" Rush Week party at the Beta Omicron Zeta (BOZ) house, the whispered comments had little to do with her intellectual abilities.

BOZ, a fraternity that had a reputation of political conservatism combined with social rowdiness, was famous for its late-night Rush parties. And this year's Wednesday-night bash seemed to exceed everyone's expectations. No one knew just how many kegs the BOZos (as most people called them) had ordered for the "Hump Day" festivities, but the beer was flowing freely. Alcohol was not the only substance being abused: the sweet smell of cannabis filled the air. Most students attending the party had cast their inhibitions to the winds, and the sight of newly formed couples disappearing into the upstairs bedrooms or onto the back patio was not unusual.

It was a little before midnight when partygoers noticed Angelica Caputo entering the house. She was almost immediately surrounded by three BOZ seniors: Marshall Stanworth, Stuart Young, and Lee Kelly. Marshall, son of a wealthy and powerful Cromwell alumnus, was one of BOZ's most influential members; Stuart and Lee were his best friends. When these young men made their interest in Angelica apparent, everyone else gave up any hope of approaching her. As far as the onlookers could tell, the three seniors spared no efforts in supplying Angelica with a steady stream of alcohol, and she was soon visibly tipsy. She talked and giggled with Marshall, Stuart, and Lee, and later, she and the three BOZ seniors disappeared upstairs.

At nine o'clock the next morning, Angelica walked into the office of Sylvia Stevens, Cromwell's dean of students, and demanded an immediate meeting, explaining that it was a matter of some urgency. The dean agreed to see her, and as soon as she sat down, Angelica came straight to the point.

"I've been raped," she said. "Last night three BOZ seniors got me drunk and took advantage of the fact that I was out of control. They took me into an empty storage room in the frat house and in spite of my repeated pleas for them to stop, they all forced me to have sex with them. After a few minutes I lost the strength to struggle. All I could do was hope it would be over quickly. As soon as they finished, I managed to leave the party and get back to my room. It's a good thing I live in Dalloway Hall, right across from the BOZ house; I couldn't have gone much farther. I immediately took a shower to wash their filth off me, and tried to get some sleep. Now I want them brought to justice."

"Have you notified the police?" inquired Dean Stevens.

"No," Angelica replied, "I'm not sure I have much of a case from a police point of view. Since I took a shower as soon as I got to my room, I washed away any physical evidence there might have been. Anyway, even if there had been evidence of intercourse, that wouldn't be enough to establish that I was raped, that the sex was without consent on my part. Although I did try to fight the guys off as forcefully as I could, I don't think there were any signs of the struggle on my body or my clothes."

Angelica continued, "It would help if someone else had seen what was going on, but as far as I know, there weren't any witnesses to what happened in the storeroom. Everyone at the party was pretty much out of it, and even if anyone had seen or heard something, I doubt their testimony would stand up in court—and I know what happens to rape victims when their cases come up for trial. The rapist's defense attorney tries to make it seem like it's the woman's fault, like she asked for it. I know what my reputation is around here because of being somewhat uninhibited in my dress and speech. I don't think I could stand the accusations that would be made against me in court.

"But I expect a better response from the Cromwell administration. Whether or not I file charges with the police, there's no doubt that college rules have been broken. Never mind the fact that BOZ was serving alcohol to minors at a Rush Week function. What I'm really outraged about is the fact that I was forced by three Cromwell seniors to have sex against my will. Doesn't this constitute a blatant case of rape, sexual misconduct, or whatever you want to call it? Isn't it a violation of college regulations?"

"It's true," said the dean, "that Cromwell policy forbids sexual coercion. Our disciplinary code states that if such coercion is proved, it can be dealt with by a range of punishments, including permanent expulsion from the college. You can rest assured that any cases of sexual misconduct that come to our attention will be dealt with seriously. Of course we'll have to investigate your accusation closely, and we'll have to hear what the BOZ men involved say about it. If it comes down to your word against theirs, we'll just have to try our best to reach a clear assessment of the situation."

Angelica nodded. "Yes, I know," she said. "All I want is a chance to state my side of the story." She left with an assurance from Dean Stevens that the matter would be dealt with immediately.

Some Questions to Consider

Given Angelica's version of the facts, has Cromwell's sexual misconduct policy indeed been violated? (See the appendix for a full statement of the policy.) Does her prior behavior, speech, or attire have any bearing on your interpretation of the case? To what extent can she be held responsible for what occurred to her at the BOZ house? To what extent should Marshall, Stuart, and Lee be held responsible? What role do you think alcohol played in this sequence of events? Should the fraternity system as a whole bear some responsibility for violating the spirit of the dry Rush agreement?

PART TWO

Before going to the dean's office on Thursday morning, Angelica had told her roommate, Kira Washington, what had happened the night before. Kira had been fast asleep when Angelica came back from the BOZ house, and so had been unaware that anything was wrong. When she heard Angelica's tale the following morning, she offered to accompany her to the dean's office to make her report, but Angelica preferred to go alone and so Kira headed for breakfast. She recounted to a couple of her friends what Angelica had told her about the previous night's events, and within half an hour—even before Angelica had left Dean Stevens' office—the news was all over campus.

When one of the BOZ brothers told Marshall, Stuart, and Lee what he had heard in the dining hall at breakfast about Angelica reporting them for rape, they laughed and told a story very different from Angelica's. "She was asking for it," all three of them maintained.

"Come on," said Lee, "you know how girls are. They put up a little token resistance, saying no even when they mean yes, just to spice things up. You've seen the way Angelica dresses; the way she talks and acts. It's true that we took her into the storeroom and had sex with her, but so what? Our frat house is private property, isn't it? What goes on there between consenting adults is our own business. After all, there's no doubt that she wanted it."

"Yeah," agreed Stuart, "the way she looked at us, she was practically begging for it. After saying 'No' a couple of times and pushing us away half-heartedly, she just shut up and lay there. I figured she was having as much fun as we were."

Marshall nodded. "If anyone's to blame," he said, "it's her. I mean, I was just trying to get to know some of the freshmen who were interested in the fraternity. I wasn't so into partying and all that. But when this babe came along and started falling all over me—well, I'm a red-blooded American male. What was I supposed to do? I'm sure the administration will see it our way when we explain all the facts. And if it looks like the dean is going to give us any serious trouble, I'll just have my father give her a call. That should straighten things out."

As the BOZ version of the facts became known, it was clear that it would come down to Angelica's word against theirs. Dean Stevens decided that in order to get to the truth of the matter, it would be best to convene a special meeting of the Judicial Advisory Committee (JAC), a group of students and faculty charged with hearing the more complex disciplinary cases. The JAC, which acts under the jurisdiction of the dean of students, would investigate the case and, in the event of a guilty verdict, recommend an appropriate penalty for the dean to approve and enforce.

By late that afternoon the dean had reached the JAC's faculty members and informed them of the particulars concerning the alleged rape. They agreed to move as quickly as possible on the case, and several members suggested the following Monday for the hearing. Philip Wong, a psychology professor who served as the JAC's chair, formalized the hearing date and immediately began contacting potential witnesses.

The JAC consisted of ten members. It included five faculty members appointed by the college provost: Professor Wong, the chair, known across campus for his fairness and his ability to see all sides of an issue; Selena Weil, a young, popular biology professor with a reputation for being liberal in her views; Duncan Connor, an aging mathematics professor who had, for the past ten years, served as faculty adviser for the relatively well-behaved Pi Epsilon Tau fraternity; Tom Sanders, a wise-cracking professor of political science who was best known among students for his anecdotes about his rowdy college days; and Anita Gupta, a newly hired English professor who was relatively unknown on campus. Also serving on the committee were five students randomly chosen from the student body on a case-by-case basis.

By the time Dean Stevens had convened the committee, rumors about Angelica's allegations and the BOZos' denial of those allegations were flying. What had actually happened last night at the BOZ party? Was Angelica really raped? Which students would be selected to serve on the JAC? Who would the committee call to testify at the hearing on Monday? The whole campus was buzzing with questions.

The leaders of the Cromwell Women's Caucus called a special meeting to consider the case, and at the same time, the members of the Cromwell Greek Council met to discuss whether they should respond to the situation in any way. From the language lab to the field house, Angelica and the BOZos were the main topic of conversation. Inevitably, sides were taken and tempers flared. Cromwell's students found themselves forced to think through their positions on a very complex and sensitive issue.

Some Questions to Consider

Is Marshall, Stuart, and Lee's version of the facts credible? Does it affect your perception of Angelica's case? Lee remarks that the BOZ house is the fraternity's private property, but in fact BOZ rents it from the university; does this have any bearing on the case? Given a situation where it's one person's word against another's, what methods could the JAC use to ascertain the truth? Should other students on the Cromwell campus be getting involved in this case? If so, how? What particular students or student groups might have an interest in the outcome of the hearing, and what forms of involvement might be appropriate for them to pursue?

SMALL-GROUP EXERCISE
Group 1 Party Witnesses

Talking It Out

One of your friends talked you into checking out the BOZ Rush scene, and so you ended up at the Hump Day festivities. You'd never seen so many people getting so drunk so quickly, but you restrained yourself.

BOZ bashes tend to draw a big crowd, and this one was no exception. However, Angelica Caputo stood out anywhere she went, and you certainly noticed when she walked in the door. You saw her come in around 11:45 P.M. and watched her, beer cup in hand, talking and laughing with Marshall, Stuart, and Lee. Then all of a sudden she and the three BOZ seniors disappeared. You wondered where they went, but you didn't spend much time thinking about it. That was the last you saw of Angelica, though you thought you caught a glimpse of Marshall, Stuart, and Lee asleep under the entrance hall table when you left the party around 2:00 A.M.

You'd never met the three seniors before the night of the party, and you don't really know Angelica either. She's in one of your classes and you occasionally see her around campus, but you've never said much more to her than "How's it going?" You've heard some of the talk about her sexual exploits—you're not sure how much of it to believe. However, as far as you could tell last night, she seemed to be getting awfully friendly with the three seniors. In fact, now that you think of it, you're sure you saw her willingly accept Marshall stroking her on the cheek, Stuart kissing her on the earlobe, and Lee patting her on the rear end. Sex? Probably. Rape? You can't see how anything could be proven conclusively. After all, it's just Angelica's word against the BOZos, isn't it?

Apparently the college administration is going to make an attempt to reach some kind of ruling. They've convened the Judicial Advisory Committee to hear evidence in the case, and you, like many of the other students present at last night's party, have been called by Prof. Wong to testify at Monday's hearing. You've heard that some of your friends who had also attended last night's party at the BOZ house have been called to testify as well, and you decide to get together to discuss the issues.

Do you really have anything to report that could affect the outcome of the hearings? What did you actually see? What do you actually know? Given what you know, what conclusions, if any, can you draw about Wednesday night's events?

Writing It Out

Prof. Wong asks all the party-going witnesses to submit a brief report outlining their interpretation of the case. He notes, "We'd like to hear exactly what you saw at Wednesday night's party, and what conclusions you draw based on your observations." What will you write in response to this request?

SMALL-GROUP EXERCISE

Group 2 Leaders of the Cromwell Women's Caucus (CWC)

Talking It Out

In your very first week at Cromwell, you had heard rumors that last year at least five cases of acquaintance rape and three cases of physical abuse of women had occurred at CC—and that only one of the victims had reported the occurrence to the college administration. Unfortunately, the one case that was reported, which involved a young man who beat up his girlfriend and broke both her arms, never went anywhere. After filing a complaint with the dean of students, the young woman became confused and changed her story so many times that it was difficult to ascertain exactly what had happened. Meanwhile, the man in question—a BOZ brother—transferred to another college, and the case fizzled out. You decided that you wanted to work to create a climate on campus that would discourage such abuse, so you joined the CWC.

Now the case of Angelica versus the BOZos has erupted. In order to discuss the issue, an emergency meeting of the CWC has been convened. It isn't immediately apparent that the group should jump to Angelica's defense. Some members claim that Angelica's appearance and behavior are demeaning to all women and a provocation to the worst possible actions on the part of men; however, other members contend that true liberation consists in women being free to dress and behave however they choose. "The bottom line," one particularly insistent CWC member maintains, "is that Angelica said no. That makes it rape, and that's all we need to know. We have to give her our support." Other members have called Angelica's veracity into question, asking, "Why should we believe her side of the story?"

When everyone decides that they need a break before continuing with the group discussion, you still aren't sure where you stand, and so you gather in a corner of the room with a few other CWC members to talk through your thoughts. How do you feel about Angelica's accusation of rape? Do you think the CWC should play a role in the case? If so, what position should the group take?

Writing It Out

After much debate, the CWC membership agrees that the organization should present a position paper to the Judicial Advisory Committee concerning Angelica's case. This paper will explain the CWC's view of the case and present relevant evidence to support that view (drawn from everything known about the case, about the participants, and about the context of harassment of women at CC). The paper will also argue for a particular judgment on the part of the JAC, and suggest what action, if any, should be taken regarding the participants in the case. Because of your excellent communication skills you are asked to come up with a rough draft of the position paper for the CWC as a whole to consider. What will you write in response to this request?

SMALL-GROUP EXERCISE

Group 3 Representatives to the Cromwell Greek Council (CGC)

Talking It Out

Before you transferred to Cromwell, you belonged to a Greek society at your previous college which also has a chapter at CC. Your new chapter has chosen you to serve on the CGC, the group of representatives from each of CC's fraternities and sororities that coordinates Greek activities and serves as a liaison between Greeks and the administration. At the first CGC meeting, held two days after the notorious BOZ bash, the CGC president notes that no BOZ representatives are present because they're busy arranging the defense of Marshall, Stuart, and Lee.

Upon hearing this, a representative from Pi Epsilon Tau (PET) exclaims, "Honestly, I've had it up to here with the BOZos. I thought things were bad when the BOZ president was busted for possession of cocaine two years ago. Then there were rumors last year that one of the BOZos had been caught beating up his girlfriend. Headaches like this we don't need, especially with some professors talking about discontinuing college support for Greek organizations. I think the CGC should stay out of this."

"I wish we could just stay out of it," the CGC president replies, "but our campus newspaper has asked us for a statement on the case. So we need to discuss where we stand."

In the ensuing debate, divergent views are aired. Some CGC representatives claim that BOZ presents the worst possible image of Greek life, and that unless the BOZos' actions are condemned, people might think the CGC condones rape. Others contend that a spirit of unity requires all Greeks to stick together, especially since no one has yet been convicted in this case. "The bottom line," one sorority representative maintains, "is that anyone is innocent till proven guilty. For now, we have to give BOZ our support."

When everyone decides they need a break before continuing with the discussion, you still aren't sure where you stand, and so you get together in a corner of the room with a few other CGC members to talk through your thoughts. How do you feel about Angelica's accusation of rape? What do you think of the defense being suggested by Marshall, Stuart, and Lee? Do you think the CGC should take a position? If so, what should it be?

Writing It Out

The CGC eventually agrees that the group must respond to the newspaper's request for a statement. The statement will present the CGC's view of the case, providing relevant evidence to support its view (drawn from everything known about the case, about the participants, and about the context of BOZ's behavior at CC), explaining what conclusions the campus community should reach after considering the facts, and suggesting what action, if any, should be taken regarding the participants. Because of your strong communication skills, you are asked to formulate a rough draft of the statement for the CGC membership to consider. What will you write in response to this request?

SMALL-GROUP EXERCISE

Group 4 Student Members of the Judicial Advisory Committee

Talking It Out

You vaguely remember reading something about the Judicial Advisory Committee in the Cromwell handbook of rules and regulations, but all you can clearly recall is that the committee's student members are randomly chosen from the student body every time a new case comes before the group. You never paid much attention to this procedure or the committee; it seemed like just another part of CC's byzantine system for overseeing student conduct. This afternoon, however, you receive a phone call from the dean of students informing you that your name has been drawn to serve on the JAC. The case you'll be hearing is the one that everyone on campus is talking about: Angelica Caputo versus the BOZ brothers. The dean provides you with a general outline of the case, and closes her conversation by admonishing you to "use the power that has been vested in you wisely, as some very grave matters are at stake."

You wish that you had never been selected for the JAC position. The last thing you want is to get embroiled in a major campus controversy, but there seems to be no escaping the luck of the draw. Well, if you have to serve on the committee, you realize you'd better serve responsibly. You decide to ask the dean who the other student members are, and to caucus with them before the formal hearing begins on Monday in order to share some ideas about the basic facts of the case.

As the five of you gather in a campus lounge early Thursday evening, you begin to sift through what you've heard about Angelica's allegations and the BOZos' responses. The discussion becomes more and more intense. After a good deal of debate and dialogue, you realize that you're just getting more and more confused, and that you need to think through the issues systematically. You know you must consider the following questions: Given what you know about the case, what initial impressions can you draw? Which facts are relevant or significant to the case, and which are extraneous? Do you have enough information on which to base a decision, or are there further matters you need to know? How might you go about gathering additional information?

Writing It Out

One of the other students chosen to serve on the JAC remarks that all the ideas might come together more clearly if they were written out as a sort of pre-hearing summation of the case, outlining exactly what is known at this point and what still remains unclear. Since you're well-known for your strong writing skills, your fellow JAC members turn to you and suggest that you be the one to draw up a draft of this summation, for all of you to examine together. What will you write in response to this request?

PART THREE

Marshall, Stuart, Lee, and Angelica all assumed that no one had actually witnessed what went on after they disappeared upstairs at the BOZ house Wednesday night. In fact, two freshmen—Samir Nasser and Henry Xavier—were in a position to shed some light on the situation.

The two freshmen were roommates, and both were considering joining BOZ. They had made a point of attending the Hump Day party to get a good look at the fraternity's fabled nightlife, and so they found themselves standing together in a corner of BOZ's main party room a little before midnight on Wednesday. They looked around longingly at the more experienced upperclassmen who, one after another, attached themselves to the attractive women who had come to party at BOZ.

"I never had any luck with the ladies in high school, but somehow I thought things would be different when I got to college. I figured that with so many more to choose from, there were bound to be at least one or two who would be interested in me. But as far as I can tell, there isn't a single unattached girl here. I think the juniors and seniors have snapped them all up," Samir lamented.

"Yeah," agreed Henry, "I wish someone really hot would walk in right now." At that very moment Angelica entered, seemingly in answer to his prayer. Before he could make a move toward her, however, she was surrounded by Marshall, Stuart, and Lee.

The two freshmen watched the three seniors eagerly supply Angelica with drink after drink. It seemed to Samir and Henry that Angelica quickly became as much "under the influence" as most of the other partygoers. They watched from a distance as she talked and giggled with the three men. Angelica's every move appeared to the innocent freshmen as an invitation to intimacy. And as far as Samir and Henry could tell, the three BOZ seniors were practically drooling in anticipation.

Marshall, Stuart, and Lee moved off with Angelica, and Samir and Henry caught a glimpse of them making their way upstairs. As if obsessed, the two freshmen followed, and saw Marshall, Stuart, and Lee guide Angelica—who appeared to be moving in an alcoholic haze—into an empty storage room. One of the men slammed the door, and Samir and Henry heard a deadbolt slide shut.

Feeling a bit foolish, Samir and Henry were about to return downstairs when they suddenly heard screams coming from behind the storeroom door. "No! No! Stop! Please stop! I don't want to do this! Leave me alone! Don't touch me!" they heard Angelica cry.

The freshmen didn't know what to do. For what seemed like hours, though in reality it was only a few moments, they felt themselves freeze as they heard Angelica shout "No! No! No!" over and over again.

Just as they had both snapped out of their paralysis and had summoned the courage to break down the door and save her, Angelica's cries ceased and nothing but heavy breathing could be heard coming from the storeroom. Samir and Henry waited outside the door another minute or two, and then—a bit frightened—they left the party.

On the way back to their room in Blaine Hall, they thought about whether or not they should do anything about what they had seen and heard. "Angelica was resisting their advances," argued Samir, "and no matter what she was wearing or how she was behaving beforehand, that makes anything they did to her in the storeroom count as rape. There *is* a policy concerning sexual misconduct here at CC, and I'm sure Marshall, Stuart, and Lee were violating it. Maybe we should report them."

Henry responded, "But she *did* stop protesting after a few minutes, so maybe she changed her mind and decided she didn't object after all."

"Maybe," replied Samir, "or maybe she just collapsed or passed out or something."

"But there's no way we can know which it was," Henry pointed out, "and anyway, if we talk, the BOZos will probably kill us or something. You know all the rumors about them being prone to violence, beating up their girlfriends, and stuff like that. Well, they'll have it in for us pretty bad. I'd like to live a little longer."

Samir nodded in agreement. After a few more minutes of conversation they agreed not to report what they had seen and heard at the BOZ house.

Some Questions to Consider

How does the testimony of Samir and Henry affect your perception of the case? Should they have intervened during the party, making their presence known to the BOZ seniors in order to stop whatever was happening to Angelica? By not intervening, do they bear any culpability for what occurred? Do they have a responsibility to report what they know to someone in authority? What should they do?

SMALL-GROUP EXERCISE

Group 1 Party Witnesses

Talking It Out

The time you had spent at the BOZ party Wednesday night should have been devoted to studying, so in order to catch up with your work, you spend much of Thursday night in the library. Finally you decide you're just too tired to think, so you head back to your residence hall with some friends who had also attended the BOZ party. As you pass Blaine Hall, you hear groans of agony emanating from an open ground floor window. You and your friends peer in and recognize Samir Nasser and Henry

Xavier, two freshmen you know from your classes who appear to be dangerously drunk and who are babbling hysterically about a terrible secret they can't reveal. Coming to the conclusion that Samir and Henry need help, you climb through the window and do your best to sober them up.

Half an hour later, they seem to have regained some measure of equilibrium. They ask you and your friends to sit down and, after swearing you to secrecy, they reveal what they witnessed at the BOZ party. You suggest that they disclose their information to the JAC, but the two freshmen categorically refuse to do so.

"If we testify, we're dead meat," says Henry. "No matter how confidential the JAC hearings are supposed to be, word will get out. Sooner or later the BOZos will know that we were the ones who ratted on them, and they'll do whatever they think is necessary to get back at us—maybe even shutting us up forever."

Samir adds, "You know how the BOZos seem to get away with anything. They'll never get punished in Angelica's case, and then when they come after us, who's going to care?"

If Samir and Henry don't intend to report to the JAC, you wonder why they revealed their observations to you. "We don't dare say anything openly, but we still don't feel right about it," explains Samir. "So we thought we'd feel better if we shared our anxieties with people we consider to be our friends."

"Remember, though," says Henry, "you're sworn to secrecy. If you say anything, it will eventually get out that the information came from us, and then our asses are grass."

After an hour of further discussion, it becomes clear that Samir and Henry won't budge in their decision to keep their observations private. After you leave, you and your friends discuss the situation. Is there anything further you could or should do? Now that you know there is firsthand testimony that could affect the outcome of this case, do you have a responsibility to report it, regardless of your promise to Samir and Henry that you would keep their secret? Are Samir and Henry justified in their fear of the BOZos? Is there any way their testimony could be heard without jeopardizing their safety?

Writing It Out

The next morning you find a memo in your mailbox from Prof. Wong, which concludes as follows: "It has occurred to us that, in the course of the last day or two, further evidence may have emerged concerning events at the BOZ house on Wednesday night. We would like to ask you to supply us with any additional information you may have come across or any further observations you may be able to recall since you submitted your initial report." What will you write in response to this request?

SMALL-GROUP EXERCISE

Group 2 Leaders of the Cromwell Women's Caucus

Talking It Out

On Friday morning you're having breakfast in the dining hall with several other CWC leaders when Lucy Donovan, a first-year student who's an active CWC member, walks over and sits down.

"I was visiting a friend in Blaine Hall last night," Lucy tells the group, "and his next-door neighbors were really noisy—I think they were drunk. After a while some people came over to visit them; we could hear a lot of talking, though we couldn't make out what was being said. Of course I wasn't supposed to be there since Blaine is an all-male residence hall and it was after visiting hours. But anyway, I decided to stay the night. My friend fell asleep. I couldn't—the noise from next door kept me up.

"The room was hot, so I opened the window and the muffled words from next door became clear. From what I overheard, the guys next door were witnesses to Angelica's rape! They saw Marshall, Stuart, and Lee lock her in the storeroom, and they heard her screaming over and over again for the BOZos to stop what they were doing. The two guys swore their friends to secrecy, but they told them the whole story."

After recounting every detail of Samir and Henry's tale, Lucy continues, "The guests took off around 1:00 A.M. Before they left, they tried to convince the guys to report what they knew, but the guys refused. They're afraid that if they testify against the BOZos, they'll get killed. My friend slept through all of this and he's still not up, so you folks are the only ones I've told."

You ask Lucy if she knows her friend's neighbors, and she replies, "Yeah, it's Samir Nasser and Henry Xavier. I know I should report what I heard them say, but then it'll come out that I stayed overnight in my friend's room. I'll get into trouble for breaking the visitation rules, and the dean will probably notify my parents. My folks will kill me if they find out I spent the night in a guy's room! What should I do?"

Before anyone gets a chance to respond, Lucy suddenly realizes she's about to be late for an exam in her American history class and leaves abruptly. Once she is gone, you and your fellow CWC leaders discuss the situation. What should you advise Lucy to do? Should she tell the JAC what she's heard and leave herself open to disciplinary action—and parental dismay? Or should she keep quiet, and pretend that she didn't hear anything? Are there any other options available to her?

Writing It Out

Since Lucy left in such a hurry you didn't get a chance to give her any advice, so you and your fellow CWC-ers decide to write her a note making some recommendations about what action she should take. Someone suggests that you should be the one to come up with a draft of the note, since you—as a fellow first-year student—know Lucy better than any of the others. What will you write in response to this request?

SMALL-GROUP EXERCISE

Group 3 Representatives to the Cromwell Greek Council

Talking It Out

On Friday morning you head to breakfast in your usual groggy state, and as you slowly awaken, you find yourself listening to your dining hall companions rehashing all the gossip about Angelica Caputo. You don't hear anything that isn't old news, so you just keep quiet and finish your third cup of coffee.

After downing about ten times the caffeine, carbohydrates, and cholesterol that a healthy person should eat, you wander toward the exit. As you pass the closed doors of the private dining room, you overhear a heated discussion concerning the alleged rape case, and your curiosity gets the better of you. You suddenly notice that you laced your shoes "incorrectly" this morning and, bending down to relace them, you stop to listen.

A few seconds are enough to reveal that you are eavesdropping on an informal meeting of the student members of the JAC, and that they have come across a startling piece of information: unbeknownst to everyone involved, there are two witnesses to what transpired between Angelica and the BOZ seniors on Wednesday night, and these witnesses have incontrovertible evidence that Angelica expressed strong and prolonged verbal resistance to the advances of Marshall, Stuart, and Lee. The one thing none of the JAC members seems to know, however, is the identity of the two witnesses.

After lacing and relacing both shoes several times, you look around and notice that a few of your fellow CGC members are standing by the doorway as well. You nod to each other and by tacit agreement move together toward one of the private, soundproof study rooms in the student union.

As you sit down to discuss what you've just heard, a couple of important questions come up: Should you warn the BOZos about the evidence against them? Does what you overheard in any way change or affect the statement of the CGC's position that you wrote last night? Together you try to figure out what course of action you should now follow.

Writing It Out

After much discussion among yourselves, you decide to write a joint memo to all CGC representatives, filling them in on what you've heard and on what you propose the CGC should do in light of the current situation. Someone suggests that since you have such a way with words, you should be the one to compose a draft of the memo. What will you write in response to this request?

SMALL-GROUP EXERCISE

Group 4 Student Members of the Judicial Advisory Committee

Talking It Out

On Friday morning you stumble off to breakfast after lying awake much of the previous night worrying about the rape case you've been called upon to adjudicate. As you absently munch your Cocoa Toasties, you mutter to yourself, "Why me? Whatever the JAC decides, half the campus is going to be furious with us."

After you pump your system sufficiently full of sugar and caffeine to get you through the day, you wander out of the dining hall and pick up your backpack, which you've left on the shelves by the door. You suddenly notice a sheet of paper sticking out of your pack's front pocket. Pulling out the paper, you begin reading the following note, which had been printed in anonymous block capitals:

> AS A STUDENT MEMBER OF THE JAC, YOU SHOULD BE MADE AWARE THAT THERE WERE TWO WITNESSES WHO HEARD EXACTLY WHAT TRANSPIRED BETWEEN ANGELICA CAPUTO AND THE THREE SENIORS SHE HAS ACCUSED OF RAPE. THROUGH A SET OF CIRCUMSTANCES I WOULD RATHER NOT DISCLOSE, I BECAME PRIVY TO THE OBSERVATIONS OF THESE WITNESSES. THEY ARE RELUCTANT TO COME FORWARD FOR FEAR OF RETALIATION, BUT BECAUSE THEIR INFORMATION IS SO CRUCIAL, I FEEL CALLED UPON TO REPORT IT.

The note goes on to describe, in precise detail, exactly what Samir and Henry saw and heard, without ever revealing the names of these two witnesses or of your informant.

After you finish reading the note, you realize that this information is clearly significant to the case, but with no names of either the note writer or the alleged witnesses, how can such hearsay evidence be considered? However, can you afford to ignore the information? If such witnesses exist, isn't it your responsibility to bring their testimony into the open?

You decide to immediately get together with your fellow-student members of the JAC to discuss the situation. Luckily, you find all of them eating breakfast at various tables in the dining hall, and you quickly persuade them to join you in the private dining room. On the way there, they stop to pick up their belongings from the front shelves and discover that each one has received an anonymous note identical to yours. Together you try to figure out what course of action you should now follow.

Writing It Out

After much discussion among yourselves, you together decide to write a joint memo to the JAC faculty members, filling them in on what you have learned from the anonymous notes and on what you propose the JAC should do in light of the current situation. Someone suggests that since you seem to know what you're talking about, you should be the one to come up with a draft of the memo. What will you write in response to this request?

PART FOUR

It sometimes seems that if anyone at Cromwell College so much as sneezes, the whole campus knows about it within minutes. Rumors certainly moved quickly in the case of Angelica versus the BOZos. By Friday night, it seemed that everyone had heard everything that had transpired in Dean Stevens' office on Thursday: what Angelica said, what the BOZos said, and what the dean herself said. Even the identity of the student members of the JAC, usually a closely guarded secret, had become public knowledge. No one could pin down the source of this information, though many speculated that word first got out through one of the more talkative faculty members of the JAC who had received a detailed briefing on the case from the dean. In any case, both Angelica and the BOZ seniors, along with the rest of the CC community, got wind of the claims made by each side, and worked hard all weekend to arrange their strategies accordingly.

Indeed, the past couple of days had been very busy ones for all the students, faculty, and administrators at CC who were involved with the alleged rape case. A number of students who had attended the BOZ Hump Day party had been called to testify at Monday afternoon's hearing, and they'd been busy preparing a couple of pre-hearing reports that the JAC requested, setting out their testimony in written form. The Cromwell Women's Caucus had been busy preparing a position paper which they submitted to the JAC, arguing for their own interpretation of the case, and they also had been advising a potential witness. The Cromwell Greek Council had been busy coming up with a statement for the Monday morning edition of *The Cromwell Clarion*, CC's student newspaper, explaining their position on the matter, and they'd had a couple of meetings over the weekend to clarify their approach to the situation. And the members of the JAC had been busy organizing their own thoughts before beginning the hearing.

Marshall, Stuart, and Lee had, of course, also been hard at work, and they'd enlisted the help of their BOZ brothers in preparing their defense. They planned to call several of their fellow BOZos to serve as character witnesses, and had also asked Duke Schuyler, a computer science professor at CC who's always been a good friend to the men of BOZ, to testify to their good will.

Prof. Schuyler had gladly agreed to perform this service, telling the young men, "Y'all have always seemed like nice boys to me, and I'm sure you wouldn't do anything ungentlemanly. Of course if an attractive girl practically propositions you, I don't expect you to turn her down—and from what I've seen of Angelica Caputo, there's no question in my mind that she'd be a willing participant in just about any wild behavior. But the bottom line is that clean-cut young fellows like you aren't the sort to *rape* a girl. I'd be more than willing to say that to the JAC on Monday. You can count on me!"

The BOZos realized, however, that character witnesses wouldn't be enough to make a strong case, so they'd asked several of their fraternity brothers who had been at the Wednesday night festivities to present testimony supporting their contention that Angelica's behavior earlier in the evening gave every indication that she would welcome intimate relations with the three seniors; and that, moreover, she was too drunk to offer any resistance, thus denying her claim that she fought off the advances of Marshall, Stuart, and Lee.

The three seniors were also considering presenting testimony that they themselves were somewhat "under the influence," and therefore not fully cognizant of their own actions. They knew this argument wouldn't really excuse any infractions of college policy, but they felt that it would win the sympathy of at least one faculty member of the JAC—Prof. Sanders, famous for his stories about his own collegiate drinking sprees—and, perhaps, might also go over well with the student JAC members.

Their star witness, though, was the president of BOZ, Dan Harris, who had sex with Angelica just two days after her arrival on the CC campus. Dan was willing to testify that on that occasion Angelica had initially murmured a few "No's" just as things were getting hot and heavy, but that she then went on to give every possible sign of enjoying herself throughout the rest of the encounter. In support of Dan's testimony, the BOZos also planned to call as witnesses Tama Gould and Yvonne Toufaian, two women who had a conversation with Angelica the day after her encounter with Dan and who heard her say that she had an "exciting" time with him the previous night.

Marshall, Stuart, and Lee felt sure that this precedent would go a long way toward substantiating their story that Angelica's initial resistance was only a token gesture to "spice things up," and that she was, in fact, a willing participant from the beginning. The three BOZ seniors anticipated that opposing testimony would be presented by Angelica and her supporters, but they felt confident that their own witnesses could shake her case enough to prevent the JAC from coming to a clear conclusion.

Angelica, in the meantime, had been equally busy. In preparation of her case, she had focused on the uncontested fact that she said "No." Of course she had already told Dean Stevens that she had done more than merely saying "No"; she had struggled with the men physically until she ran out of strength. But no one else besides Marshall, Stuart, and Lee was actually in the storeroom to witness her physical resistance and there were no signs of struggle on her clothing or her body, which made it difficult for her to substantiate this point. However, there was no question that she did indeed say "No;" even the three BOZos admitted this.

Angelica fully expected them to contend that her refusal was just a coy come-on, but she planned to argue that when a woman tells a man to leave her alone, he has no right to interpret her response in any way other than at its face value. That holds true, she would argue, whether she's drunk, whether she's naked, whether she has the reputation for being "loose," even whether she's previously had sex with the same man willingly. When she says "No," that's the end of the story. Anything that happens after that is rape. As she had remarked to one of her friends, "You shouldn't have to break a guy's arm to let him know you're not interested."

Given this line of reasoning, and going against the advice of some of her friends, Angelica did not intend to call any additional witnesses. The BOZos, she argued, were the best possible witnesses in support of her case, having already incriminated themselves in their admission to the dean that Angelica did initially express verbal resistance.

After the effort and anxiety involved in the preliminary preparations, all parties seemed almost relieved when Monday afternoon rolled around and the hearing began. This was to be a closed hearing, conducted in the strictest secrecy. The music classroom in Abbot Hall where the hearing was being held was completely soundproof. The only individuals who would be in continuous attendance were the members of the JAC, Angelica, and the three BOZos. Witnesses were being sequestered in classrooms down the hall, and would be brought in only when the time had come for them to testify.

Prof. Wong opened the hearing with a reference to the campus-wide excitement the case had generated. "What we decide here today will be examined closely by all members of the CC community," he explained, "and therefore it is incumbent upon us to act as thoughtfully as possible." As proof of the widespread interest in the case, he cited the CWC position paper and the statement made by the CGC in the pages of the *Clarion*. "Although we cannot allow such documents to influence our findings," Prof. Wong said, "we will certainly think carefully about the issues they raise as we engage in our deliberations on the case." He went on to also express his appreciation to the bystanders at the party who had submitted pre-hearing reports to the JAC. "Having their thoughts in writing beforehand will, we hope, enable us to conduct this hearing efficiently and effectively," he said.

After this preamble, the official business of the hearing began. Angelica, as the complainant, was allowed to be the first to state her case, and this she did with all the eloquence she could muster, following the strategy she had worked out over the weekend. When Angelica had completed her presentation, the JAC members asked her several questions for clarification, but no new evidence came to light.

The BOZos then countered with their defense, calling their character witnesses and a few of the Wednesday night BOZ partygoers as well as Dan, Tama, and Yvonne. Once again, the JAC followed up with additional questions and, once again, nothing further was uncovered.

The JAC then called several additional witnesses, including the students Prof. Wong had initially contacted who had been present at the BOZ party. Each of these witnesses stated precisely what they observed, including any specific behavior on the part of Angelica and the BOZos that may have had some bearing on the case. Several witnesses noted that before disappearing with Marshall, Stuart, and Lee, Angelica seemed to be willingly accepting such physical attentions from the three men as strokes on her cheek, kisses on her earlobe, and pats on her rear end.

All was going as Angelica and the BOZos had expected, until Samir and Henry were brought into the room upon Prof. Wong's request. In spite of their initial reluctance to come forward, the two freshmen had finally been persuaded to testify, though no one at the hearing knew exactly what caused this change. As they related what they saw and heard Wednesday night, Angelica thought to herself, "Well, I had a strong case without them and they really aren't adding anything new, but their testimony about the vehemence of my verbal resistance can't do anything but help my argument."

Marshall, Stuart, and Lee, in the meantime, had begun to whisper among themselves. Although they thought no one could hear them, their voices were louder than they realized, and a couple of the student members of the JAC were close enough to pick up most of what they were saying.

"This is great," Marshall began, "because they're supporting what we said about Angelica really coming on to us when we were downstairs, about her being drunk, and about us being drunk."

"Yeah," replied Stuart, "but it makes it sound like she did more than just say 'No' a couple of times. Did she really yell at us over and over again? I was too drunk to know . . . but anyway, I don't think things are looking too good for us."

"Oh, don't be such a pessimist," Lee snapped. "Sanders will vote to acquit us because he partied his way through college. Connor will vote to acquit us because even though he's the adviser for those PET wimps, he supports a strong Greek system and won't want to do anything to give any Greek organization a bad name. The five students will vote to acquit us because no one's going to mess with BOZos. Weil, that flaming liberal, will probably vote against us. It's anyone's guess where Gupta stands, but I've heard from a couple of her students that she's a real stick-in-the-mud, so I figure she'll probably vote against us, too. Wong looks like he isn't getting any, so he'll vote against us out of jealousy. But that's still seven to three in our favor! So buck up, okay?"

Stuart, shaking his head glumly, muttered, "I hope you're right, Lee, I really hope you are, but I'm not so sure. . . . "

"Jeez, Stuart, stop being such a dweeb," said Marshall. Prof. Wong targeted a dirty look in the BOZos' direction and started to lecture them on disturbing the proceedings.

Samir and Henry were, apparently, the last witnesses to testify. Once they completed recounting their story, both Angelica and the BOZos were given an opportunity to sum up their cases. Marshall, who served as spokesman for the BOZos, reiterated the points he and his co-defendants had presented concerning Angelica's background and past sexual experiences. He ended by proclaiming, "Did she really mean 'No,' or was she just teasing us? It all comes down to our word against hers. All of us here know what kind of a girl Angelica Caputo is. How can you believe anything she says? You also know what kind of guys we are: as staunch supports of the Greek system, we've been the mainstay of this campus's social life, and as proud members of BOZ, we've been an integral part of the Cromwell community for over three years. If you find us guilty of sexual misconduct, you'll just be giving carte blanche to every woman on this campus to cry rape whenever she feels like it!"

Angelica underscored her contention that her verbal resistance, corroborated by Samir and Henry, in itself rendered the situation an unquestionable case of rape. "For too long," she concluded, "Cromwell has been willing to stand by while the women of our campus are abused and harassed. It's time to resist such demeaning, degrading, and despicable behavior. I call upon you to find the BOZos guilty, and to punish them to the full extent that you are able. You must either stand firm in this regard, or else lose all respect as a judicial body. Join the vast majority of colleges and universities across the country and send a clear message that such actions will no longer be tolerated!"

Now the time had come for the members of the JAC to cast their secret ballots to determine the verdict. They asked Angelica, Marshall, Stuart, and Lee to wait down the hall. The faculty members of the committee marked their ballots quickly, as if their minds had already been made up before the conclusion of the hearing. It turned out that Lee indeed guessed correctly in his prediction of their votes: Connor and Sanders advocated acquittal for the BOZos, while Wong, Weil, and Gupta turned in verdicts of guilty. With this split in the ranks, it was now up to the student members of the JAC to decide the final outcome.

CLASS EXERCISE

The students who have been taking the role of JAC members in previous exercises now have the opportunity to vote and decide the verdict.

Some Questions to Consider

Does the testimony of Dan, Tama, and Yvonne affect your perception
of Angelica's case? Does the BOZos' apparent drunkenness during the
party excuse their behavior? Does Angelica's apparent drunkenness
implicate her? Do Marshall, Stuart, and Lee's comments during the
hearing have any bearing on your perception of the case? Has sufficient
evidence been presented for a verdict to be reached? If so, what should
that verdict be? Should any penalties be imposed?

Thinking Critically

Marshall, Stuart, and Lee raised a number of points in their defense:
everything from their contributions to the Cromwell community to
Angelica's previous encounter with Dan to Angelica's character in general. Are there any logical fallacies in their presentation, for example,
ad hominem attacks, slippery slope arguments, or red herrings? What
about in Angelica's final summation of her position? Can you locate instances of emotive language, false dilemma, appeals to common practice, or any other fallacies?

Reading Closely

Cromwell's sexual misconduct policy prohibits students from becoming sexually involved with another person "without the consent of that
person." A clear understanding of the word "consent" is crucial to the
application of this policy. What constitutes consent? How can it be determined whether or not someone has consented to a particular action? Must consent be indicated verbally in order for it to be
unambiguous, or can it be conveyed clearly through body language and
other means? Does lack of objection necessarily imply consent? How
does the issue of Angelica's consent—or lack thereof—affect your interpretation of this case?

What If

What if Angelica had initially provided Marshall, Stuart, and Lee with
clear verbal and physical indications that she was willing to have sexual
intercourse with all three of them—but then, in the course of the activity, changed her mind and conveyed a lack of consent? What if Marshall,
Stuart, and Lee disregarded this reconsideration, and proceeded? Would
this constitute a violation of Cromwell's sexual misconduct policy?

Connecting the Cases

In cases 1, 2, 3 and 4 we have seen conflicts between individuals (Frank versus Greg, Sondra versus Corinne, Dorothy versus Tama, Angelica versus Marshall, Stuart, and Lee) in which the participants on each side of the conflict perceive themselves to be in the right and the other(s) to be in the wrong. Is it all a matter of perspective, or are there "objective" standards by which we can determine who is in the right? Can such standards be applied in all four of the cases, or do some situations appear more ambiguous and open to interpretation than others? If there are such distinctions among the cases, what are they, and on what basis do they rest?

Bringing It Home

How does your own institution define sexual misconduct? What policies and procedures are in place to deal with such cases? Have there been recent cases of sexual misconduct or sexual harassment on your campus? If so, how have they been handled?

Suggestions for Writing

1. Imagine that the JAC has found the BOZos guilty and has recommended, as a penalty, a one-year suspension from Cromwell. Write a memo to the dean of students stating your opinion regarding this final decision, explaining the reasoning in support of your views, and assessing whether or not the dean should take further action in the case.

2. Now that the hearing is over, Cromwell's student newspaper, the *Clarion*, is planning a special issue on the case. They have invited all members of the campus community to submit "open letters" to any of the major participants: Angelica; Marshall, Stuart, and Lee; Samir and Henry; or any of the other witnesses and interested parties. Write an open letter to anyone of your choosing, expressing your views concerning behavior, testimony, or other relevant factors.

3. Write an essay examining the ways in which this case may illuminate, investigate, or raise questions about the issue of consent in sexual relations.

Out Loud

You are a member of the JAC, and you have been called upon to explain to the Cromwell student body the decision your group reached concerning the verdict and any appropriate penalties. Prepare and present a speech that argues convincingly for your position.

CASE 5

Down in the Dumps
Fraternity Initiation or Hazing?

Cromwell College's fraternities and sororities have long been unpopular with many CC professors. These faculty members feel that the exclusive nature of the Greek societies promotes an unhealthy social competitiveness, and they worry that the fraternities, in particular, foster a somewhat anti-intellectual attitude on the part of CC students. Other professors have staunchly defended the Greek system, citing the benefits of leadership, fellowship, and fun. Whatever their perspective, however, the faculty as a whole has recently been paying more attention to the college's Greek organizations, and with this increase in scrutiny, the various fraternities and sororities have been extra careful to stay within the confines of college policy.

Pi Epsilon Tau (PET) has been no exception. The PET officers have decided to present a reputable example to the rest of the Greek community, and more than any other fraternity they have adhered to the spirit of the recent dry Rush agreement between the Cromwell Greek Council (CGC) and the college's administration. This agreement prohibits the use of alcohol at any of the fraternities' or sororities' official Rush functions, and so PET has tamed the wild antics that usually accompany the initiation of new members. Instead the group has devised several rituals that involve less drinking—but, to compensate, a greater sense of adventure.

Among other activities, all new PET initiates must spend a night inside one of the giant garbage dumpsters behind Howell Hall. PET's

Pledge Chairman George Maruyama has been responsible for overseeing the process and has been careful to take safety measures such as propping the dumpsters open in order to ensure adequate air flow. The point of this exercise is not to endanger the prospective members, but simply to have them undergo a somewhat unpleasant experience in order to test the depth of their commitment to the fraternity. Over a period of two weeks, a different initiate has been tested each night. Of course, the process has required complete secrecy: no one other than PET members has been aware of the initiation.

The final initiate to undergo the dumpster test would be Samir Nasser. Samir, together with his roommate Henry Xavier, looked forward to entering the Greek system as a way to achieve a more active social life, and after investigating the available options at Cromwell, they both settled on PET as the most congenial fraternity for them. They knew they would have to undergo some strange and perhaps daunting initiation rites—they'd heard rumors about PET's unique rituals from other students—but they were willing to undergo a little discomfort in the spirit of brotherhood and good fun.

However, when Samir heard the details about an overnight stay in what amounted to a big garbage can, he began to be apprehensive. Unbeknownst to his future PET brothers, Samir suffered from severe migraine headaches, a condition he'd always secretly believed to be somewhat wimpy. Indeed, he'd been ashamed of his migraines ever since they began to plague him in seventh grade. And so he remained silent about his condition, quietly taking his headache medication and saying nothing about the various factors that could set off one of his attacks: anxiety, lack of sleep, poor nutrition, or any of the several allergens to which he was unusually sensitive.

Samir knew that a night in a dumpster would almost certainly bring on the dizziness and pounding head pain that symptomize one of his migraine attacks, and as his initiation date drew near, he decided to share his foreboding with his roommate Henry. Henry, whose mother also suffered from severe migraines, was familiar with their incapacitating effects, and he saw no reason why Samir should subject himself to a situation that would almost certainly cause a migraine to occur.

"The guys at PET are pretty reasonable; they're not out to hurt anyone. The dumpster thing is just supposed to be a little hurdle for us to jump over—it's not supposed to make us sick. Just tell George that you have a medical reason for wanting to opt out of this part of the initiation, and see if he can come up with some sort of substitute test that you could take without endangering your health," Henry counseled.

Samir shook his head. "I don't want to do anything that sets me apart," he said. "I already feel like enough of a nerd for getting these stupid headaches and I don't need to announce it to the rest of the world. If I ask for some sort of alternate initiation, everyone in PET will know that I have a problem. The point of joining a fraternity is to be part of a community, not to start off from the very beginning with the reputation of being some sort of geek who just can't make it like everyone else."

"It's not a question of being a geek," insisted Henry. "This is a health issue. Remember that story we heard at orientation about the guy who got so wasted at a Zeta Omicron Omicron frat initiation that he ended up in a coma? You don't want anything like that to happen, do you?"

"Well, of course not," Samir replied, "but I just can't see it coming to that. I know that there are people who do pass out from really bad migraines, but that's never happened to me before. I can't see it happening now—especially if I make sure to have my headache pills with me. They can't prevent a migraine, but they work pretty well to reduce its effects. If I end up with a bad headache, that's not such a high price to pay for being accepted by the PET community."

Henry was unconvinced. "Any organization that's really worth joining would welcome you without forcing you to endanger your health."

"That's easy for you to say. You went through the dumpster initiation the other night and got through it fine. You're part of the group now. All I want is the chance to prove I can do it, too," said Samir.

"Of course you can do it—that's not the issue. But why should you have to prove anything to anyone?" Henry asked.

"Why should any of us have to? It's a test of our loyalty to the frat. I don't want people to think that I'm a special case."

The conversation continued through the evening. Henry was unable to convince Samir that he should inform the PET pledge chairman of his susceptibility to migraines and request an alternate initiation rite. Samir was too concerned about being "one of the guys." He was sure he could get through the dumpster test, especially with the help of the pills he concealed in his jacket pocket to prevent any serious consequences. He also knew that George and the other PET officers in charge of the event would make sure nothing dangerous happened.

"Give it a rest," said Samir to Henry's continued attempts to change his mind. "I'm a big boy now, and I know what I'm doing. I appreciate your concern, but you've got to let me take charge of my own actions."

When Samir's initiation night rolled around, he entered into the ritual enthusiastically, chiming in with the songs and chants the PET brothers bellowed in the frat house living room before making a quiet trek across Longfellow Drive through the Lower Quad. After settling Samir in for the night and propping the dumpster lid open with some carefully placed bricks, George and the PET officers wandered off, intending to check on him an hour or two later.

In the meantime, Samir was pleasantly surprised to find that in spite of the foul odors surrounding him, his head was clear. He figured that the circulation of fresh air through the propped-open lid was sufficient to keep him from suffering a migraine, and as he became more and more confident of his ability to easily survive the night, he dozed off. He was peacefully dreaming of getting an A in his English composition class when a patrolling security guard noticed the bricks propping open the dumpster. The guard couldn't come up with any reason why the bricks should be there, and it never occurred to him to look inside the dumpster. He simply removed the bricks, shut the dumpster lid tightly, and moved on, continuing his rounds.

A few seconds later Samir woke up with a start, sensing the increased darkness in the dumpster. As he looked up at the now-closed lid, he began to get nervous. How had the dumpster gotten shut so tightly? Was this part of the initiation, a test of his ability to trust his PET brothers? Should he try to get the lid open again, or should he have faith that the PET officers were standing right outside, waiting to open it in a few moments?

As he wondered what he should do, Samir felt a tight throbbing sensation above the nape of his neck. The pain quickly spread to the top of his head, then to his temples and behind his eyes. His vision became blurry, his head started reeling, and he knew that an unusually severe attack was coming on. He fumbled for his bottle of pills, but realized that while he had been asleep, it had somehow rolled out of his pocket into the filthy mess at the bottom of the dumpster. He rummaged among the rotting banana peels, soggy pizza boxes, and used tissues, but his search was in vain. He tried to stand up and push the dumpster lid open, but his growing dizziness and nausea prevented him. Each time he attempted to rise, he slipped on the garbage underfoot, and at one point he fell over and knocked his head on a piece of lead pipe that had found its way to the bottom of the dumpster. A few seconds later, he lost consciousness.

By chance, the PET officers decided to return and check on Samir at that very instant. They immediately realized that the dumpster was shut, and quickly opened the lid. As they peered in, they saw Samir's limp body huddled in a corner. George immediately ran to the nearest room in Howell Hall and dialed 911, while the rest of the PET officers gently lifted Samir out of the dumpster. It was only a matter of minutes before an ambulance was able to get Samir to the emergency room, but he remained unconscious.

Henry, who had also come by to check on his roommate, rode with him in the ambulance and, upon arrival at the hospital, made a very difficult telephone call to Samir's parents. The Nassers lived about two hours' drive away, and as soon as they heard about their son's condition, they got into their car and raced to the hospital.

As he awaited their arrival, Henry was consumed by feelings of guilt. He had known about Samir's migraines and had felt that his roommate was making a big mistake by going ahead with the PET dumpster ritual, but in the end, he had let him proceed. Should he have intervened more forcibly, perhaps going to George himself and informing him of Samir's medical problem? Was Henry, by his failure to act, indirectly responsible for what had happened to Samir?

As they anxiously waited outside the emergency room, George and the other PET officers also tried to figure out who was to blame for the incident. Could they be held responsible? After all, they were the ones who had come up with the dumpster idea—but they had no way of knowing that because of his susceptibility to migraines, Samir would be at special risk during the initiation. Anyway, their intention had been to create a ritual that was relatively harmless in order to avoid the drunken initiations of years past. Shouldn't they be praised for their alcohol-free innovation?

As Samir's friends continued their ruminations, one of the emergency room doctors came out to inform them that Samir had just regained consciousness and was in stable condition. It would take some time for him to fully recover from his ordeal, but no lasting harm had been done. Everyone breathed a sigh of relief when they heard the good news—but it still wasn't going to be easy to face Samir's parents when they arrived at the hospital.

Some Questions to Consider

Who bears responsibility for what happened to Samir: Samir himself, for keeping silent about his condition? Henry, for not intervening to prevent Samir from going through with the PET initiation? The security guard, for closing the dumpster without looking inside? Whoever threw into the dumpster the lead pipe on which Samir hit his head? George and the other PET officers, for instituting the dumpster initiation? All of them? Might Cromwell's hazing policy apply to the initiation? (See the appendix for a full statement of the policy.) Could anything be done to prevent such unforeseen disasters from occurring in the future? Should the CGC become involved in the case? What about the Cromwell College administration—how should they respond? How might this incident affect faculty attitudes toward the Greek system at Cromwell?

Thinking Critically

The end result of this case is that Samir has landed in the hospital. What cause, or causes, have led to this result? For example, did the PET fraternity's initiation procedure cause Samir's loss of consciousness? To what extent are cause-and-effect arguments relevant to the question of blame or responsibility in this case? Might there be any potential fallacies (e.g., post hoc or "false cause" arguments) in such cause-and-effect reasoning?

Reading Closely

In order to determine whether PET has violated the Cromwell policy on hazing, we must examine the wording of the policy carefully, particularly the definitions of hazing as "any act involving physical mistreatment of a student, causing undue discomfort or bodily injury" or "any act that endangers the life and health of the student." Could an overnight stay in a dumpster qualify as hazing by these definitions? Was Samir at physical risk only because of his medical condition—a condition unknown to the PET officers—or would *any* student have been in physical jeopardy inside the dumpster?

What If

What if the PET dumpster ritual had not replaced alcoholic initiation rites, but was instead added on to the usual drunken revelry? What if all parties to the initiation—including the PET officers and Samir himself—were seriously drunk during the events described? Would that change your perception of this case in any way? What if, as a result of the dumpster initiation, Samir had died? Would that change your perception?

Connecting the Cases

The issue of responsibility, of who is to blame for a certain set of unfortunate circumstances, has arisen in several Cromwell cases. Often, responsibility in these cases is ambiguous or shared. Who was responsible for the conflict between Greg and Frank in case 1, or between Sondra and Corinne in case 2? Who was responsible for the alleged rape of Angelica at the BOZ house in case 4? Who was responsible for Samir's falling into a coma in case 5? Does blame fall squarely on the shoulders of particular individuals or is it shared by the various parties in each case? How is the issue of responsibility presented similarly or differently in these cases?

Bringing It Home

The desire to be accepted can often outweigh more rational concerns, including health and well-being. What situations might arise on your own campus in which the quest for acceptance might become more powerful than the promptings of common sense?

Suggestions for Writing

1. Write a letter to the editor of the *Clarion,* the student newspaper, expressing your views on the Greek system at Cromwell in the context of the dumpster incident.

2. The Cromwell administration is planning to produce a new booklet for entering students introducing them to the realities of campus life, and you have been chosen to serve as a contributing writer. Write a section for the booklet providing advice to students interested in joining one of Cromwell's Greek societies.

3. Is it possible to ascribe blame to any one individual in this case? If so, who and why? If not, why not? Write an essay exploring the issue of responsibility—individual or shared—as it appears here.

Out Loud

You are one of Samir's friends, and you have gone to visit him as he recuperates from the aftereffects of the PET initiation. With a partner playing the role of Samir, act out this scenario, letting him know how you feel about his situation and providing him with an opportunity to respond.

CASE 6

Paper Chase
Freedom of the Press and Unpopular Views

PART ONE

For years CC's campus newspaper, *The Cromwell Clarion*, had been a joke among the college's students and faculty. The paper often failed to meet its weekly publishing schedule, and when it did appear, it rarely seemed to do more than serve as a public relations tool. In the past couple of years, however, things had begun to change as the *Clarion* staff struggled to turn the paper into a solid investigative journal. Under this year's editor-in-chief, Stephanie Ziska, the *Clarion* was, as one faculty member put it, "starting to look like a real college newspaper." Everyone was delighted with the serious attitude on the part of the newspaper staff; it seemed that the entire Cromwell community had only good things to say about the journalistic strides the *Clarion* was making under Stephanie's leadership.

Until, that is, the editors decided to put together a special issue exploring allegations of racism at Cromwell. As part of this focus, Editorial Page Editor Max Urban chose to publish several drawings that visually examined the existence, or lack thereof, of racist attitudes at CC. One of these, a cartoon by Cromwell student Grace Tran, led to a heated campus controversy.

Grace had been contributing editorial cartoons to the *Clarion* since the beginning of the semester. For the issue on racism, she produced a drawing of an Asian-American student walking into a laboratory classroom with "Welcome to Chemistry 101" written in large letters on the chalkboard. Two Caucasian students seated at the back of the room were whispering to one another. The caption to the cartoon read, "Uh-oh, there goes the grading curve."

Grace's intention had been to portray the stereotyping of Asian-American students as academic superachievers, and to suggest the resentment some white students might feel toward this supposed "model minority." As she later explained to anyone who would listen, she did not wish to support or give credence to this stereotype—as an active member of Cromwell's Asian-American Alliance, she worked hard to educate the campus community about the diversity within CC's Asian-American student population. All she was trying to do in the cartoon, she said, was to show the attitudes some Caucasian students might have toward their Asian or Asian-American counterparts, attitudes that Grace believed to be fundamentally racist.

Most of the articles, editorials, photographs, and illustrations that appeared in the *Clarion*'s special issue on racism were accepted with equanimity. Grace's cartoon, however, created an uproar. It began when Professor of Psychology Philip Wong walked into the *Clarion*'s basement office early on Friday morning, waving a copy of the special issue and loudly protesting the decision to publish Grace's drawing. Prof. Wong had picked up one of the first copies of the paper that had been distributed that morning. He argued that Grace was simply perpetuating the damaging stereotype of the Asian-American as a hard-working grind who gets in the way of Caucasian success.

"You may not think of this as a damaging portrayal," said Prof. Wong. "You may say that because the Asian-American student is assumed to be bright, hard-working, and so on, it's a positive rather than a negative stereotype. But the fact of the matter is that *all* stereotypes are damaging and degrading, because they deny the uniqueness of individuals and obscure the diversity within communities."

Grace, who wasn't an early riser, hadn't made it to the newspaper office yet and therefore couldn't respond to Prof. Wong's allegations. But Stephanie and Max argued that Grace's cartoon mocked, rather than supported, the views of the white students she portrayed.

"That may have been her intention," said Prof. Wong, "but unfortunately many members of our campus community may not be as sophisticated in their senses of humor as you folks are. I think most people who look quickly through the paper will see this as a condemnation of Asian-Americans, rather than a condemnation of racist attitudes toward them. I think it was very unfortunate that this cartoon appeared in the *Clarion*, and I think that the decision to print it—a decision that ultimately rests with the newspaper's editors—was highly irresponsible.

"I intend to speak to the dean of students, who has jurisdiction over the *Clarion*. The paper is funded by the college, and the college should be able to prevent the publication of material that is in violation of the CC discriminatory harassment policy. It's my opinion that

Grace's cartoon definitely creates a 'hostile environment' for Asian-Americans at Cromwell," said the professor.

"Grace's cartoon isn't *creating* the hostile environment, it's *describing* and *critiquing* it," responded Stephanie. "Anyway, as an Asian-American herself, Grace would surely be sensitive to any potential for offense."

"Not necessarily," replied Prof. Wong. He was about to continue when Grace walked into the office. Everyone started talking at once, trying to explain to Grace the objections to her cartoon. In the midst of the hubbub, Prof. Wong left and immediately went to the office of Sylvia Stevens, Cromwell's dean of students, to lodge a complaint.

Stephanie and Max were concerned about Prof. Wong's decision to take the matter to Dean Stevens. "After all," said Max, "it isn't as if this is some hothead we're dealing with. Everyone thinks of Prof. Wong as a reasonable, fair-minded guy. If *he's* upset, things look pretty serious."

"I'm sure most people won't agree with Wong's point of view on this," Grace responded. "Anyway, doesn't freedom of speech give me the right to create whatever cartoons I want, and doesn't freedom of the press give the *Clarion* the right to print them?"

"It's not so clear-cut," Stephanie commented. "Prof. Wong is right when he points out that the paper is funded by the college administration, so they do have the right to control the publication to some extent, especially in cases when the *Clarion* can be shown to be violating college policy. But I don't understand how anyone could see your cartoon as supporting racist attitudes or creating a 'hostile environment.' And Dean Stevens has always been a strong supporter of the *Clarion*'s autonomy, as long as we use our freedom responsibly. So I agree with you, Grace—we don't have anything to worry about. Let's go get some breakfast." On that note, Stephanie, Max, and Grace headed out of the office toward the dining hall upstairs.

Some Questions to Consider

Do you see Grace's cartoon as being in support of stereotyping, in opposition, or neutral? Do you think that the *Clarion* had the right to print the cartoon? Do you think the decision to print it was a responsible one? Has the *Clarion* violated the college policy on campus publications or the discriminatory harassment policy? (See the appendix for a full statement of both policies.) What do you think the administration's role should be in overseeing a campus publication that is funded by the college?

PART TWO

As they walked out of the office toward the dining hall, Stephanie, Max, and Grace were surprised to see five angry members of the Asian-American Alliance (AAA) striding down the hallway toward them. In the forefront was Ken Hayashi, who accosted Grace with the question, "How could you do this to us?"

"What do you mean?" asked Grace.

"I mean playing into the racist stereotypes of Asian students. As if we didn't have enough problems already! For weeks now you've been working with the AAA, and we all thought you really cared about our cause. Now we find out that you're just another self-hating banana: yellow on the outside, white on the inside. And you . . . ," Ken said, turning to Max and Stephanie, "don't you read what you publish before you print it? Or are you simply so insensitive that you just don't see how offensive this cartoon is?"

"Oh, get off their cases, Ken," said Grace. "Talk about being insensitive! Before you start calling people all sorts of names, why don't you calm down and think a bit. Don't you see that I was calling the stereotype into question, not lending it my support?"

"No, I don't see that," responded Ken.

"And neither will anyone else," added Evelyn Choi, who had been standing silently at Ken's side. "All they'll see is further fuel for the prejudice that already exists on this campus."

"There's no point wasting time talking to these people, Evelyn," Ken impatiently interrupted. "It's still pretty early. Most students won't even have seen the paper yet. What we need to do is go around campus to all the places where the *Clarion* is left for distribution, and confiscate every issue we can get our hands on. The fewer people who see the cartoon, the fewer who will be affected by it."

"I don't know, Ken, that seems a bit extreme. Do we really have the right to just walk off with all the papers?" asked Evelyn.

"The papers are free, after all, and they're left out in the open for anyone to take. Besides, it's the only option available to us, Evelyn. If we don't get those papers out of circulation, the harm to people's minds will be irreversible. Surely you can see that, can't you? Now are you going to support our cause and do the right thing, or not?"

"I guess I will," said Evelyn somewhat hesitantly. With that, Ken moved swiftly down the hallway and up the stairs, closely followed by Evelyn and the three other AAA members.

"Hey, you can't do that!" exclaimed Stephanie, who started off in pursuit of Ken and his comrades.

"We can't physically stop them, Stephanie," said Max, as he laid a restraining hand on her arm. "I think we'd better head for Dean Stevens' office and put the whole situation before her. She may not be thrilled with Grace's cartoon, especially after being visited by Prof. Wong, but surely she won't go along with Ken's tactics, either. What he's proposing to do is simply theft—stealing all the copies of the paper. She'll have to intervene to prevent that." Stephanie and Grace agreed with Max, and the three of them went directly to the office of the dean.

In the meantime, Ken, Evelyn, and the three other members of the AAA were doing exactly what they had said they would. Each week the latest issue of the *Clarion* was deposited in several open boxes around Cromwell College. Ken and his comrades moved methodically across campus, removing the piles of papers from the distribution boxes and bringing them to Ken's room in Oates Hall—one of the older residence halls which had working fireplaces in the rooms. Once they gathered all the papers, they intended to burn them in Ken's fireplace. Several students saw the five AAA members removing the papers, but didn't think much of it; they just assumed that *Clarion* staffers were picking up the papers for some legitimate reason.

It wasn't until they reached the distribution box in the lobby of Abbot Hall that the AAA members were challenged. Edna Redbird, a *Clarion* reporter who was leaving the building after an early morning piano lesson, stopped and stared as Evelyn Choi filled her arms with newspapers. Edna asked Evelyn what she was doing, but she received no reply. Evelyn, Ken, and the others simply grabbed all the papers and ran as fast as they could to Oates Hall.

Edna didn't think she could catch up with them, and wasn't sure what she would do even if she could. Instead, she strode over to the department of safety and notified the officer behind the front desk that she had seen several students stealing numerous copies of this week's *Clarion*. The security officer wasn't too impressed by the gravity of the situation, and it wasn't until Edna threatened to call the college president that he agreed to investigate. Edna decided that she couldn't leave the matter entirely to the department of safety, and went to the dean of students' office to report the matter there.

When Edna reached Dean Stevens' reception area, the secretary explained that the dean was currently in conference. As she peered through the open door of the dean's office, Edna recognized Stephanie, Max, and Grace.

"Are they here on *Clarion* business?" Edna asked the secretary.

"Yes, I believe so," she replied.

"I have some information they'll want to hear," Edna said, and she walked directly into Dean Stevens' office before the secretary could stop her. Stephanie, Max, Grace, and the dean all looked up as Edna entered, and she immediately told them what she had seen in Abbot Hall.

"I'm not surprised," said Stephanie. "This is exactly what they threatened to do, and I was pretty sure they'd go ahead with it. The question is what we should do now."

Dean Stevens sighed and said, "I think it would be best for you to do nothing at present. This is now a matter for the administration to handle. Please just sit tight and let us deal with it."

Stephanie squirmed in her chair and started to protest. But Max turned to her and said, "I think we'd better go along with the dean for now. And we'd better get back to the *Clarion* office and explain what's going on to the rest of the staff."

"Good idea," said Dean Stevens. "I'll get in touch with you there as soon as I have anything to report."

Stephanie, Max, Grace and Edna headed back to the newspaper office, talking over the situation and trying to figure out what the dean would do.

The first thing Dean Stevens did was contact the department of safety. The chief of security informed her that a couple of officers had gone to investigate an allegation that the *Clarion* was being confiscated, and had apprehended five students in the act of emptying the *Clarion* distribution box in front of the computer center. The students had immediately confessed to their actions. They admitted that they were creating a cache of newspapers in a room in Oates Hall, and that their intention was to burn all existing copies of this week's paper to, as they put it, "wipe out the seeds of bigotry and prejudice."

The dean now had two complicated cases on her hands: first, she had to deal with the question of whether the *Clarion* had gotten out of line—perhaps even in violation of the college's discriminatory harassment policy—by printing Grace Tran's cartoon, or whether the cartoon merely represented a legitimate expression of opinion. If the paper's editors had acted irresponsibly or inappropriately, how should she deal with the infraction?

She then had to consider the case of the AAA's attempt to redress the situation by doing away with all copies of what was, to them, an offensive publication. The college administration had itself been known to confiscate or prevent distribution of material on the Cromwell campus that could be demonstrated to be in violation of CC codes of speech and conduct. For example, Dean Stevens recalled an incident a couple of years ago when some offensive anti-Semitic leaflets published by a national neo-Nazi organization had been left on a table in the student union lobby. The dean herself had immediately confiscated and destroyed them, without thinking twice about whether she was violating anyone's freedom of expression. After all, Cromwell was a private college and had the right to determine what pamphlets were or were not acceptable for distribution. The dean, however, had been acting as an officially designated representative of the Cromwell administration; the five AAA members were simply acting as outraged individuals. Were they justified in taking into their own hands the decision-making power of the administration?

Dean Stevens also had to consider whether the two facets of the case could be disconnected or whether they were inextricably linked. Should she view the action of the AAA members as unacceptable regardless of how she viewed Grace's cartoon, or did judgment of the AAA members' actions depend on her attitude toward the cartoon? Was the AAA eradicating racism or stifling free speech?

These were difficult questions, and the answers to them would have far-reaching effects on the *Clarion*. The dean decided that the case of the AAA members could not be entirely divorced from consideration of the nature of the cartoon, and that the entire matter needed more heads than hers to think it through. She decided to convene an ad-hoc committee of students, faculty, and administrators to investigate the intertwining situations. She knew that such a committee investigation could take days to resolve the case, but she believed it would be the method most likely to produce a fair and thoughtful conclusion.

In the meantime, Dean Stevens instructed the department of safety to impound all undistributed copies of the *Clarion* in a locked storage room, including those that the AAA members had attempted to confiscate. Although a number of members of the Cromwell community had already seen copies of the controversial edition—including Prof. Wong and the five members of the AAA—it had not been widely disseminated. The dean felt that the ad-hoc committee should decide whether or not the issue should be distributed at large.

Dean Stevens phoned the *Clarion* office to report her decision, and spoke directly to Editor-in-Chief Stephanie Ziska. Stephanie responded to the dean icily, barely speaking two words in reply to her explanation. But after hanging up the phone, Stephanie vented her anger as she addressed her fellow staffers.

"It's completely unjust!" Stephanie fumed. "The committee investigation will take forever, and in the meantime the *Clarion* is being muzzled. Ken and his friends have achieved what they wanted to—only now it's not them who have stolen the paper, it's the administration."

"Calm down, Stephanie," urged Max. "I agree that this doesn't exactly look like a victory for free speech, but we have to remember that the AAA members were doing what they thought was best for the community. They sincerely believe that we printed a racist cartoon. We may not see it that way, but they do, and they acted on their belief swiftly and surely. Whether their actions were justified—well, of course I don't think so, and of course it's frustrating to have the paper impounded, especially when a number of copies are already out there. It seems kind of pointless, doesn't it? But we have to think of this as only a temporary impasse. The committee will meet, they'll consider the situation in full, and then they'll make their recommendation to the dean. There's no point getting all fired up until we know the final decision."

Stephanie wasn't easily quieted, and she wasn't the only one to remain upset. As word of the newspaper crisis swept across campus, all *Clarion* staffers gathered in the basement office, and while some, like Max, remained calm, many others were outraged.

In the meantime, members of the Asian-American Alliance were meeting to discuss their response to the actions of Ken, Evelyn, and the others. Some AAA members were strongly in support of Ken and his comrades, arguing that the fight to eradicate racism had to be waged decisively and aggressively. However, not everyone in the AAA was in support of the attempt to confiscate the paper—in fact, many deplored it. As a copy of the *Clarion*'s special edition was passed around the group, numerous AAA members expressed the belief that Grace's cartoon was clearly an attack on stereotypes of Asians and Asian-Americans, rather than a reinforcement of these images. In any case, some members argued, whatever you thought of Grace's cartoon, stifling free speech was not the answer.

The *Clarion* and the AAA were not the only groups debating the case. In class and out, everyone on campus had become embroiled in the controversy, and those students and faculty who had managed to obtain copies of the contested paper before it was impounded were suddenly very popular. By the end of the day, the special edition of the *Clarion* had been more widely read than any previous issue. The campus community waited impatiently for the ad-hoc committee to make its report.

Some Questions to Consider

Was the action of the AAA members legitimate? Could it be viewed as theft? Were there any other steps they could have taken to act on their conviction that Grace's cartoon was an expression of racism? What do you think of Dean Stevens' decision to convene an ad-hoc committee to investigate the case? What do you think of her decision to impound all undistributed copies of the paper until the committee could reach a conclusion? What other courses of action could the dean have followed?

Thinking Critically

Ken suggests that the only valid response to the *Clarion*'s publication of Grace's cartoon is to confiscate all copies of the paper. Are there any logical fallacies in his reasoning on this matter—for example, generalization or false dilemma? Is he neglecting to explore potential negative consequences resulting from the confiscation and proposed destruction of the papers? What future ramifications might Ken and his colleagues want to consider more fully?

Reading Closely

The caption to Grace's cartoon reads, "Uh-oh, there goes the grading curve," and it is presumably spoken by the Caucasian students in reference to the Asian-American who is entering the classroom. Grace seems to believe that her cartoon is an obvious critique of the attitude being expressed by the Caucasian students, but can a disinterested viewer pick up on this just by looking at the cartoon and its caption?

Are there any hints or suggestions that would enable someone to recognize Grace's intention? For example, would the cartoon be any different if it depicted the same scene but without the white students present? Does the context in which it appeared—a special issue of the *Clarion* focusing on racism at Cromwell—affect its message?

What If

What if, instead of a cartoon that could be seen as critiquing racist attitudes, Grace had produced a cartoon that explicitly expressed racist attitudes; for example, a caricature of a Chinese-American student speaking in pidgin English and offering to do his classmates' laundry? Would it be acceptable for the *Clarion* to print such a portrayal? What if Grace were not Asian-American; would that make any difference to your perception of this case?

Connecting the Cases

This is not the first time that individual students or student groups at Cromwell have come into conflict. At what point should the college administration step into disputes or disagreements between students and/or student organizations? Does it make a difference when administrators are asked to intervene—as they were by Greg Cervenko, Corinne Stanworth, Angelica Caputo, and Philip Wong? Should they intervene even in cases where they have not been approached—for example, with the "Cosmos Cult" in case 3 or with Samir's situation in case 5?

Bringing It Home

Examine a copy of your own campus's student newspaper. Is any of the material in it potentially offensive? Are there any problems with either content or presentation—anything from subject matter to sentence-level mechanics? If there are problems, how should they be handled? What should be the role of either a faculty adviser or an administration supervisor in the production of a campus newspaper?

Suggestions for Writing

1. What do you think would be a just conclusion to this case? What would be a realistic conclusion? Write an ending that you think would be appropriate.

2. Imagine that you are a member of a student group that is concerned about the *Clarion*/AAA case. Write a leaflet on behalf of this group that explains to the campus community at large your organization's position on the case and tries to convince your readers to agree with this position.

3. Max Urban remarks that Ken and his colleagues are engaging in blatant "theft—stealing all the copies of the paper." Ken, however, notes that copies of the paper "are free, after all, and they're left out in the open for anyone to take." Write an essay exploring the question of what precisely constitutes stealing, and whether or not the action taken by Ken and his colleagues can be viewed as theft.

Out Loud

You and several of your classmates have been chosen to serve on the ad-hoc committee that will determine what to do with the impounded copies of the *Clarion* and with the *Clarion*/AAA case as a whole. Decide on individual roles that you will each play (e.g., administrators, faculty members, and students) and then enact a meeting of the committee.

CASE 7

On Your Honor
Cheating and Its Consequences

PART ONE

As the semester wore on, the students of Cromwell College focused more and more on their studies, becoming almost obsessive in their academic concern as midterm examinations approached. Cromwell's first-year students were particularly anxious about midterms, since this would be their initial experience with college-level examinations. They could be seen at all hours with textbooks spread open on their laps and highlighters in their hands as they struggled to absorb information they had neglected in the press of more exciting events.

Lucy Donovan was perhaps even more apprehensive than the rest of her classmates. The past few weeks had not been easy for her. To begin with, she had had to fight a long battle with her parents about going away to school. Although Cromwell was only an hour's drive from her hometown, Lucy's mother and father—who were very strict and, in her opinion, old-fashioned in their approach to their only daughter— were worried about what might happen if Lucy was exposed to "the wrong element" while away at college. Lucy managed to talk them into letting her attend Cromwell and live in the residence halls, but her parents made it clear that she'd have to request a room in Reynolds Hall, the all-female residence, and that they'd bring her back home at the slightest hint of a problem, whether academic or personal.

Upon her arrival at Cromwell, Lucy found that residence life had its own set of troubles. She didn't get along with her roommate, her hallway was incredibly noisy, and her resident adviser did nothing to control the chaos. At first, Lucy began to wonder whether she wouldn't be happier back home—and then she met Frank McFarland.

Lucy had never known anyone quite like Frank. Aside from a rather remarkable mechanical ineptitude (it had taken him three hours to hook up his desktop computer), he was a brilliant young man, witty and unconventional yet with a warm, sensitive, and loving side. After his first conversation with Lucy, he was determined to show her just how warm, sensitive, and loving he could be.

Frank's appearance didn't make a good first impression on Lucy: earring, ponytail, and ripped jeans were not the norm among her male friends back home. But ten minutes of whispered conversation during a particularly boring American history lecture won her over. Soon the two became "an item." And soon Lucy started doing something she had never expected to do: against residence hall visitation rules she found herself spending frequent nights in Frank's room in Blaine Hall, the all-male residence hall in the Lower Quad. Frank's roommate had dropped out of school after the second week of classes due to psychological problems, and since then Frank occupied a single room, an almost unheard-of luxury among first-year students and a setup that certainly didn't discourage Lucy's overnight visits. Meanwhile, Lucy was living in fear that her parents would phone her early in the morning and discover that she wasn't in her own room. So far she had been lucky, but she continued to be nervous about the situation. She was convinced that if her parents found out about her relationship with Frank, they would immediately pull her out of Cromwell.

Lucy's anxiety about her parents, together with her delight in spending time with Frank, had begun to get in the way of her studies. Intelligent as she was, Lucy was not quite as brilliant of a student as Frank. Although he seemed to be able to get A's in all his classes with no effort, she needed to work hard for her good grades. And lately she just hadn't been able, or willing, to work as hard as she should. She knew that it was crucial for her to do well on her midterm exams: every semester Cromwell College sent a brief report of midterm progress to the parents of each student, and if a poor midterm report were to reach Lucy's parents she was certain they would use it as an excuse to drag her back home. So Lucy started putting in a lot of study time, desperately trying to make up for all the work she hadn't done in the first weeks of the semester.

Lucy wasn't too worried about her midterm grades in most of her classes, because all that went on the midterm report was an S (satisfactory) or a U (unsatisfactory). She had been doing well in English composition, and although she had fallen behind in her reading for American history, she quickly caught up. Biology was basically a rehash of her high school Advanced Placement Biology class, and she was confident that a night or two of review would adequately prepare her for the midterm exam. Her once-a-week tutorial in violin technique wasn't a problem, either. There was no question that she'd pull S's in all these courses.

So far so good—but there was one more class to contend with. Lucy had been sure, when she'd signed up for Introduction to American Politics, that it would be one of her favorite courses. She had always been interested in politics, and spent the summer after her junior year in high school as an intern in the district office of her local congresswoman. But her expectations were dashed the first day she walked into Tom Sanders' class.

Professor Sanders spent most of the first class telling off-color jokes, recounting his collegiate exploits, and denouncing just about every politician currently in office. "These power-hungry fools in Washington have just about ruined our country!" he proclaimed, but he never offered any evidence to support his negative perspective.

Lucy tried to make the best of the situation. She kept telling herself that it was good for her to be exposed to all points of view, and tried to convince herself that she might learn something valuable from Prof. Sanders' approach to the issues. The problem, however, was that Prof. Sanders never really discussed any issues. Although their syllabus listed several required texts, students in the class didn't bother with the readings, since Prof. Sanders never referred to them. In class after class, he rarely got beyond jokes and anecdotes. His occasional treatment of concepts from the readings—federalism versus state rights, for example—was so sketchy and disorganized, and so slanted toward his own idiosyncratic viewpoint, that Lucy found herself just as uninformed after his lectures as she was before they began.

None of this would have mattered as much to Lucy if not for the fact that Prof. Sanders' tests bore no relation whatsoever to his classes. It was as if he was using the exams of some other professor who was teaching a rigorous and challenging version of the political science curriculum. Indeed, it was common knowledge that Prof. Sanders used the same exams as those given last year by another Cromwell professor, Luther Jackson, who was known to be a much more thorough instructor. Lucy would have registered for Prof. Jackson's section of the American Politics class to begin with, but he was on leave this year. By the time she realized she should drop the course and switch to something else, it was too late.

The two short tests already taken by Lucy's American Politics class would have been challenging for students who were being well-taught; for those in Prof. Sanders' class, they were virtually impossible. Some students who had access to fraternity and sorority test files or knew people who had taken Prof. Jackson's class last year managed to pass. Lucy, who had no such resources and who would have scorned them as unethical even if she did have access to them, performed miserably. She was going into the midterm with a D average. Prof. Sanders had indicated that everyone who earned a C or better on the midterm exam would receive an S on their midterm report, even if they'd done poorly on the previous tests. Lucy didn't have much hope, but figured she'd better do whatever she could to pull the crucial C.

And so she devoted most of her study time to reading and trying to understand all the material listed in the first half of the Introduction to American Politics syllabus. Frank, who wasn't taking the course, tried to help her, but there was so much to cover that Lucy was beginning to feel overwhelmed. "I'm never going to pass this exam," she moaned, "and then my parents will get my midterm grades, see the U, and it'll be good-bye Cromwell!"

By Tuesday morning, the day before the exam, Lucy was panic-stricken. She forgot to show up for her work-study job in the political science department office; when Frank dropped by her room to check on her, he found her still in her nightgown, staring blankly at the wall. He reminded her that she was supposed to be at work in ten minutes, and Lucy—who had never been late before, in spite of the fact that she was supposed to show up at the ungodly hour of 8:30 A.M.—miraculously made it on time. This feat was even more impressive because Poretski Hall, where the political science department was located, was on the opposite side of the campus from her room in Reynolds Hall.

When she made her breathless arrival at the office, she was greeted with a nod from Adele Zeller, the office manager. This was one of the busiest times of the year for Ms. Zeller, and she was trying to delegate as much work as possible to her office assistant and her two work-study employees. Lucy was the first of the employees to arrive for the day. Ms. Zeller handed her a sheaf of job application letters that had been received in answer to a recent advertisement for a faculty opening at CC, and asked her to make three copies of each. "And you'd better collate and staple them properly this time—not backwards, like you did yesterday!" commanded Ms. Zeller, as Lucy sheepishly took the letters into the photocopying room.

As she lifted the cover of the photocopying machine, Lucy realized that the previous user had left a sheet of paper there. She picked it up to get it out of the way, and glanced at it to see whose it might be. Absent-minded faculty members often left papers on the machine, and if there was a name on it, the office policy was to return the forgotten paper to the appropriate professor's mailbox. Much to her surprise, Lucy realized that she was staring at Tom Sanders' midterm exam for Introduction to American Politics.

Smack at the top of the page was the topic for an essay question that was worth 50 percent of the total exam grade. Before she was aware of what she was doing, Lucy read the question: "Briefly summarize the positions on federalism taken by Madison and Hamilton; analyze the divergences between their positions, and provide your own evaluation of which position is most convincing using specific evidence from the two authors' writings."

Once Lucy realized the nature of the document she was holding in her hand, she immediately put it facedown on the table next to her in order to keep from seeing the questions on the multiple-choice section of the exam. The essay topic, however, was already etched in her memory. She looked wildly around her, but realized she was alone in the photocopying room and no one else was aware of what she had seen. She stepped into the main office, and that, too, was deserted. Ms. Zeller must have left for a moment, and the other employees had not yet arrived.

Everything in the office—computers, bookshelves, and filing cabinets—seemed to turn into a blur before Lucy's eyes. The only objects she saw clearly were the faculty mailboxes, arranged in a phalanx on the office's back wall. She darted over to Prof. Sanders' box, slipped the exam into it, quickly scrawled a note ("I'm feeling really sick and have gone home to bed—Lucy"), and left it on Ms. Zeller's desk. She ran back to her room, locked the door behind her, got into bed, and pulled the covers up over her head.

Lucy's mind was racing. What should she do? Should she tell Prof. Sanders that she'd seen the exam? That would be the most honorable course. After all, wouldn't she be in violation of Cromwell's Honor Code, which prohibits "unauthorized assistance" on exams, if she were to go ahead and take the exam given the knowledge she had of its most significant question?

Well, actually Lucy wasn't so sure. It wasn't like she had intentionally set out to cheat, she reasoned. She wasn't *trying* to get a look at the exam, and as soon as she realized what it was, she prevented herself from seeing anything further. Besides, she'd heard what everyone said about Prof. Sanders' exams being the same as Prof. Jackson's from last year, and she knew that many students had access to those materials. Why shouldn't she have the same advantage they did? No one would ever know that she had seen the actual exam. She could spend the twenty-four hours before the test rereading *The Federalist Papers* and preparing a coherent response to the essay question. She'd still be studying for the exam—her glimpse of the essay question would just serve as a sort of study guide, prompting her in the direction she needed to take in her preparations. With any luck, she'd be able to get some of the multiple-choice questions right too. Surely she'd make a C, thereby earning the coveted midterm grade of S.

After a couple of hours of agonizing, Lucy's mind was made up. When Ms. Zeller phoned her later in the morning to see how she was feeling and ask her about putting in some work time in the afternoon, Lucy told her she had a stomach virus and wouldn't be able to come back to the office that day. She pulled out her copy of *The Federalist Papers* and began taking notes.

When Frank stopped by later to walk with her to lunch, she begged off. "I'm really not hungry," she said, "and I'd rather spend my time studying for Sanders' exam. I think I'd just like to be alone all day so that I can focus on my reading." As Frank shrugged his shoulders and left, Lucy was stung by pangs of guilt, but she put them out of her mind in order to concentrate on writing an outline for her essay.

On Wednesday morning Lucy walked into her American Politics classroom and sat down in her usual seat. As soon as Prof. Sanders handed out the exam, she glanced at the essay question, picked up her pen, opened her examination book, and began writing. Once she finished her essay, she turned to the multiple-choice section. She was sure she knew the answers to at least half of the questions. Those, together with the essay, would certainly earn her the C that she so desperately needed! By the end of the exam period, she was exhausted yet satisfied, and slowly walked back toward her room for a short rest before lunch.

As Lucy meandered along, her dormant conscience stirred. "Oh, no!" she thought to herself, "What have I done? I always swore I'd never use old exam files or anything like that, because it would give me an unfair advantage over students who didn't have access to the materials. I always thought of myself as somehow more ethical than my classmates. Now I've fallen far below them. No matter how you look at it, I've cheated on this exam. How will I ever be able to live with myself?"

After much consideration, Lucy came to a decision. She was determined to turn herself in to David Nadler, Cromwell's dean of academic affairs, and ask him to convene the honor council to hear her case. "I just don't see anything else to do," she thought. "Maybe if I turn myself in, they'll go a little easier on me—but in any case, my conscience just won't let me get away with cheating. It will probably mean that I'll have to go back home to my parents, but that can't be helped."

With those thoughts, she turned back in the direction of Vanburen Hall, where the academic dean's office was located. Dean Nadler's secretary told Lucy that he was available and immediately showed her into his office. There she told her tale.

"I have no choice but to report this infraction to the honor council," the Dean remarked after hearing her story, "though I must admit that I hope they'll show leniency in your case, given your decision to turn yourself in. We'll convene the council immediately. As you know, it consists of three faculty members selected yearly by me, as well as three students elected every spring."

The three faculty members were Selena Weil, a young, easy-going biology professor who also served on Cromwell's Judicial Advisory Committee; Hal Banner, a demanding but popular philosophy professor; and Carla Lombardo, a detail-minded sociology professor who was a stickler for rules. Dean Nadler told Lucy that the faculty and student members of the council would meet to consider the facts in her case on Thursday afternoon. She had no hope that the council would find her anything but guilty, but she was resigned to her fate and awaited the group's deliberations.

Some Questions to Consider

Has Lucy violated Cromwell's Honor Code? (See the appendix for a full statement of the code.) What should she have done when she discovered Prof. Sanders' exam on the photocopying machine? Is her viewing of the actual exam to be administered the next day any different from other students' perusal of Prof. Jackson's exams from the previous year? Could these students' use of old exams be seen as an Honor Code violation? Has Lucy done the right thing by turning herself in? Has the dean done the right thing by deciding to convene the honor council? What should Lucy do now?

SMALL-GROUP EXERCISE

Group 1 Lucy's Best Friends

Talking It Out

On the way back to her room after informing Dean Nadler of what she perceives to be her violation of the Honor Code, Lucy comes across the group of you sitting on the grass in front of Reynolds Hall. She immediately joins you and tells you the whole story.

"You folks are really my best friends here at CC," Lucy concludes. "You've stuck by me before; given me good advice on how to deal with my parents, my roommate, Frank—everything. Now it seems like it's all going up in smoke for me. I know I made a big mistake when I walked in and took that exam without telling Prof. Sanders I had seen the essay question. You may not agree, but I feel that turning myself in was the only thing I could do and still live with my conscience. I know I deserve to face the consequences of my actions.

"I also know that my life at Cromwell is over now. The honor council is sure to convict me; after all, I admitted myself that I cheated on the exam. When they reach a guilty verdict, they have no choice but to either suspend me for a year or expel me permanently—the Honor Code states that all violators must receive one of those two punishments. Even if I'm just suspended, my parents will never let me come back here. Knowing them, they probably won't even let me out of the house! I'll never be able to see Frank again, and I'll never be able to see any of you again."

You try to convince Lucy that things aren't as bleak as she perceives them, but she shakes her head. "I don't know," she says. "I can't think of any way to present my case—to the honor council, to my friends, and most of all to my parents—that doesn't make it seem like I've totally disgraced my family and everything I've ever been taught to believe. You say things might not be as bad as I picture them. Well, can you give me any concrete suggestions for how to deal with my situation so that it's survivable? What should I say at the honor council hearing tomorrow? When should I tell my parents about all this? *How* should I tell them? *What* should I tell them? You've always given me good advice before. What advice can you give me now?"

Before you have a chance to say a word, Lucy sees Frank walking by and runs over to him. As she leaves, you begin to discuss her problems among yourselves, and try to reach a consensus about what advice you should give her.

Writing It Out

As you discuss Lucy's problems, you decide it might help her if you were to write her a note, as a group, giving her the concrete suggestions she wants. What will you write in response to her request?

SMALL-GROUP EXERCISE

Group 2 Members of a Group Opposed to the Honor Code

Talking It Out

Ever since the Honor Code was implemented at Cromwell several years ago, a vocal minority of students has expressed their opposition to it. They've cited a number of reasons; some are practicality based (i.e., the code doesn't work to deter cheating), some are ethically based (i.e., the code is morally wrong), and some are logically based (i.e., the code is contradictory, hypocritical, or ambiguous).

After hearing a number of these arguments, you have begun to wonder about the Honor Code, and have even attended a few meetings of the Committee to Reconsider the Honor Code (CRHC). When rumors about Lucy's case reach the CRHC, the group decides to hold a meeting to determine whether this incident raises any questions or problems that should be addressed.

At the meeting, one group member brings up the code's inflexibility that prevents the honor council from taking extenuating factors into consideration. For example, the code states that anyone found guilty of a violation *must* receive one of two punishments: a one-year suspension or total expulsion from the college. Shouldn't it make a difference that Lucy came upon a copy of the exam inadvertently, and that she turned herself in? The code, however, allows for no consideration of such factors.

Another group member points out that at the same time the code is inflexible on the issue of punishment, it is ambiguous on the definition of a violation itself; "unauthorized assistance" is forbidden, but does that really apply to Lucy's case? How about Prof. Sanders' apparent disregard for his students' "study" methods? If he knowingly uses easily accessible tests from last year, doesn't that, in some sense, tacitly "authorize" whatever assistance students find available?

After a few minutes of discussion, it becomes clear that Lucy's case raises enough questions to justify a reconsideration of Cromwell's Honor Code. How should these questions be posed in order to convince the Cromwell Student Government (CSG) to convene an open forum so that all members of the CC community who wish to could express their sentiments about the code?

Writing It Out

You've been delegated to serve on a subcommittee to prepare a memo to the CSG explaining why the issues raised by Lucy's case are significant enough to merit a total re-examination of the Honor Code and why an open forum would be the appropriate means to begin this re-examination. The CRHC has asked you to decide together how best to persuade the CSG that the time for action on the Honor Code is now, and to jointly draw up a draft of the memo. What will you write in response to this request?

SMALL-GROUP EXERCISE

Group 3 Lucy's American Politics Classmates

Talking It Out

The American Politics exam is over and done. You have no idea how you performed on it, but at least it's behind you now. After a short nap on a sofa in the student union, you head off to the dining hall for lunch, and there you hear the rumor that's all over campus: Lucy Donovan turned herself in for cheating on the American Politics exam. It never ceases to amaze you how quickly news travels at Cromwell, and how detailed the news can be. One of your acquaintances has heard the whole story, and tells you the fine points of the scandal.

As you walk back to the serving area to get a second helping of Jello Jewels, you pass a table full of several of your American Politics classmates and their friends. "Have you heard the news about Lucy?" one of them asks. You nod and sit down, filling your classmates in on everything you've picked up.

The roommate of one of your classmates, who isn't taking American Politics but who is a close friend of Lucy's, pipes up: "As Lucy's classmates, how do you feel about this? Do you feel that she *has* cheated and betrayed the rest of the students in the class? Or do you feel what she did was justified, given Prof. Sanders' teaching incompetence and the fact that half the class makes use of 'assistance,' like test files, that isn't officially authorized by the professor?

"Have any of *you* ever used old tests to study from, without them being 'authorized'? What would *you* have done if you had been in Lucy's place? What do you think the honor council should do with her case? You know that if they find her guilty of receiving 'unauthorized assistance' they have to either suspend her from school for a year or else expel her totally—the Honor Code explicitly states that one of these two punishments *must* be implemented. What would you advise the members of the council to do?"

All thoughts of lunch are abandoned as you spend the rest of your mealtime discussing these questions with your classmates.

Writing It Out

After further discussing the case, you and your classmates agree that you should do something about Lucy's situation, but you're not sure what would be the best course of action. Lucy's friend suggests, "Why don't you try to reach some kind of consensus among yourselves, and then write a memo to the honor council? It might help them in their deliberations if you would state your feelings as Lucy's fellow classmates in the American Politics course, and make some recommendations for their interpretation of the case." What will you write in response to this request?

SMALL-GROUP EXERCISE

Group 4 *The Cromwell Clarion* Editorial Staff

Talking It Out

When you first arrived at Cromwell, you thought you were the hottest thing on earth because you had been editor of your high school newspaper. When you decided to join the staff of *The Cromwell Clarion*, you were sure the editors would recognize your potential and award you a position of prominence. But it turned out that about half the CC student body had been the editors of their high school papers, and the only thing you've been allowed to do so far has been to proofread the letters to the editor.

Now, however, it looks like you're going to get a chance to make it into the journalistic major leagues. The editorial page editor has learned about Lucy's case, and has decided that it raises issues significant enough to warrant a *Clarion* editorial. Unfortunately, he's too swamped by midterms to write it himself, so he asks you and several other *Clarion* staffers to work together as a group to produce an editorial.

To give you some background, he sits down and explains some of the doubts and questions that have surrounded the Cromwell Honor Code, many of them raised by a group called the Committee to Reconsider the Honor Code (CRHC). CRHC members have noted that the code's inflexibility prevents the honor council from taking extenuating factors into consideration. For example, the code states that anyone found guilty of a violation *must* receive one of two punishments: a one-year suspension, or total expulsion from the college. Shouldn't it make a difference that Lucy came upon Prof. Sanders' exam inadvertently, and that she turned herself in? The code, however, allows for no such considerations.

Moreover, CRHC members maintain that although the code is inflexible on the issue of punishment, it is ambiguous on the definition of a violation itself; "unauthorized assistance" is forbidden, but does that apply to Lucy's case? How about Prof. Sanders' apparent disregard for his students' "study" methods and his use of easily accessible tests from last year?

Does Lucy's case raise enough questions to justify a reconsideration of Cromwell's Honor Code? Even if a total re-evaluation of the code is not justified, are there recommendations that could be made about this individual incident? How should the honor council deal with the case?

Writing It Out

After you've had a chance to discuss Lucy's case with your fellow newspaper staffers, the editor returns and says, "You can make the editorial as broad or as specific as you like. You can make large points about the code, or just speak about the particular case at hand. But whatever you do, I want you to take a stand and argue it effectively." What will you write in response to this request?

PART TWO

By Thursday afternoon, the student members of the honor council were visibly on edge. None of them wanted Lucy thrown out of the college. In their opinion, the circumstances surrounding her case pointed to a more merciful treatment. Even the most lenient punishment available, a full year's suspension, appeared harsh to them. Knowing the reputation of Lucy's parents, the members were certain they'd never let her come back to Cromwell even after the period of suspension was over. Nevertheless, the facts in the case seemed to be incontrovertible. Lucy had seen Prof. Sanders' exam beforehand—she admitted this—and this was clearly a case of receiving "unauthorized assistance."

Or was it? Selena Weil, one of the faculty members on the honor council, had a chat with the student members on Thursday morning and made her views known to them. Prof. Weil argued that Lucy's preview of the exam was *not* in fact "unauthorized." It was her contention that Prof. Sanders' behavior throughout the course of the term—his neglect of course material, his choice to use previous exams that were easily accessible to students, his negligence in leaving the exam on the photocopying machine—pointed to an "anything goes" attitude. The fact that he had never "de-authorized" the use of past exams as study aids, even though he knew that these past exams were readily available and were identical to the ones he was going to give to his current students, seemed to Prof. Weil to be further evidence that Prof. Sanders sanctioned the use of any means whatsoever to prepare for his exams. Moreover, though almost all of the professors at Cromwell included a statement regarding the penalties for academic fraud as a part of their course syllabi, Prof. Sanders' syllabus made no mention of the issue.

Prof. Weil hypothesized that if Prof. Sanders had known that Lucy had seen the actual exam the day before it was to be administered, he wouldn't have cared. She maintained that Lucy would have been justified in assuming that he would not object, given what she already knew about Prof. Sanders' attitudes. Therefore, Prof. Weil claimed, Prof. Sanders had tacitly "authorized" Lucy's use of her exam preview by sending an unspoken message that he didn't care what his students did; academic fraud appeared to be irrelevant to him.

As a final argument, Prof. Weil pointed out that when Lucy turned herself in to Dean Nadler, she fulfilled the code's stipulation that students "have the responsibility of reporting suspected violations." By reporting her own violation, Lucy could thus be seen as ultimately upholding the code, exhibiting a sense of honor far beyond that of the vast majority of Cromwell students. Given this interpretation of the situation, Prof. Weil was prepared to find Lucy not guilty of violating the Honor Code.

Prof. Weil was not the only one considering this position. As the members of the honor council filed into Dean Nadler's office at 2:00 P.M. Thursday, several of them were thinking about the possibility of a "not guilty" verdict, though others thought that the evidence plainly indicated an Honor Code violation. All were waiting to hear the dean's statement of the case, as well as any additional remarks Lucy chose to make.

Dean Nadler had invited Prof. Sanders to make a statement as well, but he declined, maintaining that he would not be able to contribute anything significant to the hearing. After all, he pointed out, it was Lucy herself, not her professor, who had brought the case to the dean's attention. Thus it was decided that Lucy's testimony would be sufficient to lead to a verdict.

Once the council members and Lucy were present, Dean Nadler closed his office door and began recounting the details of the case to "refresh everyone's memories," as he put it. He then presented the group with a memo from Lucy's American Politics classmates and asked them to take the classmates' recommendations into consideration.

After giving the council members a few minutes to read the memo, the dean turned to Lucy and asked if she had anything to add. She looked confused, started to speak, then stopped. After a long pause, she said, "Some of my friends have urged me to speak out in my own defense, but I really don't know how that would help. There's nothing I could say that would alter the facts of the case, so I guess I'll just keep quiet." Dean Nadler waited a few moments to give her the opportunity to change her mind, but Lucy seemed determined to remain silent. He then turned to the council and informed them that it was time to reach a verdict in the case. He passed each one a slip of paper on which to record their secret vote.

Selena Weil was the first to turn in her ballot; as was expected, her verdict was "not guilty." Carla Lombardo handed in her vote almost as quickly. She later explained to several of her faculty colleagues that in her view, Lucy's exam preview was clearly unauthorized. It could only be considered legitimate if her professor had verbally authorized it, which he could not have done since he was unaware that Lucy had access to the exam. Prof. Lombardo believed that in the absence of explicit authorization, students should be expected to assume that any external assistance was unauthorized. In any case, she argued, it required only the most rudimentary grasp of common sense to realize that having a look at the next day's exam would constitute academic dishonesty. Prof. Lombardo had reached the conclusion that, by the letter of the law, Lucy was guilty, and she did not feel that the law should be bent in this or any other case.

Hal Banner was the last of the three faculty members to submit his verdict. He had genuine sympathy for Lucy and the circumstances surrounding her case, and he had long been disturbed by Prof. Sanders' questionable teaching methods. However, like Prof. Lombardo, he was concerned about setting a precedent indicating that the code could be applied elastically. After much consideration, he handed in his "guilty" vote, planning to recommend a penalty of suspension rather than expulsion.

It was now up to the student members of the council to decide the final verdict. Slowly and deliberately they marked their ballots and passed them to Dean Nadler.

Some Questions to Consider

Is Selena Weil's argument concerning Lucy's innocence convincing? Why or why not? Is Carla Lombardo's argument concerning Lucy's guilt convincing? Why or why not? Has there been any change in your perception of whether Lucy's action was an incidence of cheating, a violation of the Cromwell Honor Code preventing "unauthorized assistance" on exams? If you determine it to be a case of cheating, which of the two punishments authorized by CC's Honor Code would be most appropriate: a one-year suspension or total expulsion from the college? Why?

PART THREE

As he unfolded the secret ballots, Dean Nadler's face grew grim. When all the votes were counted, he turned to Lucy and said, "I'm sorry to inform you that the honor council has found you guilty of violating the Cromwell College Honor Code. We now ask you to leave the room while we discuss which penalty would be appropriate in your case."

Lucy left the office in a daze, and sank into a chair offered by the dean's secretary. Frank and some of her close friends had come to give her their support, and they waited with her for what seemed like an eternity. In reality, it was only a few moments before Dean Nadler opened the door and invited Lucy to re-enter the office.

She walked in, sat down, and looked blankly from one member of the council to another. The dean said, "Lucy, we've decided to give you the less severe punishment of one year's suspension from Cromwell. We believe that you've learned a good deal from this incident, and that you'll never succumb to a similar temptation again. You will not receive any credit for the current fall semester, and you will not be allowed to enroll in the spring, either. Next fall, we'll be happy to welcome you back to our community. I will speak with your parents myself and explain the situation to them as fairly and as generously as I can."

At the mention of her parents, Lucy became deathly pale. She rose from her chair, turned toward the office door, and collapsed in a faint. Dean Nadler's office was plunged into chaos as honor council members huddled around Lucy, trying to revive her. The dean's secretary called the college health center and in a few minutes a nurse arrived. As Lucy regained consciousness, Dean Nadler telephoned her parents.

The Donovans wasted no time in coming to "rescue" their daughter. By that night, all of Lucy's belongings had been packed into the family minivan. Her parents couldn't wait to get Lucy away from the den of iniquity they perceived Cromwell College to be, and they told her in no uncertain terms that they would never permit her to return or to stay in touch with any of the "evil influences" she had met during her brief stay.

Lucy sat mutely in the minivan, staring out the window at her closest friends who were waving good-bye from the front steps of Reynolds Hall. Frank was nowhere to be seen. He had been by Lucy's side throughout the afternoon, staying with her while the nurse revived her and refusing to leave her even after her parents, in the first desperate moments after their arrival, threatened to have him arrested. Lucy, who seemed to be in a state of shock, finally summoned the last dregs of energy she had remaining.

"I can't stand listening to my mom and dad rant and rave at you," she told Frank. "It's just tearing me up inside. Please leave for now, and maybe they'll calm down a bit. I'll find a way to get in touch with you soon." Lucy's parents harrumphed when they heard this, but Frank simply nodded and went on his way.

Frank spent the evening telling the rest of the campus about the outcome of the honor council's deliberations. He was determined to avenge Lucy in whatever way he could, and he chose to do this by attacking the Honor Code itself.

"What kind of justice is this, what kind of honor, when someone everyone knows did no real wrong is suspended from the college, getting the same punishment as others who commit much worse infractions?" he demanded. "We need to rethink the Honor Code and rework it so that it can respond to the circumstances of individual cases."

Many Cromwell students listened sympathetically to Frank's arguments. Members of the Cromwell Student Government (CSG), who had been considering holding an open forum to discuss the code, decided to hold the meeting the following week. As Lucy drove home with her parents, CSG members were already posting flyers across the campus, announcing the forum and inviting the full participation of the entire CC community.

Some Questions to Consider

How do you feel about the honor council's decision to convict Lucy of academic fraud? What about their decision to penalize her with a one-year suspension? What do you think of the reaction of Lucy? Of her parents? Of Frank? What impact could the open forum have on Lucy's case or on future cases of possible academic fraud?

WRITING EXERCISE

Lucy's first weekend back home was a disaster. She was in disgrace; her parents were determined that she'd never return to Cromwell, and planned to keep her from seeing any of her CC friends, especially Frank McFarland.

Lucy tried to tell them her version of the story, but they didn't seem willing to listen. They were convinced that what Lucy did *was* cheating, and that she fell to this low point because of her unfortunate association with disreputable acquaintances. One look at Frank was enough to tell them that he was *not* the kind of young man they wanted their daughter dating. They decided they would allow Lucy to enroll at Cascade Community College for the spring term, but that was the only concession they were willing to make.

Lucy had yet to fully recover from her state of shock. Aside from a few feeble attempts to explain the circumstances to her parents, she simply gave in to all their demands.

Meanwhile, word of Lucy's situation spread across campus, and many students were outraged. There appeared to be widespread sentiment for a clearer and more flexible Honor Code. The CSG decided to recommend particular revisions that would clarify the meaning of "unauthorized assistance" and that would provide a greater range of punishments depending on the circumstances surrounding a particular violation. They intended to present the exact wording of a proposed new Honor Code at next week's forum.

In the meantime, Cromwell's dean of academic affairs appointed an ad-hoc faculty committee to explore the current state of the Honor Code at Cromwell and to determine whether the current code needed reconsideration. Hal Banner, the honor council member who was serving as

chair of the ad-hoc committee, planned to attend the CSG forum in order to acquaint himself with student attitudes toward the code, and he
also invited written comments on the matter to be submitted to him as
soon as possible.

What would it take for this tale of Lucy and the Honor Code to
reach a satisfactory conclusion? Could any statements be conveyed—
to Lucy, to her parents, or to Prof. Banner in his role as chair of the ad-
hoc committee—that would lead to positive results? Decide which *one*
of these three audiences (Lucy, her parents, or Prof. Banner) you would
like to address; plan a letter to your target audience that makes a specific proposal and argues for it as clearly and concretely as possible;
and write your letter coherently, concisely, and convincingly.

PART FOUR

After being back home for a few days and wandering around the house
in a mental fog, Lucy finally shook off her lethargy and worked up the
courage to face her parents. She had received a number of encouraging calls and letters from her Cromwell friends and their words of support motivated her to confront her parents at the breakfast table on
Wednesday—exactly one week after she had taken Prof. Sanders'
midterm exam. She looked them straight in the eyes, and said, "Mom
and Dad, you know that I love you and that I appreciate all you're doing to keep me on the right path. But I've got to learn to stand on my
own two feet.

"I'm not denying that I made a mistake regarding Prof. Sanders'
exam, but you have to realize that to some extent you played a role in that
mistake. If you hadn't gotten me so afraid that you would pull me out of
school at the slightest provocation, I never would have felt the temptation to use questionable information on the test. You can't keep giving
me the message that you don't trust me to take care of myself; otherwise,
how will I ever grow or mature? After all, you're not always going to be
around to look after me. The long and the short of it is that if I'm ever going to become a responsible adult, I need the opportunity to live my own
life, to make my own decisions—and, maybe, my own mistakes.

"I guarantee you that I'll never again make the same mistake: getting so worried about my academic performance that I do something I
know is ethically wrong. But I also have to be honest with you and let
you know that I'll continue to keep in touch with my Cromwell friends.
They had nothing to do with this mistake, and I'm sure all of my
friends, especially Frank, would have counseled me to act honorably
had I asked their advice beforehand. I can't cut myself off from my
friends; they've come to mean so much to me in the past few weeks. You
have no idea what happiness Frank has brought into my life—and isn't
my happiness what you ultimately want? Please don't judge Frank and
the rest of my friends just by appearances. Give them a chance.

"I'm going to go back to Cromwell next fall, when my suspension is over. I'd like to do it with your love and approval, but I'll do without it, if I have to. If you refuse to give me your financial support I'll find a way to manage—grants, loans, extra work hours, whatever I can get."

Lucy's parents were stunned by this unaccustomed assertiveness from their daughter. But they, too, had been considering the situation and had to admit that there was some truth in what she said. Lucy had not been the only one to receive thought-provoking calls and letters; Dean Nadler had already telephoned her parents three times, and some members of the Cromwell community had written directly to the Donovans, asking them to rethink their attitude toward their daughter's circumstances.

These words of concern from outside sources had an impact on their views. They asked Lucy for a little time to think things over and later that day told her of their decision: they would allow her to stay in touch with her Cromwell friends and to take courses at nearby Cascade Community College in order to keep up with her studies. After her year of suspension, they would accept her return to Cromwell with their unconditional financial and emotional support. At the end of that second year, they would consider Lucy's situation and determine whether she could continue her education at CC.

Lucy was elated; this was a better outcome than she had expected! She rushed to the telephone to call Frank and tell him that she'd be able to see him as soon as she could talk her parents into lending her the minivan for the one-hour drive to campus. He was thrilled to hear the news, and had some good news of his own.

"The CSG's open forum on the Honor Code was held last night, and the turnout was awesome," Frank said. "A lot of the discussion focused on your case. There was talk of a boycott of Prof. Sanders' classes—some students felt he should be charged with an Honor Code violation himself because of his 'plagiarism' of Prof. Jackson's exams, and a few even argued that he should be fired for being such a negligent teacher. But there was a broader agenda, too. Dozens of students spoke in favor of reworking the code, and the CSG presented a proposal for a new Honor Code that defines 'unauthorized assistance' more precisely and that offers a greater latitude of punishments. Prof. Banner, who's heading the ad-hoc faculty committee that's been charged with re-examining the Honor Code, was also at the forum, and he had some very positive reactions to the CSG proposal. The faculty committee is meeting tomorrow, and I'm sure they're going to proceed with the process of revising the code. It looks like some good will be coming out of your situation after all!"

After a few more minutes of chatting with Frank, Lucy hung up the phone. Her year of suspension would not be easy, but she knew she could survive. By next fall, she would be back at Cromwell with Frank—once again breaking the residence hall visitation rules.

Some Questions to Consider

How do you feel about the conclusion of Lucy's case? Do you agree with Lucy's claim that her parents bear some culpability for what occurred, due to their attitudes and expectations? Do you agree with the CSG proposals for a new Honor Code at Cromwell? Do you agree with the students who called for some action to be taken against Prof. Sanders? Was he in any way responsible for what occurred, and does he deserve any penalty?

Thinking Critically

Lucy's case is rather complex and raises a number of issues, some of which relate to academic fraud, but some of which go beyond the problem of cheating into such areas as faculty obligations, parental involvement, and the question of just punishment. Can you identify all the issues raised by this case? Can you identify the theses presented by the various participants in the case in response to these issues?

Reading Closely

The phrase "unauthorized assistance" which appears in the Cromwell Honor Code is central to an assessment of Lucy's actions. For Prof. Weil, tacit authorization can be inferred from a professor's general behavior and teaching methods; for Prof. Lombardo, authorization must be granted in explicit verbal terms, and any exam "assistance" that has not been explicitly authorized must be considered unauthorized. Which of these two interpretations of "unauthorized assistance" seems more convincing to you? Why? Are there any other ways "unauthorized assistance" could be defined? If you were rewriting the Cromwell Honor Code in order to clarify the meaning of this phrase, how would you go about explaining it more precisely?

What If

What if Lucy had not turned herself in, but her viewing of Prof. Sanders' exam had been witnessed by one of the other employees in the political science department office who subsequently reported her for violating the Honor Code? Would you view Lucy's case any differently? Why or why not? What if Lucy had made a photocopy of the entire exam before replacing it in Prof. Sanders' mailbox, and used the copy as a "study guide"? Would you view Lucy's case any differently? Why or why not?

Connecting the Cases

In several Cromwell cases we have been faced with students who may have violated college policies. In some policies, such as the Honor Code, the penalties for violation are clearly delineated; in others, such as the sexual misconduct policy or the discriminatory harassment policy, there is greater flexibility, with "disciplinary action" to be determined "according to the established procedures of the college." In the event of a guilty verdict, what would constitute a just punishment for each of the potential policy violations we have encountered so far; for example, in cases 1, 2, and 4? How would these penalties compare to the penalties indicated for Honor Code violations?

Bringing It Home

What are the current student attitudes on your campus regarding academic fraud? What are your college's policies and procedures for dealing with cheating and plagiarism? Do you believe that your college's policies affect student behavior in this area? Do you support the idea of college honor codes or other academic honesty guidelines as a deterrent to cheating? Why or why not?

Suggestions for Writing

1. Write a letter to a close friend unfamiliar with the Cromwell scene, briefly explaining the facts of Lucy's case and exploring what you would have done had you been in Lucy's place and inadvertently come across a crucial exam question. How would your actions have differed from—or resembled—hers?

2. The editor of your former high school newspaper decides to do a special issue on cheating. He asks you to write a feature article on the issue from the college perspective, basing your discussion on interviews with current college students as well as on previously published material dealing with academic fraud on the university level.

3. Does Prof. Sanders bear any responsibility for Lucy's actions? To what extent can faculty teaching methods contribute to or detract from the temptation to cheat? Write an essay exploring the faculty's role in promoting academic honesty.

Out Loud

You have decided to attend the CSG's open forum on the Honor Code. Make an oral presentation to the other forum participants that conveys your own position on the code, using Lucy's case as necessary to support, illuminate, or explain your position.

CASE 8

Unite and Fight
College Employees and Student Support

PART ONE

One morning Kira Washington and several of her friends were walking to the dining hall for breakfast when they heard the sound of rhythmic chanting. As they neared the student union where the dining hall was located, the chant became intelligible: "Students and workers, unite and fight!"

What was going on? The answer presented itself when Kira and her friends reached the building. Right in front of the entrance a line of people marched back and forth, chanting and brandishing placards which declared, "Local 1339, Amalgamated Food Service Workers Union, ON STRIKE." Kira recognized a number of dining hall workers whose faces had become familiar to her. To reach the dining hall, she would have to walk through the line of pickets.

One thing Kira had absorbed from her study of American history was a deep-seated respect for the ideals of the labor movement—not to mention the fact that her father, a high school English teacher who was very active in his union, had recently participated in a controversial six-week-long strike which convinced Kira and her family even more fully of the necessity for working people to stand up for their rights. How could she bring herself to cross a picket line?

She turned to her friends to seek their advice, but most of them had already walked through the line of strikers and on into the student union without thinking twice about their actions. A couple of others were discussing the option of getting to the dining hall through the student union's side entrance, which they proceeded to do.

After considering the situation, Kira followed them. She reasoned that by using the side door she wouldn't actually be crossing the picket line. Besides, she had to eat, didn't she? Much as she would have liked to, she certainly didn't have the money to go to Pancake Heaven instead of the Cromwell dining hall. She really had no other choice, she figured.

As Kira entered the dining hall, she picked up one of the bright pink leaflets on a table beside the big double doors. Her eyes were drawn immediately to the leaflet's banner headline: "STUDENTS AND WORKERS, UNITE AND FIGHT!" As she skimmed the text, she noticed one of the dining hall managers eyeing her suspiciously.

"You're blocking the doorway," he said abruptly as he walked over to her. "Either get in the line, or leave."

"Okay, okay, I'm getting in line. I was only stopping for a second to look at this leaflet," Kira replied.

"It's just propaganda," snorted the manager.

"You mean the information here isn't correct?" Kira asked.

"Well, I wouldn't say that. Actually, I don't think there's any question about the accuracy of the statements made in the leaflet—no one is disputing the facts as they're presented here. But in today's economy, these workers are lucky to have any jobs at all. A lot of people with their level of skills are permanently unemployed. They shouldn't be complaining about the conditions here." With that remark, the manager turned away and headed for the kitchen.

The line at the serving area was unusually long this morning. While Kira waited her turn, she perused the leaflet, which explained the background to the strike that was in progress. The leaflet read:

STUDENTS AND WORKERS, UNITE AND FIGHT!

By this time, you're probably aware that Cromwell College's food service workers have gone on strike. Why are we doing this? Just to create long lines in the dining hall and make students' lives miserable? Far from it. We have good reasons for taking such serious action, and we'd like to explain them to you.

For the past three months, food service workers at Cromwell have been working without a contract. As you may know, Cromwell, unlike many other colleges and universities, does not employ an outside contractor to provide food. Meals, snacks, receptions, and so on are handled by the college itself, through its Department of Food and Beverage Services (DFBS).

In negotiations for a new contract conducted over the summer, the director of DFBS informed Cromwell food service workers that under new cost containment policies, a wage freeze would be in effect for the next two years. In addition, health benefits—already minimal— would become even more limited, with drug and alcohol treatment as well as mental health outpatient services no longer covered by the insurance plan. Furthermore, coverage for physical therapy, nutritional counseling, and other medical services would be drastically curtailed.

Cromwell's food service workers, who are members of Local 1339 of the national Amalgamated Food Service Workers Union (AFSWU), found this to be unacceptable. Currently, a typical full-time dining hall employee at Cromwell earns a mere $16,000 per year; the head chef—the highest paid of Cromwell's DFBS employees—earns only $27,000. With meager salaries like these, benefits such as medical coverage are particularly important. Therefore, we refused to sign the contract as presented. Union representatives proposed an alternate contract, which continued health benefits at their current level and provided a 3 percent annual cost-of-living wage increase across the board.

Cromwell rejected this proposal out of hand. We continued to negotiate in good faith. Eventually, we even offered to accept a one-year wage freeze, as well as cuts in mental health coverage, but our numerous overtures went nowhere. In spite of our attempts to meet DFBS halfway, it became apparent that they were unwilling to make any concessions whatsoever. After months of confronting intransigence and insensitivity, we have determined to take the only effective action available to us as workers: we are now on strike, and will remain on strike until we see some signs of compromise from DFBS.

What can students do to help us? First of all, if you see the justice of our cause, you can let DFBS and the Cromwell senior administration know that you do not support the exploitation of workers on this campus. You can let your parents know, too, and ask them to exert whatever pressure they can to put an end to this stalemate. If your own financial situation enables you to do so, you can honor our picket line and refuse to take your meals in the Cromwell dining hall. You can make whatever contributions you can afford to the AFSWU strike fund. Work in solidarity with us, and we *can* reach a fair settlement with the college!

By the time she finished reading, Kira was at the head of the line. She was surprised to see George Maruyama, a student she knew from her American history class, serving lukewarm scrambled eggs and soggy hash browns from the steam table.

"What are you doing back there?" she asked George as she held out her plate.

George smiled and replied, "Well, it's a dirty job, but someone's got to do it. Actually, I'm not complaining. You know my work-study assignment is here in the dining hall, cleaning up after breakfast every day. Well, since the strike started this morning, DFBS has offered me extra hours at extra pay to take the place of a regular dining hall worker. I can certainly use the money."

"But aren't you being a strike-breaker, a scab? Doesn't your willingness to take over the job undermine the bargaining position of the workers?" asked Kira.

"Maybe," answered George with a shrug of the shoulders, "but the students have to eat. Someone has to cook their food and serve them. Why shouldn't that someone be me? Anyway, if I didn't do it, somebody else would. There are a whole bunch of us who do work-study in the dining hall. All of us were asked to take on extra duties and extra hours during the strike, and we were offered an additional dollar per hour over our usual wages if we agreed, with the overtime and extra pay coming not from work-study funds but out of the DFBS budget. Only a couple of students have refused the extra hours. Everyone else is glad for the chance to make more money—we can all use it."

The young man behind Kira started grumbling loudly about how long she was taking to get her food, and so she walked away from the serving area and took a seat at an empty table by the window. The chants of the strikers filtered faintly through the glass. She thought about what George had said, and as she ate her unappetizing breakfast, she wondered what she would have done if she, like him, had been asked to take the position of one of the striking workers.

Some Questions to Consider

How do you feel about the food service workers' decision to go on strike? Given their statement of the issues, do you think their action is justified? What about the dining hall manager's claim that they should simply consider themselves lucky to have a paying job? How do you think Cromwell students should deal with the strike, and with the question of whether or not to cross the picket line? Do you think Kira and her friends did the right thing by going through the side door? What do you think of George's decision to take over the position of one of the striking workers? Did he make the right choice?

SMALL-GROUP EXERCISE

Talking It Out

Not many Cromwell students come from wealthy families. A majority receive some form of financial aid such as grants or low-interest loans. Over half the students participate in a federally subsidized work-study program, working on campus with wages applied directly toward tuition.

You, too, are on work-study, and upon your arrival at CC this semester, you were assigned to wash dishes in the Cromwell dining hall for ten hours a week at the minimum wage. It's not a great job, but it's less tedious than you expected since your fellow workers are a pretty fun bunch. Etta Lester, one of the dishwashers who has been working in the dining hall for years, has taken on the role of surrogate mother to you. She even remembered your birthday and got the guys in the bakery section to make you a special cake.

You've heard Etta complaining about her low wages and limited benefits, and she's mentioned some of the problems with the DFBS contract negotiations. But none of this affected you directly until yes-terday afternoon, when you received a call from one of the DFBS shift managers informing you that the dining hall workers had called a strike and would not be reporting for duty the following morning. He asked if you'd be willing to take on additional work hours, doing the same job you'd always done for work-study but adding dinnertime to your regu-lar breakfast schedule. He offered you the bonus of an extra dollar per hour for any time you worked during the strike, including your regular shift, if you were willing to commit to at least five additional hours per week. The shift manager gave you overnight to make up your mind, and told you that you had to give him an answer by noon the next day.

The offer is tempting. You're never able to get much done around dinnertime anyway and usually just spend the time chatting with your friends, so there's no question of your academic progress being dis-rupted. And since you're especially tight for money right now, you could use the extra dollars. However, you know that the only chance the food service workers have to get DFBS to listen to their demands is through an effective work stoppage. If work-study students step into their positions, that would render the strike meaningless. How could you do that to the people you work with every day?

To help sort out your thoughts, you decide to discuss the issue with a few of your friends who also have work-study jobs in the dining hall and who are faced with the same dilemma. How should you re-spond to the shift manager's offer?

Writing It Out

After spirited discussion, you realize you'll be able to articulate your position more clearly and forcefully in writing than in speech, and so you decide to give the DFBS shift manager a note. He's asked you to tell him whether you accept or reject his offer as well as how and why you've reached your conclusion. What will you write in response to this request?

PART TWO

As Kira pondered the issues raised by the food service workers' strike and slowly sipped a slightly bitter cup of coffee, she glanced at her watch and realized that she'd have to be at her American history class in about ten minutes, which would give her just enough time to walk over to her room in Dalloway Hall and pick up her books. She again went through the student union's side door, but this time she could not avoid the strikers. A few of them had brought their picket signs to this entrance, and several students had joined them as they sang the open-ing verse of "Solidarity Forever."

Among the supporting students was Sondra Johnson, whom Kira had met several weeks ago while doing volunteer work at a local shelter for homeless women and children. Sondra approached Kira and began to urge her to show her solidarity with the striking workers by joining the group of protesters, but Kira hurriedly moved away, explaining that she was about to be late for class. Sondra sadly shook her head as she watched Kira walk toward the Lower Quad.

Sondra turned to her friend Art Larson, who was standing beside her with a homemade poster that read, "Students in Solidarity with Local 1339." She sighed and said, "It never ceases to amaze me. You take someone like Kira. She's involved with the Cromwell Women's Caucus, she volunteers at the One World Shelter, and last week I saw her at a meeting of Cromwell Students for International Human Rights. But when it comes to issues of class, of workers' rights, of the rights of anyone to a fair wage and decent health care—when it comes down to the fact that workers on this very campus are being treated like dirt—she can just shrug her shoulders and go her merry way as if it's no concern of hers.

"That's the problem with the students here," Sondra continued. "They think that if they do a little community service and go to a couple of meetings, if they sign a petition protesting abuses of human rights halfway across the world, then they've done their duty, without facing up to the wrongs that are occurring daily on their very doorsteps."

"Come on, Sondra, aren't you being a little hard on these people?" asked Art. "After all, it's not always easy for college students to realize that they have anything in common with a bunch of underpaid food service workers."

"Yeah," Sondra responded, "and at first I thought that was because so many of the students here at Cromwell are white and so many of the dining hall workers are black, but the African-American students aren't really showing any more support for the workers than their Caucasian classmates are. I've realized that it isn't an issue of race, but of class, and of being willing to see things from the perspective of someone who's trying to earn a living by cleaning up the mess we leave when we walk away from our breakfast tables.

"It's a question of justice, of fairness, of giving people the opportunity to live a decent life. It just seems so obvious to me—I don't understand why everyone else can't see it. You don't have to be a rocket scientist to realize that $16,000 a year isn't much to live on, especially when you're trying to support a family," concluded Sondra.

"Of course that's true," replied Art, "but I think it's sometimes harder for people to deal with injustice in their own community than far away. After all, we've all been going to the dining hall day after day, letting the workers cook our meals and dish them out on warm, clean plates. Why do we let them serve us like that? Why aren't we cooking our own meals, cleaning our own dishes?"

Art continued, "Everyone grumbles about how much we pay for the meal plan, but we obviously aren't paying enough to guarantee the people who serve us a decent standard of living. In a way, *we're* the ones who are exploiting the workers. After all, we're the ones who are directly benefiting from their service, and we're the ones who are indirectly paying their salaries. I think a lot of Cromwell students may not want to face up to their own complicity in worker exploitation, and that's why they're so eager to avoid the issue altogether."

Sondra shook her head. "It's never crossed the minds of most Cromwell students that they might have any complicity in the plight of the dining hall workers. The fact of the matter is that most students here, like students everywhere, are selfish and self-absorbed. *That's* why they don't care about the strike."

As Sondra and Art continued their discussion, they realized that a number of other students had joined the side-door pickets, including several who sported the distinctive red and black lapel buttons of Left Out, a national student group with a militant branch at Cromwell College. The Left Out members had begun some rather vicious chants, and their overbearing voices drowned out the striking workers' lively rendition of "We Shall Not Be Moved."

The dining hall workers and their supporters continued to sing and tried to ignore the loud chants as best they could. But when Walter Dietz, one of the more bloodthirsty Left Out members, began shouting, "Kill the scabs! Kill the scabs!" one of the employees decided she had had enough.

Etta Lester was old enough to be Walter's mother, and there was a note of maternal scolding in her voice as she took his arm and said, "Young man, we don't need that kind of nonsense. This is a peaceful picket. We may not like the fact that so many of the work-study students chose to take over our jobs, but everyone has to do what they think is right, and I guess they just see the issues differently. We don't want anyone hurt, and we don't want to intimidate or harass anyone. So either you agree to join us in a nonviolent protest, or you go home."

Walter snorted derisively and replied, "You know that your strike will never be effective unless it has a major impact on the operations of the dining hall, stopping or at least drastically slowing down the meal service. That will never happen if DFBS can just get a bunch of students to step in. The students may not work as efficiently, but with the help of a few management types, they can keep things running. As long as they keep things running, you can be out on strike till you starve—it won't have any impact.

"Now, most of these students didn't even think twice about what they were doing when they agreed to take on extra work. All they had in mind was making more money. They didn't realize that the money they make comes, in a sense, out of the regular workers' pockets, since it's the money you're giving up by going out on strike. And even if they did take this into consideration, it probably wouldn't hold a lot of weight compared to their own self-interest.

"The only way to get to them," said Walter, "the only way to make them really stop and question their own actions, is to get right in their faces, to let them see that what they've done is wrong, that there are consequences—nasty consequences, frightening consequences—to the action they've taken. That's all I'm trying to do."

Etta shook her head. "You don't change anyone's mind by threatening to kill them," she said. "That may change their immediate actions, but in the long run, it'll make them even less inclined to sympathize with our cause."

"Never mind the long run," Walter interjected. "What you should be concerned about is getting DFBS to compromise with you as soon as possible. And that means keeping the work-study students out of the dining hall—by any means necessary."

At that moment, George Maruyama stepped out of the student union's side entrance. As soon as Walter caught a glimpse of him, he shouted, "Hey! It's one of the scabs! Get him!" and rushed toward George with his right hand in a fist. Art Larson moved quickly to intervene, seizing the arm of the would-be assailant and thanking his lucky stars that he'd had the self-discipline to keep up with his weight training all semester.

Who knows what mayhem might have then ensued if not for the timely appearance of four campus security officers, who shepherded the Left Out members to the department of safety. George decided not to press assault charges, but he did ask one of the security officers to escort him safely back to his residence hall.

Sondra and Art, shaken by the narrowly averted violence, thought about leaving the scene. However, after discussing the matter they decided that now more than ever the striking workers needed their support. They agreed to skip all of their classes for the next day or two and devote their time to the cause of the food service employees.

The workers continued to picket the student union, but after a couple of days most members of the Cromwell community ceased to pay attention to AFSWU Local 1339. Sondra and Art eventually had to go back to attending their classes, and although they still spent as much time as they could lending support to the strikers, only a handful of their peers joined them. Even the members of Left Out—thwarted by the workers' refusal to take a hard line against the strike-breakers, as well as by the security officers' surveillance of their activities—were keeping a low profile.

As Walter Dietz had predicted, the DFBS managers were able to keep the dining hall operating with the help of the many work-study students who had agreed to extended hours, and thus the strike was rendered ineffectual. There was no movement toward compromise on the contract. In the meantime, AFSWU's rather limited strike fund quickly ran dry. The workers had to put food on their own tables, make their rent or mortgage payments, and support their families, and they couldn't do that unless they had some money coming in. And so, just ten days after the strike had begun, Local 1339 voted to end it and to sign the contract that had been offered to them in the summer.

The union meeting during which the vote was taken was an emotional one, and Etta Lester was not the only one who left in tears. Every morning during the strike, she had read the coverage in the local newspaper, which stressed the fact that students were refusing to stand in solidarity with the workers and were instead pursuing their own financial self-interest. After a couple of days, the story was picked up nationally, and one syndicated columnist commented on the changes in the attitude of today's youth as compared to college students thirty years ago.

Etta had thought better of the Cromwell students she worked with every day. She had been sure they would never knowingly hurt her in her quest for a better way of life for herself and her family. Now her faith was shattered. As she headed back home after the meeting, Etta wondered how she would manage to keep her modest household going for the next two years without even the hope of a pay increase above her annual salary of $16,967. She wondered how she would ever be able to afford the physical therapy her daughter needed to help her recover from hip surgery, now that the treatment would no longer be covered by health insurance.

And she wondered how she could go back to work the next morning and face the work-study students with the same smile she had always greeted them with in the past.

Some Questions to Consider

What do you think about Art's contention that Cromwell students are implicated in the exploitation of the food service workers? What about Sondra's claim that the typical college student is too self-involved to care about the concerns of others? How do you feel about the behavior of the Left Out members? Do you find Walter Dietz's explanation of his actions convincing? What about Etta's point of view? Does it seem more or less convincing than Walter's? How do you feel about the conclusion of the case?

Thinking Critically

The dining hall manager admitted to Kira that the information reported in the strikers' leaflet was fundamentally accurate, and that he was not "disputing the facts as they're presented here." Can you identify which items in the leaflet are factually based? If these facts are not contested, do they provide sufficient evidence to support the strikers' position? Are there alternative interpretations of the information presented that could lead to conclusions different from the conclusions reached by the striking workers?

Reading Closely

What elements in the leaflet might contribute to the manager's sense that the document is "propaganda"? Have the workers used any strategies to slant their presentation according to their own point of view? For example, how are the union representatives portrayed in the second-to-last paragraph, and how does this compare with the portrayal of the DFBS negotiators in the same paragraph? You may also want to look closely at the use of adjectives, which are often a vehicle for conveying personal perspective; for example, what messages are conveyed through the use of such adjectives as "minimal," "limited," "mere," "only," and "meager"?

What If

What if the striking workers had decided to adopt the confrontational approach of the Left Out demonstrators, and had begun attacking people (e.g., harassing the work-study "scabs") or property (e.g., destroying dining hall equipment)? Would that change your perspective on this case? Why or why not?

Connecting the Cases

Cromwell student groups have often played a role in cases that do not directly involve their members. For example, the Cromwell Women's Caucus, the Cromwell Greek Council, the *Clarion,* the Committee to Reconsider the Honor Code, the Cromwell Student Government and, in case 8, Left Out, as well as the Students in Solidarity with Local 1339, have all intervened in campus controversies. Are such interventions justified? Is a labor dispute involving college employees any business of students? Are the proceedings of an individual case any business of the community? When is student involvement legitimate, and what form should it take?

Bringing It Home

How much do you know about the situation of employees on your own campus, particularly those who are neither faculty members nor administrators? Pick one sector of your campus workforce (maintenance personnel, clerical staff, etc.) and find out as much as you can about their working conditions.

Suggestions for Writing

1. You've heard that George Maruyama has hardly left his room all week because he's had so many doubts and conflicts about his decision to take on the work of a striking employee. Write a letter to George explaining your attitude toward his choice.

2. During the food service workers' strike, one of your close friends asks you to sign a petition in support of the striking workers. Write an entry in your personal journal that explores your thoughts in response to this request.

3. Walter Dietz argued that the goals of the striking workers should be achieved "by any means necessary"—including the threat of violence. Do you agree with this claim? Are there some situations in which violence is justified to achieve a legitimate goal? Is this such a case? Why or why not? Write an essay explaining and supporting your point of view.

Out Loud

A prime-time television news show is coming to Cromwell to cover the food service workers' strike. For some background on the case, the producers have randomly contacted a group of "typical" CC students—including you and several of your classmates—to gain a student perspective on the strike. Have one of your classmates play the role of a television reporter, and conduct a roundtable discussion with the reporter in which you present your views.

CASE 9

Core Wars
Conflicting Views of General Education

As he sat with a couple of his friends over a dining hall dinner of mystery meat and unidentified greens, Victor Barrera could hardly bring himself to put a forkful of food into his mouth.

"What's the matter, Victor?" asked Irene Oban, one of his dining companions. "I know the food is awful, but that's never stopped you before."

"Yeah," added Henry Xavier, the third student at the table. "Usually the amount you put away is incredible. Is something bothering you?"

Victor put down his fork and nodded. "It's this core curriculum business that's gotten me all tied up in knots. You know I'm serving on the student-faculty committee that's examining Cromwell's core of required general education courses. Well, we've been getting together every week since the semester began, and we had yet another meeting this afternoon. Lately our sessions have been really frustrating. We've been meeting for weeks now without making much progress. So far, the only thing we've settled on is that we have to do something more than the current structure of vague distribution requirements from the different academic areas. We need to create a more coherent core experience shared by all students."

While Victor was explaining the issues to Irene and Henry, they were joined by Grace Tran, another student member of the Core Curriculum Committee. As she sat down and began eating her salad, Grace picked up the thread of the discussion, pointing out that it was one thing to come up with the idea of a more coherent core experience, and another thing to put it into practice.

"At first," Grace said, "I didn't like Professor Banner's suggestion of an introductory core course that all students would have to take. But when I thought about it, I saw the value of a required interdisciplinary course that would encourage students to think critically about significant issues and that would give us a common intellectual experience as a basis for our later studies. I guess the rest of the committee saw the value of it, too, since we were quickly able to reach consensus on the need to develop such a course."

"Yes," agreed Victor, "but what we haven't been able to agree on is what the course should consist of. How would we structure a one-semester introductory core course? It seems like everyone you ask has a different idea. When we first started exploring the possibility, Prof. Wong proposed an issue-based approach: in other words, we'd look at a particular issue—say, obedience to authority—and read works from different disciplines that would shed light on the issue. Then Prof. Weil wanted us to take a more historical approach: for example, focusing on a single decade in American history, and exploring the intellectual, scientific, political, economic, and artistic forces that shaped that period of time.

"Once the ball started rolling, the ideas kept coming. Prof. Gupta suggested we do something more in-depth: choosing one complex and meaningful text—something like the biblical Book of Genesis—and really giving it a close reading, approaching it from all points of view and examining its significance as an account of creation, a literary work, a basis for religious faith, a philosophical disquisition on human nature, and so on. And just a couple of weeks ago, Prof. Lombardo came up with what she called the local approach: focusing on a particular spot in our immediate community, something like the block of State Street directly across from the Cromwell front gates, and examining that particular plot of land from a range of perspectives: environmental, historical, sociological, economic, aesthetic, whatever."

"You know," Grace remarked, "all the approaches seemed interesting as the various professors explained them, and I started to get really excited about the idea of this core course. Then came Professors Connor and Hunt, who got everyone in a tizzy by insisting that the course needed to be an overview of the great ideas of Western civilization: everything from Sophocles' *Oedipus Rex* to Freud's Oedipus complex."

Grace smiled, and then continued, "My feeling was that a course like that crammed into one semester would be pretty superficial, and wouldn't really be relevant to most students' lives. But a couple of the other student members of the committee said that they felt deprived and impoverished because they had never been required to read Plato's *Republic*. When I pointed out that if they wanted to read it so badly they could go off and do it on their own without forcing everyone else to read it, too, they got ticked off at me and said that my laissez-faire attitude was an example of the worst kind of moral relativism."

"You've got to admit, though," said Henry, "that those two professors do have a point. How can you say that the works of intellectual giants like Plato or Freud are irrelevant to students' lives? How can we call ourselves educated if we haven't read some of the central works that have shaped our culture? If we don't know something about the intellectual background of our civilization, how can we participate in it thoughtfully? For example, wouldn't our understanding of the Declaration of Independence, and thus our country's political system, be enhanced by reading John Locke?"

"Maybe," replied Grace, "but if you think Locke is so valuable, why not just check the *Essay Concerning Human Understanding* out of the library? Why do you need a course to force you to read it? Anyway, we can't read everything. How do we choose what to include and what to exclude? You may want us to read John Locke, but perhaps we'd gain a fuller perspective on the Declaration of Independence by reading texts by Mary Wollstonecraft, Frederick Douglass, Thomas Paine—people who talk about rights that are *not* necessarily addressed in the Declaration. These authors aren't always included in lists of the great books, but surely their perspective is just as valid as John Locke's."

"I don't deny that Mary Wollstonecraft and Frederick Douglass can offer us valuable perspectives," said Henry, "but their views are the opposition ones. The dominant views are the ones that have shaped our society, and those are the ones we need to become familiar with first, before we explore the minority positions."

"Why can't we look at the two together?" Victor interjected.

"The question is, who should be deciding what's worth looking at?" said Irene. "Do you trust the members of the Core Curriculum Committee to determine what you need to know? No offense to Victor and Grace, but I certainly don't. Frankly, I'm not convinced that the idea of requiring everyone to take a single core course is such a good one.

"Cromwell students aren't all identical," Irene continued. "We're unique individuals with unique educational goals, and no one—certainly not a student-faculty committee—knows us as well as we know ourselves. I'd like to have more of a say in my own education, and pick the courses that I think will work for me personally, given my needs and interests. Maybe I'm just contrary by nature, but I can't stand being forced to do things 'for my own good,' and I'm sure a lot of other students feel that way, too. When we're made to take a required course we end up with a hostile attitude to the class we're stuck in, which makes it impossible to learn effectively."

"I may not think the core committee has all the answers," Henry replied, "but I have to admit that most of the professors at Cromwell have a lot more knowledge and experience than I do. To be honest with you, I'm not really sure what my educational needs and interests are— I just don't know enough yet to decide what would be best for me. Given my natural laziness and that of most students I know, if we were left to our own devices, we'd all probably just pick the easiest classes, not necessarily the most beneficial ones. I know that's not the right thing to do, but I'm not sure I'd have the self-discipline to act otherwise. So I'm willing to let my professors make some educational decisions for me."

"But the professors themselves can't even agree," Victor pointed out. "When Connor and Hunt first made their great books proposal, Prof. Weil immediately asked them if they had considered the inclusion of texts by women, and by writers and thinkers from marginalized groups like Native Americans and African-Americans. Remember, Grace, that speech she made about diversity and inclusiveness? I thought Prof. Connor was going to explode. That's when he made his comment about being opposed to affirmative action for books. Things really started getting ugly then."

"Yeah," said Grace, "like when Prof. Weil called Prof. Hunt an intellectual imperialist. Every session we've had lately has ended up with someone walking out in a huff. When I tell my roommate some of the stuff that's been going on, she just laughs and says, 'Another battle in the core wars!'"

"Well," offered Irene, "I guess it's not hard to see how emotions could be running pretty high. After all, it's a really fundamental dispute you're embroiled in about the basis of a liberal arts education. I think it must be especially tough for professors to deal with the discussion calmly, since they've staked their careers on one or another view of what a college education should be."

"Yes," agreed Grace, "these are fundamental issues we're addressing. And though the meetings are taking up a lot of time, I'm glad we have all year before we have to report our progress to the dean of academic affairs. We still have a lot of work ahead of us. We haven't even decided yet whether we need to make our core course knowledge-based, covering a particular set of texts or ideas that every educated person should be exposed to, or skill-based, focusing on the analytical skills that are crucial to a college education.

"If you follow the skill-based schema," Grace explained, "the actual content of the course—the reading list, the syllabus, and so on— can be pretty flexible, as long as what you're doing is meaty enough to require serious analysis and synthesis. You could take Wong's issues approach, Weil's historical approach, Gupta's in-depth approach, Lombardo's local approach, or even Connor and Hunt's great books approach; any one of them could work to get us to examine things closely and make connections between different points. The choice of subject matter isn't all that crucial."

"But if you follow the knowledge-based schema," said Victor, "then you have to decide what material, given the limits of a one-semester course, really needs to be covered—and that's hard to do."

"It may be hard," said Henry, "but isn't that what needs to be done if we're going to be educated in a responsible manner? It *does* matter what the content of a required core course should be—you can't just say that the subject matter is irrelevant as long as we get the necessary skills. Would a course analyzing TV sitcoms be as valuable as a course examining the works of Aristotle, Hobbes, Marx, and so on? Both would encourage students to use their analytical skills, but in the second case we'd be applying these skills to something really worth studying, and we'd also be learning about important texts for our culture."

"For *whose* culture?" Irene asked.

"American culture," Henry responded. "We may all have different backgrounds, but we do share a common political and economic system; we all participate in the social fabric of American life. Shouldn't we read works by the people who have done the most to shape American society?"

"But the authors you're mentioning are all white European males. Are they the only ones who have shaped American society? Doesn't focusing on the so-called 'great books' exclude a whole set of perspectives that have been marginalized for too long? Besides, I could argue that TV sitcoms are actually more important to contemporary culture than any of the authors you've mentioned," Irene responded.

"Sitcoms may be more prominent in current American culture than political philosophy, but their influence isn't going to last very long," said Henry. "The thing that sets the great books apart is that they've stood the test of time. They have a universal significance that can appeal to all readers in all ages and all cultures—not just white European males."

Grace snorted. "Hmph. The texts you're talking about have stood the test of time because the educational establishment has been governed by white European males for hundreds of years. They're the ones who have determined what's worth knowing, so of course they've preserved texts that serve their interests. But who's to say that the works of John Locke are any more valuable than Native American myths and legends?"

"We have to make some tough choices," said Henry, "but that doesn't mean we should just say the choices don't matter, that whatever we study is okay as long as we practice our analytical skills."

The four dinner-table companions fell silent as they pondered the matter at hand. Just then, their friend Art Larson approached the table. "Why so thoughtful?" asked Art, sitting down to join them.

Victor turned to Art and asked, "If you had to design a single course that every Cromwell student had to take—not a particular requirement like computer literacy or composition or a foreign language, but a more broad-based core course that would serve as a sort of introduction to a liberal arts education—what would that course look like?"

"Wow," said Art, "no wonder you were all so quiet just now. Coming up with a course like that is a pretty tall order. Is that what the Core Curriculum Committee is working on these days?"

"Yes," said Grace, "and I think it would be helpful if we had more student input on the subject. We've got to find a way to get more students involved in the discussion."

"I'm afraid," said Art, "that the apathy around here is especially strong when it comes to the curriculum. It's funny—we spend so much time on academics at Cromwell that you'd think it would be the one thing we'd be most concerned about, the one issue we all have a stake in. But I've noticed that most Cromwell students haven't thought very much about what or how or why they're learning.

"It's a shame," Art lamented, "but we never seem to question the prevailing assumptions about curriculum or pedagogy. We may complain a little bit about the teaching methods of one professor or another, especially the ones whose courses are difficult, but we never get beyond superficial griping. We just say to ourselves—well, this is another hoop I have to jump through on the way to becoming a doctor, or lawyer, or whatever."

"I have to agree with you, Art," said Victor. "After all, when the Core Curriculum Committee asked for student volunteers to help determine the future of Cromwell's curriculum, only five of us opted to serve. That doesn't say much for the level of interest in curricular matters from the student body at large."

Irene and Grace shook their heads sadly. "It's too bad," said Grace. "But if students aren't willing to stand up and make their voices heard on this issue, they'll just have to learn to live with whatever decisions are made for them."

Some Questions to Consider

What do you think about the notion of a required core curriculum? Does such a shared academic experience help or hinder the overall education of individual students? How would you respond to the various professors' suggestions for an introductory core course? Can you think of a required core course that you would be excited about taking? Do you agree with Henry about the content of such a course? If so, why? If not, why not? Why do you think so few students at Cromwell seem to care about curricular issues?

Thinking Critically

Victor, Irene, Henry, and Grace all approach their discussion of a required core course with certain assumptions about the goals and purposes of education. Examine the comments they make throughout their discussion and try to identify the assumptions underlying their positions. For example, what is Henry assuming about what constitutes an educated person when he asks, "How can we call ourselves educated if we haven't read some of the central works that have shaped our culture?"

Reading Closely

In their discussion of what would constitute appropriate reading material for a core course, Grace and Henry each offer suggestions of authors or texts to consider for inclusion. Just by looking at the names offered by each of these students, what can you tell about their perspectives?

What If

What if Cromwell were to offer a course that served as an interdisciplinary introduction to the liberal arts, but did not make it a requirement? Would a majority of students take such a course of their own volition? Would this result in the "coherent core experience" favored by the Core Curriculum Committee?

Connecting the Cases

When only a small number of students are willing to make themselves heard on an issue that concerns the student body at large, it becomes questionable whether the vocal minority is truly representative of student opinion. In several of the cases we've read, a small group of students has taken it upon themselves to address matters of widespread importance. Do you see any problem with this? If you feel that broader student input should be encouraged, how could this be achieved?

Bringing It Home

Does your own college have general education or core requirements? Does it have a required course or set of courses that all students must take? If so, explore the rationale provided by the faculty for the existence of these requirements, and investigate the attitudes of students toward the required courses. If not, explore the rationale for *not* mandating core requirements.

Suggestions for Writing

1. Think of a course you took in high school that you feel prepared you especially well for college-level academics. Write a letter to the teacher of that class, explaining why you believe the class was so useful.

2. Present a proposal to the Core Curriculum Committee for a required core course. In your proposal you should include the rationale and goals for the specific course you're proposing, a brief

description of the course (subject matter, format, etc.), and some discussion of readings and/or assignments.

3. Irene rejects the notion of a required core course, believing that she should "have more of a say" in her curricular choices; Henry, however, welcomes the guidance of the Cromwell faculty in determining his curricular needs. Should students be left free to make all their own curricular choices? Write an essay that presents a well-supported argument in response to this question.

Out Loud

The general student body at Cromwell doesn't seem particularly concerned about the college curriculum. What would it take to convince them that academic matters such as the proposed core course are significant? Deliver a statement to your classmates that will stimulate interest and involvement in this issue.

CASE 10

It's a Riot
Same-Sex Relationships and Public Opinion

The current semester at Cromwell College seems destined to be an unusually turbulent one, as one controversy after another has rocked the CC student body. This time, the commotion has focused on Cromwell's Gay and Lesbian Association (GALA).

Many colleges and universities have had such support groups for years, but conservative Cromwell had been a particularly late bloomer in this respect. GALA only came into existence last year, and had since fought an uphill battle for acceptance on the Cromwell campus. Whenever the group posted leaflets announcing organizational meetings, the leaflets were immediately torn down or defaced with obscene and insulting graffiti. A small but influential coalition of students, parents, and alumni loudly proclaimed their dismay that an organization like GALA should be allowed to exist at such a venerable institution as Cromwell College.

But GALA was now a fact of life at CC, largely thanks to Paul Vega and Irene Oban—two sophomores who were among the handful of openly gay or lesbian students at the college. Paul and Irene had agreed that the time was ripe for a support group at Cromwell for gay, lesbian, bisexual, and transgendered students, and they had been instrumental in making the group a reality.

In the past, Cromwell had not been a hospitable place for gays and lesbians. The few Cromwell students who were open about their non-heterosexual orientation had been frequently subjected to verbal harassment. Whistles, catcalls, and objectionable epithets would erupt as they walked across the dining hall to sit at their usual table. Most of this harassment came from the members of the Beta Omicron Zeta (BOZ) fraternity, though other groups also were occasionally heard to mutter insults as Paul and other openly gay men walked by.

Paul, who had an unusually strong sense of self, had never been intimidated by the verbal harassment; he just laughed. He did, however, become angry when he went to the student parking lot one morning last fall and found that his car was sporting the word "faggot" spray-painted in large white letters. He became even angrier when an off-campus group of gay men, who had rented Cromwell's facilities for a weekend retreat over winter break, stepped off their bus upon first arriving on the campus to be greeted by a barrage of rotten tomatoes. Paul himself had witnessed the assault, but no one was able to identify the perpetrators.

It was events such as these that had prompted Paul and Irene to form GALA. They persuaded biology professor Selena Weil to serve as their faculty adviser; they had approached Professor Weil first because of her widespread popularity, second because of her well-known sympathy for all marginalized student groups, and third because they felt that her marital status (she was happily married to a physics professor and had two young children) would help to protect her from uncomfortable allegations that might be made against any unmarried faculty members who allied themselves with the group. With the help of Prof. Weil, last January Paul and Irene prepared all the paperwork necessary to establish GALA and presented a proposed constitution for approval by the Cromwell Student Government (CSG). At their first meeting of the spring semester, the CSG voted to grant GALA recognition as an official student organization.

With the group officially recognized by the CSG, GALA was able to participate fully in this year's orientation events along with the other student organizations, and both Paul and Irene expressed high hopes for a successful year ahead. So far, their optimism seemed justified. The fall semester's first organizational meeting drew twenty students, and by the third weekly get-together that number almost doubled. Everyone involved in the group agreed that GALA needed to pursue two purposes: support (providing emotional and psychological assistance to group members), and outreach (raising the awareness of the Cromwell student body to the presence of gay, lesbian, bisexual, and transgendered students on campus and to a range of relevant issues).

The support activities, consisting of weekly meetings for the discussion of such problems as coming out to your parents, had been conducted quietly, and caused little controversy. The outreach activities, however, were by their nature more open. In the first few weeks of the semester, GALA sponsored a free condom giveaway program, a lecture by a noted lesbian poet, a publicity campaign to help defeat a local "family values" congressman who was running for re-election, and a Friday night dance party that was, by all reports, one of the hottest social events ever to occur on the Cromwell campus.

At the same time, GALA had managed to upset a significant portion of the Cromwell student body. "I don't care what they do, as long as they're not in my face," seemed to be the viewpoint of many CC students. But with a different public event every week, GALA had forced the Cromwell community to take notice of the presence of gay and lesbian students on campus. Moreover, with the support of the group, many students who had been closeted worked up the courage to come out. Suddenly, as one shocked first-year student was heard to exclaim, "It seems like everyone at CC is gay!"

This was, of course, an exaggeration. But on a small campus like Cromwell's, even a couple of dozen openly gay or lesbian students might seem like a lot to students who were uncomfortable about same-sex relationships. As the gay and lesbian couples at CC had become more unabashed about their sexual orientation, more conflicts ensued.

When Irene and her friend Vivian were seen walking around campus with their arms around each other, they were conscious of half-suppressed sniggering and occasional obscenities being targeted in their direction. In spite of occasional heckling, however, most Cromwell students seemed willing to ignore public displays of affection on the part of lesbians. More controversial, however, were signs of physical intimacy between homosexual men. It was over just such an issue that Cromwell College witnessed its first riot.

It began at a GALA support meeting, when several group members started complaining about feeling physically constrained in public. "It's not fair," commented one young man. "I see straight couples practically having intercourse on the dance floor, and nobody seems to care. But if I so much as touch my lover's arm, I feel like I'm violating the sensibilities of the entire community."

Irene nodded. "Look at the crap Vivian and I have to put up with—and we're women, which for some reason makes people more willing to accept physical contact. Imagine what would happen if a couple of gay *men* walked around campus holding hands—or kissing!"

Most of the GALA members just shook their heads sadly. Paul, however, always the most confrontational and aggressive member of the group, immediately broke into the conversation: "Well, you're probably right that people would be outraged at the sight of two gay men openly expressing their affection for each other. But why should we let their outrage control our behavior? Don't we all know that they'd be *wrong* to be outraged, that we're not doing anything evil, that we have as much right to love, happiness, and self-expression as anyone else? I for one am sick of worrying about whether or not I'm going to disgust some homophobic goon. I deserve to live my life freely and openly."

Paul turned to his lover, Jeffrey Abrams, and asked, "Jeffrey, how would you feel if from now on you and I were to behave just like any straight couple? You know, holding hands if we feel like it, or whatever? Do you think you could handle the consequences we might face on this reactionary campus?"

Jeffrey, not quite as confrontational as Paul, was silent for a few moments. Finally he nodded his head and said, "Well, Paul, I have to admit that I'm afraid of how people will react, but I'm also getting sick of constantly having to hold back from even the most trivial public expression of my feelings for you. You and I have already come out openly—everyone at Cromwell and everyone back home knows we're gay. I don't think we'd have anything to lose by doing what lovers everywhere do: proclaiming our love for each other by signs of physical affection."

"Way to go!" exclaimed Paul. The next day, Paul appeared casual and comfortable as he sat with some friends at his usual table in the dining hall, complaining about the inedible CC lunch fare. When Jeffrey came into view by the salad bar, Paul smiled and waved at him.

That simple action was enough to generate a series of mutterings from a group of BOZ brothers seated a couple of tables away. "Hey, faggot! Waving to your sweetheart?" they jeered. Paul merely smiled, but by this time most of the people at the surrounding tables had focused their attention on Paul and the BOZos, and watched to see what would happen next.

When Jeffrey walked over to Paul's table and sat down beside him, the BOZos' taunting became even louder. Paying no attention to their jeers, Paul leaned over, put his arm around Jeffrey's shoulder, and gave him a kiss on the cheek.

That was too much for the BOZ brothers. The muttering escalated into loud insults. One young man, Zeke Edwards, rose out of his chair and started striding toward Paul and Jeffrey's table, all the while uttering threats about what would happen to "perverts who do things that make decent folks want to puke." A couple of Zeke's fraternity brothers tried rather ineffectually to hold him back, while some of the other BOZos cheered him on.

Other Cromwell students at the surrounding tables had a variety of reactions. Some, equally disturbed by Paul and Jeffrey's behavior but not as open in their disgust as the BOZos, sat back to watch Zeke in action. A few, sensing a potential conflagration and not wanting to take part in it, quickly got up and left the dining hall. Others, who may or may not have been in sympathy with Zeke and his brothers but who felt the need to deter a fight, tried to convince the BOZos to calm down. Still others took Paul and Jeffrey's side, walking over to their table to help defend them, if necessary.

In the meantime, Zeke had reached Paul and grabbed him by the arm. "You'd better not display any more of this repulsive behavior," Zeke demanded. "Otherwise, I'll have to teach you a lesson you won't forget!"

Paul, however, was not about to let Zeke practice his unique methods of education. Just as Zeke lifted a clenched fist and started to wave it in front of Paul's face, Paul quickly punched Zeke in the stomach with enough force to make him wince and stagger.

It wasn't easy to tell exactly what happened next, but within minutes there were at least thirty Cromwell students doing their best to beat each other up. Paul and Jeffrey had focused on Zeke, and were pounding him with their fists while he attempted to execute a series of well-aimed kicks. Some of Zeke's fraternity brothers began by attacking Jeffrey and Paul, but then moved on to the others at their table who had plunged into the fray.

Irene and Vivian tried to hold back a couple of the participants but ended up getting drawn into the melee as well. A number of bystanders then jumped in to assist them. In no time at all, the uproar had resulted in five bloody noses, four black eyes, three sprained ankles, two broken fingers, and a dislocated knee. And that was just the beginning.

In the meantime, someone had called the department of safety and alerted the security officers to the fight in the dining hall. When a group of four officers arrived on the scene, the place was a shambles. A number of dishes, cups, and glasses had been broken in the brawl, posing a serious danger to anyone who happened to slip onto the floor. Several students were already sporting bleeding gashes in their arms, legs, and faces as a result of falling on broken glass or crockery. A few of them—including Zeke, Paul, Jeffrey, Irene, and Vivian—were so bruised and beaten that they were only semiconscious. They lay sprawled on the floor, moaning softly.

At the sight of the uniformed officers, a sudden hush fell upon the mob. Those who were still capable of movement sank into the nearest chairs and looked around silently. No one wanted to suffer any legal charges or even any college disciplinary action, and no one had considered this possibility when the throwing of punches began. Now the realization of what they had done started to dawn on all parties. Sheepishly, they gazed at the mess they had created. The security officers began taking statements from the participants and a hastily summoned nurse from the health center attended to the injuries. Slowly the dining hall emptied as the officers completed their interrogations.

When word spread across campus of what had happened, reactions ranged from shock to anger to disbelief. The cuts and bruises that had been sustained in the dining hall riot were quick to heal, but the tattered emotions of the Cromwell community could not be mended so easily. For weeks after the brawl, students and faculty alike eyed each other suspiciously.

"Is she bisexual?" a student might ask himself as he sat in GALA adviser Selena Weil's Introduction to Biology class. "Is he a gay-basher?" another student might ask herself as she sat beside a classmate who had come to Zeke's assistance in the fight. Although no one had pressed legal charges in the case, college disciplinary proceedings had gone forward and tensions still lingered.

The dean of students had listened to the opinions of the various parties involved. Paul Vega had argued that he and Jeffrey Abrams had only acted in self-defense, and that Zeke Edwards, as the true instigator of the brawl, should receive the most stringent punishment. It was Paul's contention that he and Jeffrey had done nothing that should have disturbed Zeke, but that Zeke had threatened them verbally and that his fist-waving was clearly a prelude to violence. "He was about to hit me," said Paul. "What was I supposed to do, just stand there and let him?" Paul also emphasized the history of harassment he had encountered as a gay man at Cromwell, and insisted that the BOZ brothers' behavior in the dining hall—and Zeke's behavior in particular—constituted a clear violation of Cromwell's discriminatory harassment policy.

Zeke, however, had argued that it was in fact Paul who had thrown the first punch, and that his own fist-waving was merely a figurative gesture intended to impress upon Paul the extent of Zeke's disgust. "I don't see how he can claim he was acting in self-defense. After all, I had no intention of actually hitting him. I'm entitled to express my opinion about behavior that is morally repugnant to me, and that's all I was doing," Zeke maintained. Moreover, he claimed that Paul and Jeffrey had deliberately attempted to provoke violence by engaging in flagrant homosexual behavior directly in front of a group of students whom they knew would be highly disturbed by it; therefore, Zeke asserted, Paul and Jeffrey should be punished most severely.

In the end, however, Dean Stevens ignored all pleas, and meted out punishment uniformly. She decided to place *everyone* who had been involved in the brawl on disciplinary probation. A couple of the participants had already been on probation previous to the dining hall incident. In their cases, the dean imposed an immediate one-semester suspension from Cromwell.

Although a few students expressed the opinion that Dean Stevens' actions were too harsh and a few others maintained that they were not harsh enough, most members of the CC community were willing to let the matter rest. Only a few weeks were left of the semester, and students and faculty alike were beginning to feel the inevitable end-of-term pressure. Consequently, almost everyone seemed to want to ignore the brawl and the ensuing tension, and focus on academic matters instead. Whatever went on inside people's heads, the campus was outwardly quiet.

In the meantime, GALA continued to hold weekly support meetings and public outreach events which included a well-attended self-defense workshop. The CC community seemed to have become more tolerant; the graffiti and verbal abuse had abated. Although demonstrative same-sex couples continued to attract inquiring or openly disapproving looks from bystanders, no one confronted them either verbally or physically, perhaps afraid of setting off another riot.

When the GALA members gathered for their regular meeting a month before the semester's end, their conversation was full of hope. "Maybe we're finally changing people's attitudes," Irene remarked. "I feel like the whole campus has become more tolerant of us." Vivian and Jeffrey nodded in agreement.

Paul, however, felt differently. "I wouldn't be so sure," he warned. "Just because they're not yelling at us or beating us up doesn't mean that they really accept us. I think they're just afraid of starting another fight and getting into trouble.

"You know, I think that Zeke and the other BOZos were pretty shocked when Jeffrey and I fought back. I think they expected gay men to just sit there and take whatever got dished out. I'm glad we put up a struggle—at least we helped to destroy that one particular stereotype. But homophobic attitudes are built up over a lifetime. It would take years to really change the way that people look at us. We can make them think twice before expressing their true feelings—I think we've already achieved that. But as for *changing* their feelings . . . well, I guess I'm not as optimistic as you seem to be."

Whether or not Paul was accurate in his cynicism, it was fortunately the fact that no further riots erupted that semester.

Some Questions to Consider

How do you feel about the existence of GALA at Cromwell College? Do you agree with Zeke that Paul and Jeffrey deliberately instigated a violent response? Is there any evidence in the case that might support or refute this charge? If you had been in the dining hall during the riot, how would you have responded—when the jeering began, when Zeke approached Paul and Jeffrey, and when large-scale violence subsequently erupted? Who do you think was to blame for what ensued? How do you feel about the disciplinary action taken by the dean?

Thinking Critically

Paul and Jeffrey apparently see their kiss as a legitimate expression of their affection for one another; Zeke apparently sees it as a deliberate provocation. To what extent are these different positions on the same event a result of differing sets of assumptions? Can you identify the assumptions underlying Paul's position? What about Zeke's?

Reading Closely

Paul maintains that Zeke and the BOZos violated the discriminatory harassment policy. (See the appendix for a full statement of the policy.) The policy identifies several forms of conduct that could constitute discriminatory harassment, including "objectionable epithets, demeaning depictions or treatment, and threatened or actual abuse or harm." Does anything that was said or done in the dining hall fall under this definition? Can it be argued that the remarks made by Zeke and the BOZos were directed against Paul and Jeffrey "because of their...sexual orientation"? Can it be argued that these remarks had "the purpose or reasonably foreseeable effect of creating an offensive, demeaning, intimidating, or hostile environment" for Paul and Jeffrey?

What If

What if no violence or physical interaction had in fact occurred, and the BOZos' response to Paul and Jeffrey's kiss had instead been limited to verbal reactions? Would that change your views on this case? If so, how? If not, why not? What if Paul and Jeffrey had sat down at the BOZos' table instead of their usual one, and kissed within inches of Zeke and his fraternity brothers? Would that change your views on this case?

Connecting the Cases

We have examined the issue of freedom of expression in earlier cases; do you see it as an issue here as well? Do Paul and Jeffrey have a right to express their affection for one another just as Corinne or Lizette or Grace might have had the right to express their beliefs by displaying the Confederate flag, practicing an individual version of spirituality, or drawing a controversial cartoon for the campus newspaper? Should there be limits to physical means of self-expression? If so, why, and how would you determine such limits? If not, why not? Does physical self-expression differ from verbal or pictorial forms of expression? Why or why not?

Bringing It Home

Cromwell is not the only campus where the presence of gay and lesbian students has caused controversy. Through textual research, field observation, or personal interviews, investigate and report on the situation of gay, lesbian, bisexual, and transgendered students on your own campus. How strong is the presence of gay and lesbian students? How welcome are they made to feel by other members of the campus community?

Suggestions for Writing

1. Imagine that you were sitting in the dining hall at the time of the commotion, and that you witnessed the events leading to the violent confrontation. Write an entry in your personal journal that explores your reactions to the situation.

2. The Cromwell Alumni Magazine occasionally publishes "point of view" columns written by current CC students to inform alumni

about contemporary campus issues. Write an article for the magazine explaining the response of a typical Cromwell student (i.e., you) to the general situation of gay and lesbian students at Cromwell and to the dining hall incident in particular.

3. When people are deeply offended by something, they may respond violently. In such a case, who is to blame: the person who committed the allegedly offensive act, or the person who responded violently? Is the blame shared? Write an essay that explores this question as it relates to the dining hall incident and as it may relate to other such incidents you know about from your reading or personal experience.

Out Loud

Your roommate, who has recently become an active member of GALA and is slowly beginning the process of "coming out," feels that it is only fair for you to know about this. You had never previously suspected that your roommate might not be heterosexual. With one of your classmates as a partner, enact a conversation between yourself and your roommate in which you express your feelings about the information you have just received.

CASE 11

Speak Up
Controversial Speakers and College Policies

PART ONE

As the members of Beta Omicron Zeta (BOZ) gathered for their regular Monday night chapter meeting, an unaccustomed sense of seriousness filled the air. The fraternity was in trouble, and it was time to take stock and take action.

BOZ President Dan Harris called the meeting to order by assertively banging on the edge of the Ping-Pong table. "Listen, BOZos," he began. "You know I'm the last guy to try to keep you all from having a little innocent fun. But I had a chat with our faculty friend Duke Schuyler the other day, and he said that he's heard some of the other professors talking about trying to shut us down.

"Although we have some strong supporters on the faculty, unfortunately we have a lot of enemies, too," Dan went on, "especially that biology professor Selena Weil, who I hear is leading the forces against us. Apparently she and her faculty buddies think that we've gotten out of hand. They're saying that all we do is get rowdy and cause trouble, that we don't contribute anything positive to Cromwell. Schuyler suggested that we'd better act quickly to salvage our reputation by doing something to make us look good. You know, some high-profile community service thing, or a campus work project, or tutoring the basketball team, or bringing some impressive speaker to campus, or something like that. Any ideas?"

The BOZos were silent. The sorts of activities Dan had just mentioned were not exactly up their alley. They gave great parties, and their "Beach Blanket Weekend"—a springtime extravaganza that featured truckloads of sand and culminated with the crowning of the Bikini Queen—was, in their view, the highlight of Cromwell's social calendar. But BOZ members were not known for their commitment to improving the intellectual and moral tone of their community.

Finally, Zeke Edwards spoke up: "Well, Dan, you're right that we probably need to do something to spruce up our image, but what kind of community service did you have in mind? I'm not about to go delivering meals to AIDS patients, like those Pi Epsilon Tau idiots do. I joined BOZ to help take my mind off my own problems, not to wallow in other people's."

"Yeah," agreed BOZ junior Joe Kalidis, "and I don't know about a work project, either. Remember last spring, when we tried to be nice and give Coach Herron a pleasant surprise by repainting the women's locker room? We weren't exactly greeted with open arms. I'm not all that eager to undertake any other campus beautification projects."

The negativity continued as another BOZ junior, Brent Ingram, commented, "Tutoring won't work, either, since us BOZos aren't exactly famous for having high GPAs. Not that I'm ashamed of that—I certainly wouldn't want anyone to think that we're a bunch of nerds. But the basketball team isn't going to want any academic assistance from *us*, and neither is anyone else.

"However," Brent continued, "I think there is one option open to us that we can be a little more positive about, and that's the idea of bringing a speaker to campus—someone with a big name and someone serious, maybe someone involved in government or politics. We get him to come here, we pay him out of the money in our Education Fund, we publicize the event, and we open it up to the whole Cromwell community. All of a sudden people will start thinking about BOZ as a bunch of responsible, civic-minded men with a strong interest in public affairs. If our first event goes well, we could even think about sponsoring a whole series of talks."

"You're right," said Joe, "and we wouldn't really have to do much ourselves—just line up the speaker, reserve the Abbot Hall auditorium, and then plaster the campus with posters."

"But how could we get anyone impressive to come here? We could never afford the speaking fee. How much money do we have in the Education Fund, anyway?" asked Zeke.

"Not a whole lot," replied Dan. "We did some creative bookkeeping to help finance last week's 'Space Odyssey' party, so now we only have around $300 left for education."

"That's about one-tenth of what we'd need to get anyone halfway decent!" lamented Zeke.

"I don't know about that," said Brent. "I think I might be able to help us out here. You know Bailey Blanchard, who just lost the election for state lieutenant-governor?"

"Of course I know him. His face has been all over the media for the past six months. Don't tell me you have some kind of connection to him!" exclaimed Zeke.

"Uh huh," assented Brent. "He was my father's college roommate. I never wanted to say anything about it before because frankly, I can't stand the guy—too full of himself, and all he ever wants to talk about is politics. No fun, you know? But he and my dad are still close, and I'm sure that if my dad asked him, he'd be happy to speak at Cromwell, maybe even for free—which would mean that we'd still have $300 to spend on something else, like another party."

"That's a great idea, Brent," said Dan. "How soon can you talk to your father?"

"I'll call him right now," Brent offered.

"Wait a second," interjected Joe. "Aren't you all forgetting that the reason Bailey Blanchard got so much media attention is because he used to be involved in some kind of white supremacist group, and that he still makes a lot of outrageous statements? There was a big controversy just a few weeks ago when he said that immigrants who may get U.S. citizenship on paper still aren't 'real Americans.' And what about all those comments he makes about how 'Anglo-Saxon values' are morally superior? Is this the kind of speaker we want to sponsor?"

"Oh, come on, Joe," said Zeke. "What are you, a champion of political correctness all of a sudden? Bailey Blanchard is famous, he's a politician, he ran for lieutenant-governor and got a respectable percentage of the votes. It's not like he's some gas station attendant dressed in a white sheet. He's legit. And since Brent has a connection to him, we actually have a chance to get him."

"Anyway," Brent added, "isn't college supposed to be a place for the free exchange of ideas, with all points of view represented? The more controversial Blanchard is, the better. Here we are, BOZ, champions of free speech and free thought!"

"I like it!" said Dan. "Let's go for it!"

Brent called his father immediately, and asked him to put in a good word with Bailey Blanchard. Mr. Ingram contacted his old roommate that evening; Blanchard, glad to do his friend a favor, readily agreed to speak at Cromwell for a token fee of $100, leaving the BOZos with $200 in their Education Fund. The speaking date was set for 8:00 P.M. the following Monday—just one week away—and the boys of BOZ got busy.

Some Questions to Consider

How do you feel about Brent's contention that it's important for all points of view to be presented on a college campus? Are there any views that should not be permitted to be aired? The BOZos propose to reserve the Abbot Hall auditorium for Blanchard's speech; should the Cromwell administration have some say in what is presented on private college grounds, or should recognized student groups have autonomy in such cases? Given what you know so far about Bailey Blanchard, would you support him being permitted to speak on campus?

PART TWO

The BOZ brothers unanimously elected Brent Ingram as coordinator of the Bailey Blanchard event. Brent decided to skip all his Tuesday classes and devote the day to organizational activities, beginning by reserving the Abbot Hall auditorium. As an official student organization, BOZ could request the use of campus facilities, but first Brent had to obtain a facilities request form from the dean of students' office. On the form, he entered information concerning the date, time, nature of the event, and expected attendance.

Brent also had to obtain the signature of a faculty or staff member who would agree to sponsor the event, so he headed to Duke Schuyler's office in the Gilman Annex. Professor Schuyler was more than happy to affix his signature, congratulating Brent on obtaining such a distinguished speaker as Bailey Blanchard to initiate what Brent had grandiosely dubbed "Which Way America?: The BOZ Lecture Series on Economics, Politics, and Society."

Brent's next move was to return to the dean's office and submit the facilities request form to the administrative assistant in charge of scheduling campus events. As she glanced at the form, she said, "Bailey Blanchard. . . that's a familiar name, but I can't place it right now."

"He ran for lieutenant-governor, but lost," said Brent.

"Oh," said the assistant. "I had no idea that BOZ was so interested in public affairs. I'm glad to see you guys taking a more serious turn."

"Thanks," said Brent, smiling as he thought of how quickly the Blanchard scheme was working to improve BOZ's reputation.

After checking the availability of the auditorium, the administrative assistant turned to Brent and said, "Well, this all looks okay. The auditorium is free Monday night, and I can't see any problem. Speaking engagements proceed pretty routinely here. It's not like sponsoring a dance or concert, which would require special safety and security measures. Of course, facility requests are subject to review by Dean Stevens, and I'll run yours by her along with the others I received today." She continued, "You may as well go ahead with your plans. The dean will be in touch with you if she has any questions."

Brent decided that his next move would be to grab a quick lunch and then track down his friend Yvonne Toufaian, who was an excellent artist. He was hoping that Yvonne would design a poster advertising the Blanchard talk, and that she'd be able to do it immediately so that he could get copies made as soon as possible. He wanted to have the posters plastered all over campus no later than Wednesday afternoon, to give the Cromwell community ample notice.

As he patiently awaited his order of a cheeseburger and fries at the dining hall's grill counter, Brent spotted Yvonne at the salad bar. As soon as his burger was ready, he walked over and invited her to join him for lunch. The two of them strolled to an empty table, chatting about this and that. When they were seated, Brent got down to business.

"I need your help, Yvonne," he said. "Well, actually, BOZ needs your help. We're sponsoring a talk by Bailey Blanchard in the Abbot Hall auditorium next Monday, and we were wondering if you'd design a poster for us to advertise the event."

"Bailey Blanchard?" queried Yvonne with an incredulous stare. "*The* Bailey Blanchard, who ran for lieutenant-governor? You're bringing him here to Cromwell?"

"Yep," Brent answered smugly. "Pretty cool, huh?"

Yvonne shook her head. "I don't know, Brent. I mean, not only does Blanchard come off as incredibly racist, but don't you remember that speech he made during the campaign about how the large-scale entrance of married women into the workforce has ruined American life? I may not be Ms. Radical Feminist, but even I get turned off by that kind of nonsense. What made you decide to invite him, of all people, to speak here?"

Brent shrugged his shoulders. "Frankly, we were able to get him cheap. Besides," he added, "it's crucial to have all points of view represented in the marketplace of ideas. Think of the speakers we've had on campus recently: a bunch of left-wing extremists! Isn't it about time we brought some balance to the discussion?"

Brent was warming to his subject and his voice took on a declamatory tone as he continued, "I may not agree with everything Bailey Blanchard says, but I welcome diversity of opinion, especially on a college campus, and BOZ is proud to champion the right of free expression for all. It's a basic matter of First Amendment rights. Bailey Blanchard isn't hurting anyone, he's just expressing his opinions. He has just as much of a right to do that as anyone else. It's like that famous quotation—I forget who said it, but it goes something like this: I may not like what you say, but I'll defend to the death your right to say it."

Yvonne remained unconvinced. "I don't deny Blanchard the right to express his views," she said, "but I just don't think we need to provide a forum for him here at Cromwell. After all, it's not like the guy hasn't had a chance to get his ideas across anywhere else—he got more coverage than any other candidate during the campaign. Why make our college facilities available to him to spout his brand of idiocy?"

"It may be idiocy to you, but it obviously seems a lot more reasonable to all the people who supported him in the lieutenant-governor's race. I was just reading some of the materials distributed by his campaign office, and they say that two weeks before the election, immediately after one of Blanchard's televised speeches, a random survey of voters indicated a 59 percent approval rate of his message to the people. He did pretty well by the time the election came around, too: he carried overwhelming majorities in four counties, and if you discount the five biggest urban areas he had 51 percent of the state's popular vote. Even with the urban areas in the picture, he ended up with 29 percent of the electorate voting for him, which is a pretty significant proportion." Brent—who had clearly done his homework—concluded, "This isn't some fringe lunatic we're talking about. Bailey Blanchard has a lot of popular support both in and out of this state. Isn't it worth hearing what he has to say, even if only for that reason?"

"I've already heard what Bailey Blanchard has to say," Yvonne remarked. "Just because 29 percent of the voters in this state are bigots doesn't mean that those of us who are more enlightened need to support racism, sexism, and all the other forms of prejudice Blanchard espouses. You know, our student activity fees help to pay for events like this. When they have to rent sound equipment and stuff like that for programs sponsored by student organizations, they take the money right out of our activity fund. Well, I don't fork over fifty dollars every year to provide a microphone for Bailey Blanchard."

"We've had other speakers here whose views I haven't agreed with," said Brent, "but I'm willing to let my activity fee help support these events because I think it's important to have as many different viewpoints aired as possible—even viewpoints that are offensive to me. Can't you grant the same courtesy to Bailey Blanchard that I've granted to Green Party radicals?"

"I don't like the Green Party either," responded Yvonne, "but there's a big difference between them and Bailey Blanchard. If you want to extend the boundaries of discussion on this campus, why not bring a legitimate representative of conservative thought who can present us with some ideas, instead of just a bunch of offensive remarks putting down anyone who isn't a white Anglo-Saxon male?"

"Hey," said Brent, "excuse me for breathing! Take it easy, Yvonne. I always thought you were reasonable, which is why I asked you to help. If I had known you were one of those knee-jerk PC liberals, I never would have approached you about it."

"I am so sick of that term 'PC'—and the same goes for 'liberal,' which are both vague labels that people like you use to condemn anything you don't agree with. Anyway, if you really want to know, I consider myself to be a libertarian. Libertarians are concerned about encouraging a free market—in intellectual as well as economic matters. I'm not interested in denying anyone the right to speak. But I don't see why I should have to pay for it—I don't want my activity fee to finance bigotry and hatred. And I think you'd better find someone else to design your poster." Yvonne got up and walked away.

Brent was stunned. He knew that Bailey Blanchard was controversial, but he had never expected Yvonne to react so strongly to the mere mention of his appearance at Cromwell. "She sure is being touchy—must have her period or something," Brent muttered. Well, Yvonne was not irreplaceable. Brent decided to rely on his computer's desktop publishing software to create a design for the poster, so he went off to see what he could do with some creative pointing and clicking.

In the meantime, Yvonne had run across a couple of her friends, and had filled them in on the BOZ plan to bring Bailey Blanchard to the Cromwell campus. Soon word of mouth had done a better job of publicizing the event than any poster could. By late afternoon, almost everyone knew about Blanchard's upcoming visit, and reactions were mixed. Only a handful of CC students actually admitted to supporting Blanchard's views, but many who indicated revulsion for his ideas were still adamant that he be allowed to speak on campus for some of the same reasons that Brent had presented to Yvonne: they saw it as a free speech issue, and as a way to encourage the presentation of a full range of political views at Cromwell College.

Moreover, they pointed out that BOZ, as a recognized student organization, should have the right to plan whatever events they felt were appropriate. Any attempt on the part of the CC administration to prevent BOZ from following through on the Blanchard event would be an attack on the autonomy of student groups and could set a dangerous precedent for the future. Rather than muzzling Blanchard and interfering with a student-initiated event, these students asserted, opponents of Blanchard should simply exercise their own rights of free speech and openly express their rejection of Blanchard's views. Besides, they pointed out, there was no way to know exactly what Blanchard would say during his Cromwell appearance. Was it fair to object to his speaking before the fact?

Other students responded that as a private institution, Cromwell had the right and even the duty to choose who should be allowed to speak on campus. As one sophomore put it, "Would you let just any idiot into your living room?" While supporting the principle of free speech, these students saw Blanchard as going beyond the boundaries of responsible discourse. They felt that there was no need to have foreknowledge of precisely what Blanchard would say at Cromwell; his previous record provided enough of a precedent by which to judge him. They feared that his Cromwell presentation might constitute a form of hate speech, the kind of verbal abuse prohibited by Cromwell's discriminatory harassment policy. There are limits to permissible speech, these students maintained: you shouldn't be allowed to shout "Fire!" in a crowded theater, and you shouldn't be permitted to spout "fighting words" that could provoke violent reactions—which, they argued, was just what Bailey Blanchard was in the habit of doing.

CC freshman Art Larson had heard the news of Blanchard's visit to Cromwell. Along with many other students, he was disturbed by the thought that campus facilities would be given over to a man like Bailey Blanchard. Determined to prevent this from happening, Art decided to gather a coalition of student leaders to approach Dean Stevens and ask her to bar Blanchard from speaking at Cromwell. He immediately began making phone calls, and by ten o'clock that night he had brought together representatives from fourteen different campus organizations—from the Gay and Lesbian Association to the Asian-American Alliance—for a meeting in the Howell Hall lounge. All present agreed to appear en masse at the dean's open office hour the following morning.

Some Questions to Consider

Do you see the Blanchard controversy as a free speech issue? Do you find Brent's argument concerning the need for political balance to be convincing? What do you think about Yvonne's resistance to having her student activity fee used to support Blanchard's speech? Do you think Art and his coalition of student leaders are right in their decision to ask for Blanchard to be barred from Cromwell? Are there other actions they could or should have taken to express their own views, in addition to or instead of preventing Blanchard from expressing his?

PART THREE

When Art's coalition showed up in Dean Stevens' office at nine o'clock on Wednesday morning, she was already on her fourth cup of coffee and her second dose of aspirin. She had spent a sleepless night concerned about the Bailey Blanchard situation.

Blanchard's name had caught her eye while she was hastily skimming facility requests on Tuesday afternoon, and she had put all her other work on the back burner while she considered how she should proceed. Blanchard, in her view, was an unapologetic racist, not to mention being sexist, xenophobic, and homophobic. Should CC permit such a man to use college facilities? The dean's initial response was negative.

However, Blanchard's talk was being sponsored by an official student organization, and Dean Stevens was wary of appearing to censor the activities of a student group. She knew that, were she to forbid the use of the Abbot Hall auditorium for this event, BOZ would charge her with shackling freedom of expression on the Cromwell campus. She shuddered to think what the local radio talk show hosts would say about "political correctness" at CC. What should she do?

She decided that the safest course would be to turn the matter over to her superior, the college provost. She caught him just as he was leaving his office for the day; he, in turn, decided that the matter was serious enough to involve the college president. As the three conferred in the president's office, they concluded that the Cromwell administration had the right and the responsibility to decide who would and would not be permitted to speak on campus. It was their collective view that Blanchard's statements did not constitute legitimate political discourse. Moreover, given the volatile nature of most of his previous speeches, there was the possibility that Blanchard's talk would provoke violence—and they did not feel they could guarantee the security of such a speaker on the Cromwell campus.

On Wednesday morning, half an hour before Art's delegation arrived at her office, Dean Stevens had called BOZ President Dan Harris, waking him up from a very deep sleep, and informed him of the decision to forbid Blanchard from speaking at Cromwell. Dan was furious, and pointed out to the dean that Blanchard had already been invited to Cromwell; how could BOZ disinvite him? Dean Stevens suggested that BOZ find an off-campus facility where the Blanchard speech could be held.

Dan, who had by this time managed to rouse the BOZ brothers who lived at the fraternity house, thrust the phone into the hands of a rather dazed Brent Ingram. Brent summoned up his mental resources and began to lecture the dean on the sanctity of the First Amendment. When it became clear that the Cromwell administration would not back down, Brent hung up abruptly—and then decided to follow Dean Stevens' suggestion. After a few more phone calls, he found a nearby meeting hall that was willing to host the Blanchard speech for a fee of two hundred dollars: exactly what BOZ had left in its Education Fund. The speech could go on as planned.

When Art and his supporters arrived at the dean's office and demanded that Blanchard be banned from speaking on the Cromwell campus, the dean was able to tell the group that Blanchard had already been forbidden from speaking in the Abbot Hall auditorium. She mentioned that she was unsure whether BOZ was arranging for the talk to be held off campus, but she assured the assembled students that Blanchard would not appear on CC property, and the group left satisfied.

By noon Wednesday Brent's posters had sprouted up on bulletin boards across the campus, announcing that Bailey Blanchard would be speaking the following Monday at the Crosstown Community Center. It didn't take Art's coalition of campus leaders long to respond. Each representative met with his or her constituency. The consensus among the groups was that a strong showing should be made outside the community center, protesting Blanchard's talk and repudiating his views. Plans for a massive demonstration went forward, with hundreds of Cromwell students pledging to participate.

When Monday evening arrived, around one hundred people were seated in the community center's meeting hall waiting for Bailey Blanchard to appear. Approximately one-fourth of this number were

BOZ brothers; many other Cromwell students had come out of sympathy with Blanchard's message or merely out of curiosity, as had some members of the neighboring community and representatives of the local press. Outside the center, about four hundred CC students brandished placards condemning Blanchard's point of view. A sizable number of signs also faulted BOZ for sponsoring the talk ("Why do you think they call them BOZos?" read one poster, illustrated with a picture of Bozo the Clown).

Blanchard's speech followed his usual pattern. He began by bemoaning what he perceived to be the country's financial instability and moral malaise, and then went on to present a list of villains responsible for the nation's woes: illegal immigrants, welfare cheats, working mothers, atheists, anti-family activists, conniving corporate money-men, lax public school teachers, and a host of other scapegoats. As Blanchard's rhetoric grew increasingly vitriolic, some of the BOZ brothers grew visibly uncomfortable, and many audience members walked out on the speech. By the end, only about sixty people remained.

Back at the BOZ house later that night, a group of the fraternity members huddled around the TV to watch the coverage of Blanchard's talk on the eleven o'clock news. The report began, "Earlier this evening Cromwell College's chapter of the Beta Omicron Zeta fraternity defied hundreds of protesting students as they presented a talk by Bailey Blanchard, former white supremacist leader and failed candidate for state lieutenant-governor. The BOZ brothers were apparently so eager to hear Blanchard's message that when the college administration prevented them from hosting him on the Cromwell campus, they rented an off-campus facility for the event."

The voice-over was accompanied by the image of hundreds of demonstrators outside the community center, with the camera zooming in on the "Why do you think they call them BOZos?" sign. What had initially seemed like an image-enhancing coup for BOZ now appeared to be a public relations disaster.

Brent Ingram seemed depressed as he started in on his second six-pack of beer. "I feel like it's all my fault," he said to Dan Harris. "The whole thing was my idea to begin with. I thought I could really help BOZ, but in the end I let the frat down. I'm sorry."

"Hey, don't worry about it. If anyone's to blame, it's me, suggesting that we try to get serious all of a sudden. I let Prof. Schuyler talk me into taking on something completely out of our line. We should have stuck to what we do best."

"You're right," agreed Brent. "The one thing that's kept us going all these years, that's always gotten us plenty of pledges, and that's made us the most talked-about frat on campus, has been our ability to let loose and have fun. That's what we've always based our reputation on, and that's what students expect of us. If a bunch of stuffy faculty members don't see the value in a little innocent recreation, that's their problem. We know we haven't done anything to deserve being shut down—we just need to stand firm on our own belief in ourselves."

"Right on, brother," said Dan. "Let's party!"

Some Questions to Consider

Do you think the Cromwell administrators did the right thing in forbidding Blanchard to speak on campus? What other options could or should they have pursued? Do you think the coalition of campus groups did the right thing in deciding to protest the talk? Is there anything else they could or should have done? Would you have attended Blanchard's talk? Would you have participated in the protest outside the center?

Thinking Critically

In his conversation with Yvonne, Brent presents numerical data to indicate Blanchard's popular support. What point is Brent trying to make through his use of this data? Is his statistical evidence convincing? Are there any potential problems with the figures he presents? Is Brent's discussion of Blanchard's support relevant to his argument concerning Blanchard's right to be heard at Cromwell? If so, why? If not, why not?

Reading Closely

"Immigrants who may get U.S. citizenship on paper still aren't real Americans." "Anglo-Saxon values are morally superior." "The large-scale entrance of married women into the workforce has ruined American life." Some opponents of Bailey Blanchard maintain that remarks such as these, which Blanchard apparently uttered prior to his speaking engagement at Cromwell, could be seen as constituting hate speech or "fighting words" and could provide evidence of Blanchard's potential for violating Cromwell's discriminatory harassment policy. (See the appendix for a full statement of the policy.) Do you agree that the comments quoted above are in fact hate speech, or do they remain within the boundaries of legitimate political discourse? Do you agree that they violate Cromwell policy? Why or why not?

What If

What if the Cromwell administration had decided to allow Blanchard to speak on campus? What action, if any, do you think Art's coalition of student groups should have taken in response? Should it have been any different from the action they took in opposition to the speech at the Crosstown Community Center? What would your own reaction have been to Blanchard's on-campus appearance, if you were a Cromwell student?

Connecting the Cases

In several of the cases that we've read, individual students or student groups have taken actions that may not be in the best interest of the campus community at large. How much autonomy should students have? At what point—if any—should the college administration intervene in such matters as, say, spiritual practices, fraternity initiation rites, or organization-sponsored speaking engagements? Does it make a difference whether activities sponsored by a Cromwell student organization occur on campus or off?

Bringing It Home

Is your own campus a public or a private institution? How does the public or private nature of a college campus affect its ability to restrict speech? Does your campus have any restrictions on invited speakers? Have there ever been problems surrounding controversial speakers at your school?

Suggestions for Writing

1. Imagine that you are a member of a student organization which has decided to produce a leaflet stating the group's views regarding whether or not Blanchard should be allowed to speak on the Cromwell campus. You have been assigned to write the text for this leaflet, explaining why the particular organization you represent is taking the particular position you are supporting.

2. What with all the excitement surrounding the Blanchard speech, you completely forgot that you had an assignment due in your English composition class. Your instructor has graciously allowed you to make it up by writing a paper explaining why you found this controversy so engrossing that it temporarily eclipsed your academic concerns.

3. How does the Blanchard incident at Cromwell relate to situations involving inflammatory speakers at other colleges or universities? Use textual research and/or interviews to find out about related events at other institutions of higher learning, explaining their relevance to the case at hand.

Out Loud

How do you think Cromwell students should have responded to the presence of Blanchard at the Crosstown Community Center? Make a speech to your classmates urging them to take whatever action you think would be appropriate, such as attending Blanchard's talk, attending the rally outside the talk, or ignoring the event altogether, and present a well-reasoned argument for your position.

CASE 12

With Child

Dealing with Unplanned Pregnancy

It was just after daybreak on a crisp Thursday morning, and Kira Washington lay in her narrow bunk bed staring at the cracks on the ceiling. She hadn't had much sleep, and her tangled sheets bore testimony to the tossing and turning which had occupied most of the night. Now that some weak rays of sun were making their way past the window shades, Kira felt she had to get out of bed. She climbed down the side as quietly as possible so as not to wake her roommate in the lower bunk.

But Kira's roommate was a light sleeper, and stirred as she sensed someone moving beside her. "Kira?" she mumbled groggily.

"Yes, Angelica, it's just me. Go back to sleep," whispered Kira.

Angelica Caputo sat up in bed and looked at the alarm clock on the dresser. "It's only 6:30. What are you doing up at this hour?"

"I just couldn't sleep, and I couldn't stand staying in bed any longer. I didn't mean to wake you—sorry," said Kira.

"That's okay. I've got to get up early anyway—I promised I'd help set up the Safe Sex information table for the Health Fair today, and I'm supposed to be there before breakfast," explained Angelica.

"I'm worried about you, though, Kira," Angelica continued as she rubbed the sleep out of her eyes. "You've hardly slept the past three nights, and you seem awfully preoccupied. I know you don't like anyone prying into your life, but I want to help you. Is it more trouble with Conrad?"

Kira sighed. "No, Angelica, it's not Conrad. I already told you that he and I have agreed to never speak to each other or see each other again, and this time I really mean to stick to it. That man is completely out of my life—for good, forever."

Conrad Joyner was Kira's hometown boyfriend, or to be more precise, ex-boyfriend. After two years of rousing fights, regrets, and reconciliations, their roller-coaster relationship had finally come to an end a couple of weeks ago. Kira had told Angelica the details of her years with Conrad, of the frequent emotional and occasional physical abuse she had endured, of the few good times and the many bad ones, of her repeated attempts to leave him and her inability to do so. Even though she knew that Conrad would only continue to cause her pain, she kept going back to him, perhaps because she was afraid that no one else would have her. But as she went off to college and made new friends, she saw new opportunities and new hope. Finally Kira had insisted, and Conrad had reluctantly agreed, that it was time to call it quits completely, to close that chapter of their lives.

"No, it isn't Conrad," repeated Kira.

"Well, then, what is it?" asked Angelica.

Kira was silent for a few moments. She pulled on her bathrobe and busied herself rearranging the odds and ends on top of her dresser. Then she suddenly turned to Angelica and blurted, "My period is more than a week late. I'm never late, it's always like clockwork, and now it's been days, and I don't know what to do." With those words, Kira burst into tears.

"Oh, Kira! I wish you had told me right away. Don't worry; I'll help you however I can, and we'll work everything out together," said Angelica as she hugged her roommate.

Kira and Angelica stayed in their room and talked for another half an hour before Angelica hurried to the Health Fair and Kira headed to the Lebowitz Language Center to listen to the assigned tapes for her introductory Japanese class. In the course of the conversation, Kira revealed that about three weeks previously, shortly before the final decision to part, she and Conrad had spent an intimate weekend together and had, in a moment of uncharacteristic carelessness, neglected to use the condom that served as their usual mode of contraception. Kira had not yet taken a pregnancy test and had not communicated any of her anxiety to Conrad. She was now in an agony of uncertainty about how she should proceed.

Angelica, too, had some revelations to make. She told Kira about her own unplanned pregnancy, which had occurred only a few months previously, right after her high school graduation.

"I was careless and thoughtless," Angelica had said, "and I have no one to blame but myself and my own stupidity for ending up in such a situation. I can't make any excuses. I knew what I was doing. I just didn't think beyond the moment. So there I was, high school valedictorian, all set to distinguish myself in college, and then I had to go and get pregnant. Well, it seemed to me that there was only one thing to do, and that was to have an abortion. It may sound like a selfish decision, but I knew that I couldn't bear a child, that I couldn't let a brief indiscretion ruin my life, my goals, my ambitions. I felt awful, but I had to do it.

"The guy I was involved with at the time was really immature and basically a jerk. He would have been no help at all, so I just never told him about it. And my family—well, believe it or not, they think I'm a good little girl, and it would have broken my mother's heart if I had told her I was pregnant. So I had to do it all on my own, and all in secret.

"It was a miserable experience. When I got to the clinic that morning there was a crowd of anti-abortion demonstrators outside, holding up placards with incredibly graphic pictures of aborted fetuses. Once I got inside I could see that the staff was doing their best to ignore what was going on out front, but I talked to a few of the other patients while we were waiting, and we were all pretty shook up. It was a hard enough situation anyway and having to walk past those demonstrators didn't help.

"The clinic was antiseptically clean, and everyone on the staff was efficient and professional, but I felt like I was on an assembly line; it was all so cold and impersonal. It was as if the main goal was to get everything over with as soon as possible. Maybe that was because of the commotion outside—I guess they didn't want us to be exposed to it any longer than necessary—or maybe they always work that way.

"I still feel terrible about it all. I learned some things, though: that I need to be extra-careful to protect myself from another unplanned pregnancy and that I should do my best to keep other young women from going through what I went through. That's why I spend so much time volunteering for family planning and birth control organizations. But I can't say that I regret the choice I made to end the pregnancy—it was the best option for me at that time in my life.

"You'll have to decide what's right for you. But before you start making any decisions," Angelica counseled, "you'd better make sure you're really pregnant. The health center will test you for free, and they'll keep it all confidential. Or you can get a home pregnancy test kit, if you'd rather do that. They're pretty accurate."

Kira agreed that she couldn't put it off any longer, and decided that she'd buy a pregnancy test kit at the drugstore in the Crosstown Mall. She assured Angelica that she'd take the bus to the mall later that morning, and that she'd know for sure about her condition by the end of the afternoon.

Kira did as she had promised, and when Angelica stopped back at the residence hall before dinner, she found her roommate anxiously pacing back and forth across their narrow room.

"Positive," said Kira, before Angelica even had a chance to ask. "If I've counted correctly, this means that I'm due to have a baby next summer. What do I do now?"

"What do you want to do?" asked Angelica.

"I don't know," said Kira. "That's the problem. I'm so confused—about everything. I don't even know whether I should tell Conrad what's going on, much less what I should do about the pregnancy. How could I have a baby, now, at this point in my life? How could I face my family? My mom would have a heart attack if I told her I was pregnant, and my father would probably disown me or something. And anyway, I'm not in any shape, financially or psychologically, to take care of a baby. What would it do to all my hopes and dreams for the future?

"I don't think I could give it up for adoption, either—how could I just say good-bye to a baby who I had carried inside me for nine months? So then do I go ahead and have an abortion? It's not like I have religious scruples against it, or anything like that—you know I'm not exactly devout, and I've never been one of those people who believes abortion is murder—but it seems so awful, so selfish, so wrong. Oh, Angelica, I don't know how I can face this!"

"Well," said Angelica practically, "you're going to have to face it. You don't have a choice. As far as telling Conrad is concerned, you'd better think long and hard about it. After all, it was his sperm that got you into this situation, and you may feel that he has a right to know what's going on. But I know that you're thankful you've finally put your relationship with him behind you, and it would be really painful to connect with him again. Given his history of abuse, what kind of a father would he make? You've just got to weigh the alternatives, and see what feels right.

"As for sorting through the options that are open to you," Angelica continued, "I think you need to begin by gathering as much information as possible. You know, it might be an idea for you to talk to Claudia Balthazar."

Claudia was a young woman whom Angelica and Kira knew from their English composition class. She seemed like a typical first-year student at Cromwell, but there was one major difference: Claudia had an eight-month-old daughter, Tessa, whom she sometimes brought to campus. Kira agreed that a serious conversation with Claudia could be very useful, and she decided to approach her after class the next morning.

That night Kira actually managed to get a few hours of sleep. She woke early the next morning feeling focused and purposeful. She had decided to follow Angelica's advice and get as much information as she could before coming to any decision about the course of action she should follow.

The first item on Kira's agenda for the day was a stop at the health center to pick up the various leaflets they distributed regarding abortion, adoption, prenatal care, and other related matters. Kira discovered

that the college health insurance would cover the costs of routine ob-
stetric and gynecological visits throughout pregnancy, as well as the de-
livery of the baby and well-child care for one month after the birth.
Abortion, however, was not covered by the insurance plan, although the
health center would assist in referring students to local clinics and
would provide free counseling through its psychological services department. The health center also maintained listings of local adoption
agencies and other support services.

After perusing the health center materials, Kira headed to her
English composition class. She was a few minutes late, so she entered
as unobtrusively as possible, nodding quietly to Angelica who was sitting in her usual seat by the window.

Although she was generally an attentive student, Kira couldn't
keep her mind on the essay that was the subject of the day's discussion.
She was grateful when the instructor decided to give the students the
last twenty minutes of class time to begin work on their next writing
assignment; then she could disguise her inattention by scribbling random notes on a legal pad.

As soon as class was over, Kira approached Claudia and asked if
she could speak to her for a few minutes.

"Sure," replied Claudia. "I don't have any other classes till the afternoon, so I'm not in a hurry. I haven't had a chance to get breakfast
yet, though—would you mind if I have a bite to eat while we chat?"

"No problem. As a matter of fact, I haven't eaten yet either," said
Kira, and the two of them made small talk as they walked down to the coffeehouse in the student union basement. Finally, after fortifying themselves with herbal tea and blueberry muffins, their talk turned serious.

"Claudia, I know we don't know each other very well," began Kira,
"but you're the only person I know here who has a baby, and I need to
talk to you about it."

Claudia smiled. "Yeah, I guess Tessa does make me sort of unique
here. Most first-year students at traditional colleges like Cromwell
don't have kids."

"What is it like?" asked Kira.

"What is what like?" responded Claudia.

"You know, trying to survive college and be a mother at the same
time."

"Well, it isn't easy," Claudia admitted. "You know I'm not married.
The relationship I had with Brian, Tessa's father, fizzled out about
halfway into the pregnancy. He's been pretty decent about things. He
lives here in town, working part-time and taking a couple of classes at
the Crosstown Institute of Fine Arts, so he doesn't have a lot of money,
but he helps out financially as much as he can. He comes to visit Tessa
every week or so, takes her out in her stroller, and walks her over to the
park. But I can't really count on him for day-to-day support."

"My own family hasn't been all that much help, either," Claudia went on. "When I told them I was pregnant, they were pretty upset, and they immediately tried to push me into having an abortion. I couldn't see doing that—it wasn't right for me. I just felt it was impossible to put an end to the life I carried inside me. I couldn't see putting the baby up for adoption, either; I just didn't want to give her up. When I made it clear that I was going to have the baby and keep her, my dad agreed to pay the rent on a small apartment for me and the baby to live in, but that was it. My parents have barely spoken to me since Tessa was born.

"I'm on a full scholarship, so at least I don't have to worry about tuition, and I get an additional stipend from Cromwell that helps to cover my living expenses, but still it's a tight squeeze to make ends meet. You wouldn't believe how expensive diapers and baby food are!

"The real lifesaver in all this has been Brian's mother. She understood my decision to have the baby, and she's made it possible for me to be a mother and still stay in school. She looks after three other kids at her house—two of her neighbor's children, along with Brian's sister's baby. She offered to take care of Tessa, too, for free. She's wonderful with kids, and she really loves Tessa. So at least I don't have to worry about day care.

"But even though Tessa and I are getting by okay, my life is very different from the average college student. I'm up with Tessa at 6:00 every morning. On weekdays I take her to Brian's mom at 8:00, and then I've got to pick her up by 4:30 in the afternoon. She pretty much takes up all my evening and weekend time. She doesn't sleep solidly through the night yet, so I don't either, and I end up always feeling tired. I get my schoolwork done when I can—mostly between classes. I used to try to study after getting Tessa to bed at night, but by then I'm so brain-dead that I can't absorb anything significant. Of course I have no social life, and I feel pretty distant from the campus action at CC.

"Regardless of all that, though, I've never regretted my choice to carry my pregnancy to term and to keep Tessa. I want her to have a mother she can be proud of, and that's what keeps me in college. But I have to say that I've learned more—about myself and about the world around me— from her and from my decision to have and keep her than I have from any of my classes. These are life lessons that I'll never forget. Tessa has become the center of my existence. She's turned everything upside down, but she's also given me more joy and fulfillment than I ever thought possible," concluded Claudia as she drained the last drops of tea from her mug.

Kira said softly, "If someone like me were to tell you that she was pregnant, what would you advise her to do?"

Claudia shook her head. "I wouldn't give any advice at all. There's no right and wrong in this kind of situation, and there's no easy answer: each of the options presents its own trials and tribulations. It's a decision that a woman has to make on her own. But once the decision had been made, whatever it was, I would try to support the woman and help

her in any way I could. That is, if I actually knew anyone in that position." As she said those last words, Claudia placed her hand on Kira's
arm in a warm and reassuring gesture.

Kira, who was close to tears, remained silent. After a few moments, Claudia interrupted the silence by saying, "There's someone else
you might want to talk to. Do you know Yvonne Toufaian? She's in our
English class, too."

Kira nodded. "She's the tall one with the really long hair, isn't she?"

"That's right," said Claudia. "Yvonne has a baby, too, a baby boy.
He's over a year old now. Yvonne made a different decision from mine,
though: she gave her baby up for adoption. She's pretty open about it,
and I'm sure she'd be willing to discuss her choice with you."

"I'll see if I can find her," said Kira, as she stood up. "Thank you,"
she added, as she made her way out of the coffeehouse and back outside.

As she walked toward the Academic Quad, Kira caught a glimpse
of Yvonne sitting on the steps in front of the library and leafing through
a biology textbook. She headed over to her and tentatively sat down beside her.

"Excuse me," Kira began, "aren't you Yvonne? We're in the same
English composition class."

"Yes, of course," said Yvonne. "I recognize you. Kira, right?"

"That's me," said Kira. "Claudia Balthazar suggested that I talk to
you. We were discussing children, and she mentioned that you have a
baby boy."

"Well," said Yvonne, "I don't really have him. I mean, I did give birth
to a baby over a year ago, but I gave him up for adoption right away."

"Do you mind telling me about it?" Kira asked.

Yvonne looked at Kira questioningly for a few seconds, then
shrugged her shoulders and responded, "I don't see why not. It's not
anything I'm embarrassed about or ashamed of. After all, I'm not the
first young woman to find herself unintentionally pregnant. I won't go
into the sorry tale of how I ended up in that predicament—it was just
a combination of ignorance and denial. But when the time came to face
up to reality, it was clear to me what I needed to do.

"There was no way I could have an abortion; given my beliefs and
my upbringing, it just wasn't an option. That meant I'd have to share
the problem with my parents, since they were obviously going to find
out eventually. They were furious with me at first, but after a while they
calmed down and ended up being really helpful and supportive, especially my mom. I couldn't have faced it all without her.

"We talked about keeping the baby, and they said they'd be willing
to help me care for him, but I knew that even with their help I just was-
n't ready to be a mother. There are so many childless couples who
would make wonderful parents—adoption seemed like it would be the
best way to give my child a secure and happy life. So my parents took

care of all the legal arrangements, and they helped me to find the right adoptive family. The day my son was born, I put him into the arms of his new mother. I haven't seen him since."

"Wasn't it hard to give him up?" Kira asked softly.

"It was incredibly hard," Yvonne answered. "But whenever I get depressed about it, I remind myself that he's much better off in a stable family with two loving parents. I know I did the right thing for him, and for me, too."

The two young women sat together in silence. A minute or two later, Yvonne said, "I won't ask why you wanted to know about this, but I hope it helped."

"Yes, it did. Thank you," Kira replied. She slowly rose from the library steps and walked away.

When Angelica stopped back at the room later that morning, she found Kira packing a few clothes into a duffel bag. "Hey, what's going on?" she asked. "Are you going away somewhere?"

Kira nodded. "I'm going home for the weekend. If I leave now, I can make the 12:30 train. I'm not sure yet whether I'm going to tell my parents about my situation, or even whether I'm going to tell Conrad. But I know I need to think clearly about everything, and I don't think I can do it here."

Angelica hugged her roommate and said, "I'm here for you whatever you decide." She helped Kira pack the rest of her clothes and walked with her to the bus stop across from the main entrance to the campus. As they waited for the bus that would take Kira to the train station, both young women were quiet. The bus approached and Angelica gave Kira one last hug. Kira picked up her bag and purposefully climbed onto the bus. Angelica's final glimpse of her roommate was of a thoughtful face staring straight ahead.

Some Questions to Consider

What do you think Kira should do? Should she tell Conrad that she's pregnant? Should she tell her parents? How should she proceed with the pregnancy? What do you think of the choices made by Angelica, Claudia, and Yvonne? Are any other options available to Kira? What do you think about the Cromwell health insurance covering the costs of childbirth, but not of abortion? Is this appropriate? Why or why not?

Thinking Critically

Claudia asserts that "there's no right and wrong in this kind of situation." Do you agree with her statement? Is it all just a matter of personal opinion and belief, or are some solutions more "right" than others? Is there any way to come to a reasoned conclusion in a case such as this? If so, how? To what extent and in what ways could descriptive or prescriptive assumptions affect the conclusions reached?

Reading Closely

Angelica speaks of her choice to "end the pregnancy," and Claudia speaks of being unable to "put an end to the life I felt inside me." What are the connotations of the words they are each using to describe their situations? In their descriptions of the decisions they faced, are there any examples of words or expressions that are slanted or loaded? How does their choice of language reflect their perspectives?

What If

What if Kira and Conrad were in a loving, committed relationship with one another? Would that change your perspective on this case? Would it create any additional options for Kira? Would marrying Conrad and raising a child together provide a positive solution to Kira's dilemma? Why or why not?

Connecting the Cases

In some of the cases we've read, personal matters seem to affect students' lives more than academic ones. Claudia even remarks that she's learned more from her baby than from any of her classes. What lessons are being learned from the extracurricular events we've read about? Are these lessons as important as the more academic subject matter students are expected to learn in college? Should a school like Cromwell encourage, discourage, or remain indifferent to the learning of "life lessons" like those that Claudia mentions?

Bringing It Home

Do you have student health insurance through your college? If not, do you think it should be made available? Why or why not? If you do, do you know the details of your coverage? What conditions are or are not covered? Do you think your coverage is adequate? Why or why not?

Suggestions for Writing

1. Imagine that you are one of Kira's close friends, and that she has confided in you about her situation. Write a letter in which you advise her regarding her current dilemma.

2. Write a memo to the director of Cromwell's health center, presenting detailed and well-supported suggestions for the services that should be available to CC students faced with unplanned pregnancies.

3. Have you learned any important "life lessons" at college? Has the college environment helped you or hindered you from such learning? Write an essay that explores these questions as they relate to your own experiences.

Out Loud

You are a volunteer for Cromwell's peer counseling service, and Kira has asked you to help her clarify her thoughts and feelings. With one of your classmates playing the role of Kira, act out a meeting between the two of you that would help her work through her situation without explicitly telling her what to do.

CASE 13

Technical Difficulties
Financial Aid and Computer Fraud

PART ONE

"It's outrageous! It's unbelievable! It's a crime!" exclaimed Claire Legrand, slamming the door shut and throwing her backpack down on her desk.

Her roommate, Edna Redbird, looked up from her studying. "Been to the financial aid office?" she asked sympathetically.

"Yes," Claire replied. "You know how I got my award letter for next semester and it said my aid was cut by nine hundred dollars? Well, I went to talk to someone in the office to find out why. I had written them a letter a couple of months ago explaining that my mom's company had reduced her hours as part of their downsizing, and that because of that I was requesting *more* aid for next semester, not *less*! Then they gave me all sorts of new forms to fill out and took forever to process them. So anyway, I figured the nine hundred dollar cut was just some stupid error, a minus sign instead of a plus, and all I would need to do would be to point it out to them and they would fix it.

"Well, after being kept waiting in the office for forty-five minutes, I finally got to see a financial aid counselor, and she told me that according to their records the nine hundred dollar cut was accurate. She called up my file on the computer and showed me all the information they had supposedly taken from the new financial aid forms my mom and I had turned in. What they had on file was that my mom's salary was

164

going *up*, not down! I told the counselor that it was a mistake, and asked her to look up the information on the actual forms we had submitted.

"You're not going to believe this, but it turns out that after they enter the information on the computer, they get rid of the original forms, so they have no record of the new salary information my mom submitted! The counselor kept saying 'We're very careful about entering information correctly. You must be mistaken in your understanding of the facts.' Honestly! As if I don't know that my mom's salary has been cut by 20 percent, and that this is going to create serious problems for us—she was barely keeping things going as it was.

"So after blowing off some steam and getting the counselor totally ticked off at me, I asked her what I could do to convince her that I need more money. She said that all the aid money for next semester had already been given out, and that there's none left whether I need it or not. At that point I really started screaming, so she went off to get her supervisor.

"There I was, steam practically coming out of my ears, when the director of financial aid walked in. You known what he's like—cold as ice. I explained my problem as calmly as I could, but he didn't seem to care. I said that my mom and I would be willing to fill out the forms again with the current information, but he said that even if we did that, it would take another couple of months to process it—in other words, after next semester's tuition is due. Then he repeated that anyway, like the counselor said, all the aid money has already been allocated to other students and there just wasn't anything they could do. He suggested that maybe I could work more hours each week or apply for a private loan from our home bank, and then he left.

"Work more hours! I'm already doing the maximum number of hours per week of work-study, plus an additional fifteen hours dealing with the stupid customers over at Earring Extravaganza. I barely have enough time to study as it is, much less have a life. And I already have a huge amount of money out on loan; I can't take out any more.

"Anyway, it doesn't seem fair that I should add to my loan burden because of the F.A. office's error—if they had entered my information correctly, I *would* be getting more money next semester. I don't buy that nonsense of theirs about how they're so careful inputting the data. So now, because of their incompetence, I'm screwed. I don't know how I can afford to come back to school next term." With that final comment, Claire burst into tears.

Edna didn't know what she could say to comfort her roommate. The account she had given of the mix-up in her financial aid package certainly was outrageous, but no more outrageous than some other stories Edna had heard recently. As a reporter for Cromwell's campus newspaper, the *Clarion*, Edna had been working on an investigative news article concerning the college's Office of Financial Aid, and she had discovered that there were a number of apparent errors in the aid letters that had been sent out to students in the past week. In many cases, the aid packages offered for next semester were just a few dollars less than what had been expected, so the students simply shrugged their shoulders and made no complaints. But a few situations like Claire's had also occurred, involving discrepancies of hundreds of dollars.

"You're not the only one facing this problem," Edna said to Claire. "There have been so many mix-ups with financial aid, I don't think it can be attributed to random errors or run-of-the-mill carelessness. There's something rotten going on, and I'm going to find out what it is."

"Okay, I know you want to do your hotshot reporter thing," responded Claire, "but I don't see how that's going to make my own situation any better. I still don't know how I'm going to be able to pay next semester's tuition."

"If we can figure out what's happening in the F.A. office and expose whatever has gone wrong, then the college will have to rectify the situation. They'll have to re-examine the cases of everyone whose aid package has been messed up, and give them a new deal," Edna explained.

"Yeah, right," muttered Claire, unconvinced.

Edna, however, optimistic about the power of the press, was sure that the only way to solve Claire's problem—and the problems of the other students whose aid had been inexplicably reduced—was to continue her investigations of the F.A. office. She already had in her possession copies of several apparently erroneous financial aid award letters given to her by irate students, along with their copies of the financial aid forms they had submitted to the office (even though the F.A. office did not keep copies of the forms after they inputted the information, a few students had been careful enough to retain copies for themselves). She intended to present the director of financial aid with these materials, and ask him to justify the apparent discrepancies between the level of expressed need and the level of aid awarded.

This was not, however, a simple task. It took Edna days to get to see the director, Russell Munk, who (with the help of his secretary) was an expert at avoiding students—especially student journalists. The secretary managed to put off every one of Edna's phone calls, telling her that the director was in a meeting, at a conference, or on the other line; and he never responded to any of the messages she left. When Edna asked to make an appointment with Mr. Munk, the secretary indicated that he was fully booked for the next three weeks.

Edna tried hanging around in the hallway outside Mr. Munk's second-floor office, but the secretary came out and told her that all financial aid inquiries had to proceed through the proper channels, and that if she had something to discuss she needed to make an appointment with one of the counselors. Edna explained that she didn't want to talk to a financial aid counselor, she wanted to talk to the director. The secretary threatened to call security if Edna didn't leave.

Next, Edna tried waiting outside the main entrance of Vanburen Hall, the administration building where the financial aid office was located, in order to catch Mr. Munk on his way out at the end of the day. But even after standing there for hours she never saw him leave—he either stayed in his office *very* late, or managed to slip out unobserved through the side door. Finally Edna decided to stake out the men's room on the ground floor of Vanburen Hall, the only men's bathroom in the building. She figured Mr. Munk would have to relieve himself sometime, and she was right; she caught him on the way in and demanded that he speak with her, indicating that she would follow him into the rest room if necessary.

A somewhat embarrassed Mr. Munk agreed to give Edna five minutes of his time, and after visiting the men's room, he walked back to his office with her. She produced the documents that pointed to disparities in several students' award packages and asked him to comment.

Mr. Munk brushed off Edna's inquiries. "Students always think they deserve more money than they're getting," he remarked dismissively. "That's nothing new. Unfortunately our resources are limited, and we have to do the best we can to distribute money fairly."

"But next semester's allocations *haven't* been fair," interjected Edna. "In several cases, students who have demonstrated increased financial need have actually received significant *decreases* in the amount of aid they're getting. Many students whose needs have remained the same have also received decreases ranging from a few dollars to a few hundred dollars. What's your explanation for this? Has the overall amount of aid money available decreased for next semester, necessitating these individual decreases?"

"No," responded Mr. Munk, "there's been no overall decrease—the total amount of available aid has actually increased slightly. We consider each case individually, and distribute as much money as we determine is needed. We recalculate need every semester because family situations change constantly. We're very careful in our computations, and I trust that my employees have been correct in their assessments. I have complete confidence in their abilities.

"But I'm afraid I don't have as much confidence in students. Have you considered that the copies of student financial aid forms that you're showing me—copies given to you by displeased students who haven't received as much money as they want—might have been falsified? How can you be sure that you're getting the true story? The information we have in our computers differs from the information they've provided you on these forms, but what makes you think that the forms they've given you are correct, and that the data in our computer files is erroneous?"

"Are you saying that the students who gave me copies of these forms to illustrate the discrepancies between their financial need and their aid awards deliberately tampered with the forms after the fact to make it look like their need is greater than it really is?" Edna asked.

"I'm simply suggesting that student fraud is perhaps a greater possibility than error on the part of my financial aid employees," Mr. Munk responded.

Edna was so enraged by this implied accusation that she was struck speechless. After a few moments, however, she regained her voice. She pointed out that computer files are just as open to tampering as photocopies of forms, and asked Mr. Munk if he would take any steps to review the computer records to check their accuracy.

"I see no reason to do that," Mr. Munk replied. "I have no cause to believe that there is any problem with the computer files, and so I don't see why I should expend precious time and resources on such an investigation. And now, young lady, I would appreciate it if you would leave my office. If you don't go immediately I'll be forced to call a campus security officer."

Edna left Mr. Munk's office angry and frustrated. The more she thought about it, the more convinced she became that someone must have tampered with the financial aid files, reducing the need amounts recorded and thus causing a decrease in aid awarded. But why? And how could she prove that this kind of tampering had, in fact, occurred?

Some Questions to Consider

If the financial aid office has erred—innocently or otherwise—in their recording of Claire's financial need, should they be responsible for correcting the error in the amount of aid awarded? If all available money has already been allocated to other students, would it be fair to take money away from these students in order to increase Claire's award? Is there anything more Claire could or should do to solve her financial problems? Is there anything more Edna could or should do to determine the source of the apparent discrepancies in financial aid awards?

PART TWO

Edna continued to ponder the problem of gaining proof of her suspicions as she walked to the student union for dinner that evening. On her way, she ran into two of her best friends: Rachel Fromm and Jamal Porter, the computer whizzes who, among other things, managed the *Clarion*'s financial accounts. The three of them went in to the dining hall together, and Edna decided to ask Rachel and Jamal for some technical information. As they chowed down on creamed chicken, she explained her suspicions about the financial aid computer files and inquired whether it would be possible to tell if someone had in fact altered information that had been keyed into the computer.

Jamal launched into a technical discussion of the ways in which an experienced computer expert, like himself, could detect such an intervention. "It could be done," he concluded, "but the problem would be getting access to the computer files. From what you're telling me, Mr. Munk isn't about to authorize an investigation like that, which makes finding any proof impossible."

Rachel interjected, "Nothing is impossible if you set your mind to it, as my mother always says. Just because Munk isn't opening the door for us doesn't mean we can't get in."

"What are you suggesting?" inquired a wary Edna.

"Oh, come on, Edna, don't be naive," Rachel responded. "You know Jamal and I are good. Hacking into the financial aid system should be easy—we've gotten into much more complex and more carefully protected systems before."

"I know you have, but I don't want to hear about it," said Edna. "Hacking into the system would be like breaking and entering. It's illegal, and it's wrong."

"Well, la-di-da, Little Miss Do-Right," Rachel responded. "You've done all sorts of stuff before to get a news story—eavesdropping on meetings, stalking administrators, whatever. Now all of a sudden you're afraid of a little technical investigation? Besides, this isn't just a simple news story. It's a very serious matter: the misallocation of financial aid funds. We're not talking about breaking into the F.A. office with a crowbar—just using our technical know-how to find out some information that should be public knowledge anyway."

Edna continued to resist Rachel's arguments, but finally Rachel and Jamal managed to convince her that hacking into the F.A. system would be the only way to protect students from unfair financial assessments.

"Don't worry," Jamal reassured her. "You don't need to know anything about what we're doing. We'll just let you know when we've got some results to report."

Edna tried to put the whole financial aid story out of her mind for a while, concentrating on studying for an upcoming psychology exam. It was hard to ignore the depression her roommate, Claire, had sunk into, but Edna avoided the issue by plunging into her schoolwork with single-minded absorption. When Rachel and Jamal came up behind her in the library a couple of days after their dinnertime conversation and tapped her on the shoulder, she almost jumped out of her chair.

"What is it?" asked a flustered Edna.

"We have some information for you," said Rachel.

"Very interesting information," added Jamal. "Let's get out of here and go somewhere we can talk privately."

They made their way to Edna's residence hall. Claire was out, so they had the room to themselves. Jamal and Rachel proceeded to tell Edna that they indeed had discovered evidence of tampering with the financial aid computer files.

"It's clear that a number of files have been affected," said Jamal. "We were even able to find our way back to the original entries, and compare them with the changed ones. The really interesting thing is that of those files that were altered, all but one resulted in a decrease in aid. Only one ended up with an increase—and the increase in that one exactly adds up to the decreases in all the others. So it would seem that money has been taken away from a number of individual students—a few dollars here, a few hundred dollars there—in order to provide a dramatic increase in funds for one lucky fellow."

"And," Rachel interjected, "you'll never guess who the person is who ended up with thousands of extra dollars in his financial aid package."

"Who?" asked Edna breathlessly.

"Ted Stanworth!" proclaimed Jamal.

Edna was puzzled. "Ted Stanworth? One of Peter Stanworth's children?" she asked.

Jamal and Rachel nodded.

"But that can't be right," Edna said. "Ted Stanworth's father is one of Cromwell's richest alumni. He's donated tons of money to the school—they even named the field house after him in honor of all the money he's given to the athletic programs. I can't believe that his kids would be eligible for *any* financial aid—let alone thousands of extra dollars."

Rachel explained, "It seems that Ted actually has a brain, and managed to win a two thousand dollar merit scholarship for an essay he wrote on ethics and technology. That *should* be the only tuition assistance he's getting, but somehow he's ended up with over six thousand dollars in extra financial aid."

"Do you think someone in the financial aid office decided to get in good with the famous Stanworth family by helping out one of the kids?" Edna inquired.

Jamal shook his head. "We don't exactly have a smoking gun or fingerprints, but we do have evidence that indicates where the computer that was used to do the tampering is located." He explained the technical subtleties that enabled him to trace the source of the intervention. "There's no doubt about it," he concluded. "The person who hacked into the system used a pretty sophisticated PC, operating out of Blaine Hall—which is where Ted lives. I'm assuming that Ted managed to get into the financial aid system and tampered with other people's accounts to give himself some extra spending money. After all, he is majoring in computer science and could have the knowledge to do something like that."

"But what do we do now?" asked Edna. "To bring Ted Stanworth's computer fraud out into the open, we'll have to disclose the fact that you two hacked into the system, too—which could get you into big trouble."

Rachel and Jamal shrugged in unison. "Everyone will have to understand that we had to do what we did in order to get at the truth,"

Rachel reasoned. "Sometimes you have to break a few rules in the interest of justice."

Edna, Jamal and Rachel walked purposefully to Vanburen Hall, prepared to confront the financial aid director with their new information and to demand that immediate action be taken. The forcefulness of their presentation convinced Mr. Munk's secretary that her boss had better see them immediately. To their surprise, Mr. Munk listened thoughtfully to their account and watched carefully as Rachel and Jamal used his computer to demonstrate how they had discovered the presence of an online interloper in the financial aid accounts.

"I'm stunned," Mr. Munk admitted, "but not too stunned to take action. You can rest assured that this situation will be dealt with fairly and firmly. The perpetrator of this fraud—no matter who his father is—will be apprehended and brought to justice, and those students who have had their awards tampered with will have their accounts corrected immediately. I will, however, also have to take action against Rachel and Jamal for entering the system without authorization. I intend to report you immediately to the dean of students. But since you did what you did for the greater good, I will recommend to her that she exercise leniency in her dealings with you."

With that remark, the financial aid director dismissed the three students from his office, and set about cleaning up the mess.

Some Questions to Consider

Did Jamal and Rachel do the right thing? Is Edna implicated in their actions as well, since she knew what they were planning to do and did nothing to stop them? Does one suspected act of computer hacking justify another? What about the privacy of students whose files Jamal and Rachel examined? Was there any other action they could have taken? What punishment, if any, do you think the dean of students should impose upon Jamal and Rachel? If it is proven incontrovertibly that Ted Stanworth committed an act of computer fraud, transferring other students' money into his own financial aid account, what punishment should be imposed upon him by the college? Should legal charges be filed against him? Should the important position of his family be taken into consideration?

Thinking Critically

Jamal, Rachel, and Edna seem fairly sure that Ted Stanworth is the perpetrator of the financial aid fraud. Do they have sufficient evidence to reach this conclusion? What is the nature of their evidence? What other knowledge or information could contribute to an incontrovertible conclusion regarding the perpetrator?

Reading Closely

Edna initially asserts, "Hacking into the system would be like breaking and entering. It's illegal, and it's wrong." Rachel, however, points out, "We're not talking about breaking into the F.A. office with a crowbar— just using our technical know-how to find out some information that should be public knowledge anyway." Is there any difference between the kind of computer "break-in" that Rachel and Jamal committed and a physical act of breaking and entering? If so, what is the basis for the distinction between them? If not, why not?

What If

What if, instead of Ted Stanworth hacking into the financial aid files to further enrich himself from other students' money, someone else had hacked into the system in order to redistribute Ted Stanworth's two thousand dollar merit scholarship to other students in dire financial need? Would that be any more acceptable than the situation presented in this case? Why or why not?

Connecting the Cases

In several cases, we have seen a questionable means used to achieve a valuable end: for example, the separation of Sondra and Corinne as roommates to preclude unpleasantness and possible abuse, the members of the Asian-American Alliance seizing copies of the *Clarion* in order to prevent potential offense, Lucy's use of an exam "preview" to improve her academic performance, or, in this case, hacking into a computer system in order to expose a case of fraud. Does the end justify the means? If so, when and why?

Bringing It Home

Claire and Edna faced problems when they tried to obtain information from the financial aid office. On many college campuses, students find it difficult to gain immediate access to administrators and staff in various departments. Is this a problem on your own campus? Use interview material and personal observations to explore this issue.

Suggestions for Writing

1. You should be writing a paper for your English composition class, but as you sit staring at your blank computer screen, you suddenly find yourself typing out your thoughts concerning Jamal and Rachel's unauthorized entry into the files of the financial aid office— files that include your own financial aid accounts, along with those of many other students. Did they do the right thing?

2. Assume that Ted Stanworth is found guilty of tampering with the financial aid files, and that Rachel and Jamal are also found guilty of hacking into the financial aid system. Do they all deserve the same punishment? Write a memo to the dean of students presenting your opinion on appropriate penalties in this case.

3. Use newspaper accounts to acquaint yourself with recent cases of hacking incidents on other college campuses. Based on this background research as well as the events presented in this case, write an essay that proposes a set of guidelines for Cromwell administrators to use in dealing with hacking and computer fraud.

Out Loud

You have been chosen to serve on the Judicial Advisory Committee (JAC) that has been convened to determine whether Jamal and Rachel have done anything wrong by hacking into the financial aid computer files, and whether they deserve any punishment. Together with several of your classmates, enact a meeting of the JAC in which you try to reach consensus on this case.

CASE 14

Lights Out
Living and Learning Off Campus

Ramón Nabuco unlocked his apartment door and dropped his back-pack in the entryway. It had been another exhausting day—three classes back-to-back in the morning, a quick lunch in the student union's base-ment coffeehouse, and five hours of work at Media Mania in the Crosstown Mall, trying to explain the fine points of digital technology to clueless customers. Now that he was back home in Apartment 7H, he could look forward to a couple of hours of peace and quiet, since his two roommates had informed him earlier that they'd be gone for dinner.

As he walked into the living room and kicked off his shoes, he headed over to the switch that would turn on the overhead light and gave it a quick flick upwards. Nothing happened.

"The bulb's burned out," he muttered to himself. "I thought these compact fluorescents were supposed to last forever." Too tired to do anything about the light, Ramón collapsed onto the sofa and reached for the lamp that sat on a small side table. He clicked the switch at the base only to discover that, once again, there was no light. Ramón was beginning to get the feeling that it wasn't just a matter of burned-out bulbs; when repeated jabbing at the television and stereo controls had no effect, he reluctantly came to the conclusion that power to the apartment had been disrupted.

Since the building's flimsy construction allowed him to hear a good deal of what transpired in neighboring apartments, Ramón was aware that the people next door had their TV on, and that the residents across the hall were once again playing their favorite CD at full volume. The power outage was apparently limited to Apartment 7H. Was it possible that the electric company had shut off their power for failure to settle the account on time?

Ramón and his two roommates had agreed to divide the day-to-day duties of apartment dwelling. His roommate Mike was the one responsible for handling the electric bills—though perhaps responsible was not the best word to use in conjunction with Mike. Twice so far he had been egregiously late in paying the bills, in spite of the fact that Ramón and their third roommate, Brian, were scrupulous about contributing their share of what was owed in plenty of time to meet the deadline. The last time Mike submitted a late payment, they had received a nasty letter from the power company informing them that one more failure to settle their account in a timely manner would result in termination of service. It seemed that this dreaded eventuality had come to pass.

Outside, it was getting dark. Inside, Ramón was getting angry— very angry. He had a paper due in his English composition class the next morning; although he had an almost-completed version on disk, he had been planning to do some last-minute polishing this evening before printing it out. Without power, this would be impossible. He'd either have to head all the way back to campus to use one of the college computer labs, or else forego the final revisions and print out his current far-from-perfect draft when he went to campus in the morning. Mike's irresponsibility had left him in a sorry mess. As he stumbled into the kitchen to hunt for matches and the candles he usually saved for his girl-friend's visits, Ramón mumbled unprintable epithets under his breath.

Ramón had known Mike since they were fellow ninth graders at Hawthorne High School, when the nickname "Mellow Mike" was coined to describe his laid-back, who-cares attitude. If not for his phenomenal talent for last-minute cramming, Mike would probably have flunked out of high school. As it was, he managed to maintain a respectable grade point average while doing virtually no work. When the time came to apply to college, he, like Ramón, managed to get into Cromwell—but Ramón had worked hard to achieve his college acceptance letter, whereas Mike seemed to get his with no effort at all.

Mike's doting, well-to-do parents didn't seem to be aware that their son was a total slacker. All they knew was that Mike was succeeding academically, and they rewarded him for his good high school grades and his admission to a selective college by buying him pretty much anything he wanted—all of which did nothing to change Mike's inherent laziness and lack of motivation.

At first Mike's lackadaisical approach to life had seemed harmless to Ramón, even amusing. But by the time high school graduation rolled around, Ramón was beginning to adopt a more serious attitude. He knew that he would have to work hard to get through college, and that his parents—who were less financially secure than Mike's—could not give him much support. He gradually came to resent Mike's irresponsible attitude and his sense of entitlement.

Old friendships die hard, however, and when Ramón was searching for a couple of roommates to share Apartment 7H with him, he decided he would feel safer with someone familiar. He had taken a chance with Brian, whom he barely knew when they agreed to room together; at least with Mike he knew what he was getting. Now that Mike, like Ramón, was attending Cromwell and living more-or-less independently, Ramón hoped that the rigors of "real life" would force Mike to take a more practical approach.

What Ramón had not foreseen was that the qualities that had seemed merely irritating in Mike the high school classmate would be disastrous in Mike the college roommate. Not only had he failed to pay the bills on time, he never did any of his share of the other apartment duties, and spent most of his time lying on the sofa watching TV. Mike had managed to survive his midterm exams through his usual cramming, but since then school had fallen completely by the wayside. Although Mike was still officially enrolled at Cromwell, Ramón couldn't remember the last time Mike had actually been to one of his classes.

In fact, Brian—who initially had been an unknown entity—had turned out to be a much better roommate. He was an avid photographer, and determined to make a career of it. In the meantime, he worked long hours as a waiter while taking as many photography classes as he could afford at the Crosstown Institute of Fine Arts. Brian had fathered a child with his former girlfriend, Claudia. Although the romance had ended, Brian was determined to keep a strong relationship with his eight-month-old daughter. He spent time with her every week, and contributed as much money as he could toward her support. Although he may have made some mistakes in the past, the Brian of today was mature, hard-working, quiet, and dependable. Ramón often found himself wondering how Brian put up with Mike.

Ramón himself had tolerated Mike's negligence in part because he was too tired and overwhelmed by his own daily struggles to do anything about it—but the power cut-off was too much. Perhaps it had been his own fault for rooming with an irresponsible jerk, but Ramón had finally had enough. He resolved to tell Mike at the earliest possible opportunity that he would have to move out.

Just as he reached this resolution, Ramón heard a key turning in the apartment lock. He assumed Mike and Brian were returning from dinner, and summoned up his anger in preparation for a confrontation. As the door opened, he was surprised to see Brian entering the apartment alone.

"Hey, what's going on?" Brian immediately asked. "What's with the candlelight? I'm not interrupting a romantic interlude, am I?"

"I wish you were," replied Ramón, and he proceeded to explain to Brian the reason for the dim lighting. He then asked, "Where is Mike, anyway? I thought you two went to dinner together."

"We did. I won two free meals at the Chelsea Café, remember? I decided to treat Mike to dinner there—you know he hasn't eaten anything but ramen noodles for days. He hit it off really well with our waitress, and it just so happened that her shift was about to end. I left the two of them discussing which movie they were going to see. I presume she's paying, since he doesn't have a penny in his pocket."

"How can he be broke? His parents just sent him two hundred dollars a couple of days ago."

Brian shrugged. "He's wearing new running shoes."

At this point Ramón exploded. "I've had it! Every day, day in and day out, no matter how tired I am or how lousy I feel, I go to class, I go to work, I come home, I do my schoolwork, I clean up the kitchen, and I pay my share of the bills. You too—you hold down a thankless job, you work hard at your photography, you try to be a good father, and you keep your eyes on your future goals. In the meantime Mike just slacks off, doing nothing, living off everyone around him—and doing pretty well, thank you! He even gets more dates than I do."

"Yeah, but you don't need dates, remember? You have a girlfriend!" responded Brian, trying to change the subject to deflect Ramón's anger.

Ramón, however, was not so easily distracted. He continued his tirade, exclaiming, "Honestly, Brian, it's infuriating! You know Mike's parents send him money all the time—the monthly check that's supposed to cover his rent and food, and the odd couple of hundred dollars here and there for what his dad likes to call 'incidentals.' But instead of using it for living expenses, he blows it on a pair of sneakers. I wish I had two hundred dollars to spend on shoes, but I'm lucky if I can squirrel away enough money to rent a video.

"And even though his parents' money means that he doesn't have to work all day like we do, he doesn't have the energy to lift a finger around here. He can't be bothered to pick up his towels from the bathroom floor. He can't be bothered to buy his own toothpaste instead of using yours or mine. He can't be bothered to write a check to the electric company and mail it on time. Never mind that he can't be bothered to go to class—it's his business if he wants to flunk out of Cromwell. But I'm sick and tired of being used and abused by Mellow Mike!"

Thoroughly drained, Ramón collapsed on the sofa. After a moment of silence, Brian picked up the thread of the conversation. "You know," he said, "it may not be just Mike's business if he wants to flunk out of Cromwell. It may be his parents' business, too. Wait till you hear what he told me at dinner tonight."

Ramón looked up wearily. "What, that he's acing all his courses?"

Brian shook his head. "No, he really is failing everything. And he's not planning to register for classes next semester."

"What's he going to do?" asked Ramón. "Get a job?"

"Are you kidding? Mellow Mike? No way—it would cut into his favorite afternoon TV shows. His parents will keep on sending him money to live on, and he'll keep on taking it."

"They won't keep on sending him money," Ramón interjected. "You don't know Mike's parents. They're totally focused on success. As long as they can brag to all their friends that Mike got into Cromwell and that he's doing well, they'll hand him everything on a silver platter. But if they hear that he's flunking out and not taking classes next semester, they'll be furious, and they won't give him a penny."

"That's just the point," said Brian. "They're not going to hear that he's flunking out. He's not going to tell them. He's going to let them go on thinking he's doing well in school."

"He can't do that! They'll have to find out. After all, won't the college send Mike's grades home to his parents at the end of the semester?"

"Well," Brian said, "he's got that angle covered. Apparently, when you register at Cromwell you need to fill out a form that says where you want your grades and other information sent, and of course at the beginning his parents insisted that he put their address on the form. But he told me he went to the registrar's office last week and put in an address change for all official communications, including grade reports—now it's all going to come here to good old Apartment 7H."

"But he can't keep his parents in the dark forever," Ramón objected. "At some point they're going to contact the college about something or other, or else Cromwell will contact them about Mike's failure to register for next semester. It's not like a public college where there are all sorts of privacy guidelines that keep your parents out of your business—Cromwell gets in touch with parents at the drop of a hat."

"I told Mike all that," responded Brian. "He admitted that his parents will probably find out sooner or later, but as he put it, 'Better later than sooner.' He says he's going to keep the charade going as long as he can."

"That's what he thinks!" exclaimed Ramón. "He's assuming that we're just going to go along with all this, right?"

"Yeah, I guess so," replied Brian. "It's his life, isn't it?"

"He's ripping off his parents, Brian! I think we need to tell them what's really going on. After all, I've known Mike's mom and dad for years. Though I don't like the way they've spoiled Mike rotten, I still don't think they deserve this. It was one thing for him to take whatever they gave him when it was all open and above board, but now he's planning to take their money under false pretenses."

"Is it any of our business? He's not ripping us off, after all, is he? I know you want him out of the apartment, and I agree with you about that—it's time for us to find a new roommate. The power getting turned off because of his negligence really is the last straw. I'm not convinced, though, that it's our responsibility to say anything to his parents about his scheme to live off them a while longer. It's between him and them; we should just stay out of it."

"How can you say that?" Ramón asked. "If we let him go ahead and take his parents' money without intervening, then we're just as bad as he is. We know a wrong is being committed, and we're not doing anything to prevent it. That makes us his accomplices!"

"I don't know," said Brian, shaking his head dubiously. "It's his parents he's taking money from, and they're not hurting for funds. This is a family issue. And even if I did agree with you that we have a responsibility to let Mike's parents know what's going on, what makes you think they'd want to hear the information we have to offer? They may not even believe us. From what you've told me, they seem to have turned a blind eye on Mike's problems in the past."

"Well, maybe we shouldn't tell them outright," Ramón offered. "Maybe we should just suggest to his parents that it would be a good idea to inquire into Mike's current academic standing, and then put the ball in their court."

"Or maybe you could find a way to get the college to intervene," Brian said. "Isn't there anyone over there you could talk to? You could explain how Mike is duping his parents and ask them to do something about it, couldn't you? All they'd have to do would be to let Mike's mom and dad know that their son hasn't registered for next semester. Didn't you just say that Cromwell contacts people's parents at the drop of a hat?"

"You may have an idea there," said Ramón, nodding his head, "but I'm still not convinced that it isn't our personal responsibility to talk to Mike's parents. After all, we're the ones who know about his scheme."

"You know," said Brian, "I think you want to tell Mike's parents what's going on just because you're ticked off at him and you want to make sure they realize what a slacker he is. You want to punish him for being such an irresponsible idiot. Okay, I can see that. I do too. So we've already agreed to punish him by booting him out of here. I don't think we need to go any further and get him in trouble with his parents just to get revenge."

"It's not a question of getting him into trouble or getting revenge. I admit that I'm more willing to tell his parents after seeing what a disaster he's been as a roommate; he's proven that he doesn't deserve for anyone to cut him any slack. But that's not really the point. The point is that I can't just stand by and watch while a crime gets committed."

"What crime?" inquired Brian.

"Stealing!" Ramón replied.

"Oh, come on. Can you really consider this to be stealing? It's not like he's breaking into someone's house. His parents have always been happy to give him money before, so maybe he's justified in assuming that they'll want to go on giving it to him," Brian argued.

At that moment the phone rang. Brian picked up the receiver and after saying a polite "Hello, how are you?" he covered the mouthpiece and whispered to Ramón, "It's Mike's mom!"

Ramón stared at Brian, momentarily speechless with surprise. Here was the opportunity to reveal the truth. Should he take this opportunity, grab the phone from Brian, and tell Mike's mother in no uncertain terms exactly what her son was doing? Should he proceed more delicately, just dropping a few broad hints? Should he wait until he had a chance to prod the college authorities to take some action? Or should he just stay out of it? Ramón wanted to do the right thing, but the more he thought about it, the less he was sure what the right thing would be.

Some Questions to Consider

Do you agree with Brian and Ramón's decision to ask Mike to move out? Do they have a responsibility to tell Mike's parents about their son's plans to take their money under false pretenses? Should Ramón's long-standing friendship with Mike and his family have any bearing on his response to the situation? Should Mike's negligence as a roommate have any bearing on how Brian and Ramón react to the situation involving Mike's parents?

Thinking Critically

Brian and Ramón seem to have different opinions concerning the need to confront Mike's parents with their son's actions. To what extent might these differences in opinion be the result of different assumptions, as well as a different attitude or perspective toward Mike and his family (for example, Ramón's previous friendship as opposed to Brian's more distant relationship)?

Reading Closely

According to Ramón, Mike is about to commit the crime of stealing, and he and Brian will become accomplices to this crime if they "just stand by and watch." Is what Mike plans to do actually stealing? How would you define the word? What is its dictionary definition? What is its legal definition? Does Mike's intended action fall under any of these definitions? Might that affect the way in which you perceive Ramón and Brian's responsibility in this situation?

What If

What if Ramón and Brian decide to say nothing to Mike's parents about their son's scheme, but Mike's mother then asks Ramón directly if he knows how her son is doing in school? Should he lie, tell the truth, or somehow avoid the question? Would avoiding an answer to a direct question be the same as not saying anything to begin with, before being asked? If there is a difference between these two situations, how would you explain the distinction?

Connecting the Cases

Several of the cases we've read deal with the question of whether an individual has the right or responsibility to intervene in another individual's life. At what point is such intervention necessary or justifiable? For example, would Samir and Henry in case 4 have been justified in intervening when Angelica cried out from behind the locked storeroom door? In case 5, would Henry have been justified in interfering with Samir's dumpster initiation? In the current case, would Ramón and Brian be justified in intervening? Would they bear any culpability if they did not intervene?

Bringing It Home

Mike's plan to deceive his parents is made possible, in part, by Cromwell's policy of letting students decide where they want their grade reports and other important information sent. What is the policy on such matters at your own institution? Would your college contact your parents if you failed to register for the following semester? Do you agree with this policy?

Suggestions for Writing

1. If you were one of Ramón's close friends, what advice would you give him regarding his roommate situation as well as the deception of Mike's parents? Write a note to Ramón telling him how you think he should proceed, and why.

2. Should student transcripts be a private matter, accessible only to the individual student unless the student releases the information? Or do parents and guardians have a right to receive such information without the student's consent? Write a letter to the editor of the *Clarion*, the student newspaper, expressing your views on this issue.

3. Mike has apparently had a long-standing pattern of irresponsible behavior, which may affect the way we perceive his current plan to deceive his parents. Write an essay exploring the question of whether prior behavior can legitimately be taken into account when judging a current situation.

Out Loud

Together with two of your classmates (with one of you taking the role of Brian, one taking the role of Ramón, and one taking the role of Mike's mother), enact the phone call at the end of this case. How do you think it should or would develop?

CASE 15

Saturday Night Fever
Faculty-Student Romance

PART ONE

Art Larson breathed a sigh of relief as he joined the crowd streaming out of the American history lecture. It was his last class meeting of the semester, and now he had a few days to catch up on sleep and do some studying before his first final exam next Tuesday afternoon. He appreciated Cromwell's policy of ending classes on a Wednesday and waiting until Tuesday to begin exams, giving students a five-day reading period to prepare for finals.

Actually, reflected Art, most of his friends weren't planning on doing that much reading. Their energy was being directed toward this Saturday's Holiday Happening, an annual extravaganza sponsored by the Cromwell Student Government. Every December, this event brought together all elements of the CC community for one last end-of-term bash. Following the usual tradition, the evening would begin with a special candlelight buffet supper in the elaborately decorated dining hall. The spacious student union lobby would be converted into a dance floor for the after-dinner festivities, with music provided by two live bands as well as a popular local deejay.

The Holiday Happening was always the most eagerly anticipated event of the fall semester. Everyone went, even the younger faculty members—and some of the older ones, too. The students, who should have been reviewing their organic chemistry notes or trying to figure out exactly what's going on in Book IV of *Paradise Lost*, instead spent their time trying to decide what to wear Saturday night, since part of the Holiday Happening tradition included the display of unusual or elaborate attire.

Like everyone else, Art was planning to attend the Holiday Happening, but he wasn't particularly concerned about what he should wear. He was nervous enough about the party; he didn't need to add clothing anxiety to his problems.

The source of Art's nervousness was his next-door neighbor, Sondra Johnson. Art and Sondra had become good friends over the course of the semester. They were both taking introductory Japanese, and had spent many hours side by side in the language lab. They had worked closely together in various campus organizations and had discovered that they shared similar views about politics and social change. Art found that he could tell Sondra things about himself that he'd never before dared to reveal, and Sondra seemed equally willing to confide in him. Gradually they spent more and more time together, and lately their friends had been teasing them about being "an item."

Were they an item? Art wasn't sure. He and Sondra had gone to campus movie screenings together, had hung out in the student union's basement coffeehouse for hours on end, had shared vegetable samosas at the local Indian restaurant, had stayed up into the wee hours of the morning discussing everything from political candidates to their favorite ice cream flavors—but they'd never touched, never kissed, never said a romantic word to one another. It wasn't that Art didn't want to take the relationship beyond the realm of mere friendship. He was in touch with his body enough to know that he was intensely attracted to Sondra, and he was in touch with his emotions enough to know that he was falling in love with her. But how could he know whether she felt the same way about him? What if he declared his feelings for her and she reacted with outrage or embarrassment?

There was a further problem lurking in the background: Sondra was not entirely unattached. She had been involved in a serious relationship throughout her junior and senior years of high school, and although her high school boyfriend had enrolled at a university far away from Cromwell, he and Sondra were still in touch. Sondra had told Art enough about this relationship to make it clear that it was on its last legs, but Ed Franklin had not disappeared from her life and Art was reluctant to approach Sondra romantically until he was clearly out of the picture.

There was also the question of race. Ed, like Sondra, was African-American. Art was not. He knew that Sondra had close friends of all races and ethnicities, but he also knew that she felt strongly about preserving African-American culture. He'd never explicitly discussed with her how she felt about interracial dating. Would she be willing to become romantically involved with someone who was of Scandinavian descent and who had lived all his life in a lily-white suburb? Would her family accept him? Would his family, for all their avowed tolerance and open-mindedness, really be willing to accept her? What kinds of problems might they face as an interracial couple?

Art's mind was filled with questions, doubts, and hesitations, but he realized that if he didn't try to resolve his confused emotions soon, he'd go crazy. Sondra had mentioned that she didn't have any plans for the Holiday Happening, and so at dinner on Wednesday he casually asked her to join him and was glad when she accepted. In the Happening's wild and unpredictable atmosphere, he intended to let matters take their course.

When Saturday evening rolled around, Art nonchalantly popped into Sondra's room and asked if she was ready to walk over to the Holiday Happening buffet. She nodded and gave him a warm smile. Art's sartorial ambitions had reached no further than the addition of a black leather vest and a hand-tooled belt to his everyday attire of jeans and a denim shirt, but Sondra told him that he looked great. He returned the compliment, lavishing praise on the richly embroidered Moroccan caftan she had bought at the Global Market downtown. Both of them felt that something was in the air; there was an unaccustomed tension between them that heightened as they walked across the quad.

The tension dissipated when Art and Sondra reached the student union. They were so busy gawking at what everyone was wearing and commenting on who was arm-in-arm with whom that they forgot their nervousness. The Cromwell dining hall had never looked so attractive, and the chefs had produced a wonderful meal. The vegetarian entree, tortellini with artichoke hearts and sun-dried tomatoes, was delicious. As they tucked into their tortellini, Sondra and Art fell into their usual easy camaraderie, gossiping about the sights and sounds around them.

"Look at that—Greg Cervenko in sequins!" exclaimed Sondra. Indeed, the usually nondescript Greg had managed to find a sequined black and gold cape to throw over a black turtleneck and slacks. He was sitting at a crowded table across the room, laughing and joking with several other first-year students.

"I never expected to see him dressed like that," Art said, "but I guess it just goes to show how much he's loosened up this semester. Remember what a jerk he was at the beginning?"

"Uh huh," assented Sondra. "And speaking of jerks, there's Corinne."

Art turned to get a glimpse of Sondra's former roommate swathed in a cloud of pink chiffon, drifting into the dining hall on the arm of Beta Omicron Zeta President Dan Harris. They disappeared into a crowd of BOZ fraternity members, and Art turned his gaze elsewhere.

"Oh, look," said Sondra, directing his attention to the other side of the room. "Stephanie and Max look great—so elegant. And there's Samir and Henry."

"That's something that hasn't changed all semester—those guys still can't get dates. Well, at least they have each other." As soon as the words were out of his mouth, Art became self-conscious. After all, he wasn't sure that he really had a date, either. Were he and Sondra just buddies, like Samir and Henry? Or was there more to it than that?

In the meantime, Sondra was continuing to check out the scene. "Wow, look at that outfit Grace is wearing. And Dorothy—I haven't seen her so relaxed in ages. Don't you love Jamal's suit? Oh, Irene and Vivian just arrived, both in tuxedos. They look sharp, don't they?"

"Absolutely," Art replied. "And check out Tama—I never knew you could get so many zippers onto one dress. Hey, is that Victor over there? With the feathers?"

"I think so. And . . . no, it can't be."

"What?" asked Art, craning his neck to see who Sondra was staring at through the open door of the dining hall. Out in the lobby the deejay had started playing some music, and many of the people pouring into the dining hall had momentarily stopped to listen. One couple had caught Sondra's eye, but Art didn't have the clear view she did and couldn't understand why she was so mesmerized.

"Professor Banner," she whispered.

"Oh," said Art, a bit huffily. Sondra had taken Hal Banner's Introduction to Philosophy class this semester, and she had never tired of telling Art about the professor's incisive mind, his quick wit, his captivating smile, and his lean athletic frame. Prof. Banner was a big favorite across campus, popular with students and respected by his colleagues, but Art was getting a little sick of Sondra's fascination with him. He turned his back on the doorway and shoved another forkful of tortellini into his mouth.

Sondra kept staring. "Art," she said, "you'll never guess who he's got as his date."

"I don't care," said Art. "Professors are boring."

"It's not a professor, it's a student," Sondra remarked.

"So?" said Art, finishing his last bite of tortellini and starting in on the hazelnut torte he had selected for dessert.

"Come on. Aren't you just a little curious?" asked Sondra.

"Oh, all right, I give in," said Art. "Who is it?"

"Angelica Caputo," Sondra replied.

"No way. Hal Banner couldn't actually have brought Angelica as his date," Art maintained. "Angelica may be brilliant—I've heard all the rumors about her test scores being the highest of any entering student this year. But given her wild social reputation, I can't believe that any faculty member would be seen with her. Besides, student-faculty dating is just not done at Cromwell. She and Banner may be standing next to each other, but I'm sure it's a coincidence."

"Take one look at them, and you'll see there's no question that they've come together," Sondra insisted. "And you should see what Angelica's wearing!"

Now Art was curious, and he tipped his chair back to see if he could catch a glimpse of Angelica's get-up. Unfortunately he leaned a little too far and ended up sprawled on the dining hall's industrial gray carpeting. After standing up and dusting himself off, he felt too foolish to continue the conversation. He was sure that his clumsiness had ruined any chance he might have had with Sondra, but Sondra treated the incident matter-of-factly, setting Art's chair upright and helping him clean up the cake that he had knocked onto the floor.

When everything was again in order, Sondra reached over and brushed back the lock of hair that had fallen across Art's forehead. Suddenly, the tension that had been present between them earlier in the evening returned. Neither of them could think of anything to say, and the uncomfortable silence continued until Sondra abruptly interrupted it.

"I just can't resist dancing to this song. Come on," she said, moving out of the dining hall and into the lobby. As Art followed her, he noticed that the music had energized a number of other couples. Dozens of students were now on the dance floor, and so were a few faculty members. But Art hardly noticed them—he was having too good a time dancing with Sondra.

The deejay's selections were eclectic but exciting, and they danced to just about every musical style imaginable. Art's energy seemed boundless, and Sondra matched him step for step. By the time the second live band took the stage, the two had been dancing nonstop for over two hours. The student union lobby had become so crowded that there wasn't much room to cut loose, but Art and Sondra found enough space to move their feet.

All of a sudden, Art noticed that just a few feet away from him Hal Banner had reappeared. Dancing with him—yes, Sondra had been right—was Angelica Caputo, one of the most flamboyant, most intelligent, and most talked-about members of Cromwell's first-year class.

When Art saw Angelica, he couldn't help staring. She had forgone her usual black lace and leather, and instead had chosen to wear a diaphanous white gown that looked like something out of a Botticelli painting. It wasn't her attire that caught Art's attention, though. It was the fact that she and Hal Banner were looking into each other's eyes as if they were the only two people on earth. Suddenly, Angelica and Prof. Banner turned and walked off the dance floor together.

Art danced a little closer to Sondra. "Did you see that?" he asked her.

"You mean the sparks flying between Angelica Caputo and Hal Banner?" replied Sondra. "Hard not to notice, wasn't it? Pretty bold of them, considering Cromwell's policy forbidding any kind of sexual involvement between faculty and students. They could get into a lot of trouble."

"Only if someone reports them to the provost, which I can't imagine anybody doing," said Art. "Anyway, all that anyone really saw was that they were dancing together, which isn't against any rules."

"I guess not," said Sondra, "but I still think they should watch out."

"Umhm," agreed Art distractedly. The band's lead singer had just begun a credible imitation of Percy Sledge crooning his classic "When a Man Loves a Woman." It was a slow song, a quintessentially romantic song, the kind of song you danced to with a lover, not a friend. Sondra put her arms around Art's shoulders; he put his arms around her waist. Soon they, too, were looking soulfully into each other's eyes.

"I guess we really are an item," Art murmured.

Some Questions to Consider

What do you think about Art and Sondra's relationship? Do you think race is or should be a factor between them? If Art had asked you for advice about how to proceed with Sondra, what would you have told him? What do you think about the apparent connection between Angelica and Prof. Banner? Do you agree with the Cromwell policy forbidding sexual relationships between students and faculty? (For a full statement of the policy, see the appendix.) From what Art and Sondra saw on the dance floor, do you think this policy applies to what was going on between Angelica Caputo and Hal Banner?

PART TWO

When Sondra woke up the next day, she was shocked to see how late she had slept. Her roommate Odette was obviously already up and out. By the time she showered and dressed, Sondra had only ten minutes to make it to the dining hall before brunch would be over. She stopped at Art's room to see if he was up. When she knocked, he came to the door in sweat clothes that had obviously been thrown on quickly—he was still struggling to tie the drawstring at his waist.

"Ready to get something to eat?" Sondra asked.

"Sure," said Art.

They made it to the dining hall just as the meal card checker was about to close up her station. As they sat down to eat and chat, they noticed Angelica Caputo sitting a few tables away, accompanied by Nora Quinn, one of the leaders of the Cromwell Women's Caucus (CWC). Angelica had gotten to know several CWC members earlier in the semester and had become close friends with one or two of them. But Nora came off as stodgy and self-righteous, so Angelica had always steered clear of her. Sondra and Art, who knew about the two women's differences, didn't understand why Angelica and Nora would be having brunch together.

Angelica didn't understand it, either. Until just a few moments ago she had been sitting by herself in the near-empty dining hall, reading the newspaper and drinking a cup of coffee. Then she looked up and saw Nora standing next to her.

"Mind if I sit down?" asked Nora.

"If I said that I did mind, I doubt that you'd go away and leave me alone—you'd probably sit down anyway," Angelica said.

"You're right," Nora admitted. "I've got something very important to discuss with you."

"Oh? And what might that be?" queried Angelica, looking at Nora dubiously.

Nora leaned toward Angelica and lowered her voice. "I saw you and Hal Banner together last night."

Angelica shrugged unconcernedly. "So? We danced. What's the big deal?"

"You did more than dance," said Nora. "I left the party the same time you two did. I watched you get into Banner's car."

"Is that a crime?" asked Angelica.

"Of course not. But as you recall, Banner didn't start the ignition immediately. There was a lull of a minute or two—and before the car windows got totally steamed up, I managed to catch a glimpse of what was going on in there," Nora said.

Angelica tossed her head angrily. "What I do in my private life is no business of yours."

"In general, I would agree with you," said Nora. "When a man and a woman have their hands down each others' underwear in a parked car, I usually just look the other way. But you seem to be forgetting one crucial fact: Hal Banner is a Cromwell professor. Last year I spent months working with other members of the women's caucus to get the administration to institute a policy governing faculty-student relationships, and I did it for some very good reasons. You may not realize it, but students on college campuses are very vulnerable. Faculty members can find them easy prey, and can use their power and prestige to influence students to do things that aren't in their best interests."

"Oh, cut the patronizing tone. I'm eighteen, and I'm not some naive little airhead who's never been kissed. I don't need to go around peeping into other people's cars to get my thrills. Hal isn't pushing me to do anything I don't want to do. I'm perfectly capable of taking care of myself," Angelica responded.

Nora shook her head. "You may think you know it all, but you don't. You've never been in a college environment before, and you don't know everything that can happen. The policy we worked for was put in place to protect young women like you."

"Protect me from what?" asked Angelica indignantly. "Hal is one of the most decent guys I've come across in a long time—he treats me a lot better than most of the jerks I've known."

"Maybe so—though that may reflect more on your previous relationships than on your current one," Nora responded. "But the point is that as a matter of principle, sexual relationships between faculty and students are unethical. The power dynamic is unequal, with all the control being in the hands of the professor. The student in such a case can't help but be the weaker party, and where such an imbalance exists, there's a strong possibility of being taken advantage of. As a feminist, I hate to see women students put in a vulnerable position, and so the safest and most responsible course is to prevent such situations from occurring altogether."

"How can you make so many generalizations?" Angelica demanded. "Some professors may take advantage of their students, but that's not the case with all of them. As far as I'm concerned, whatever two consenting adults want to do in the privacy of their bedrooms is nobody else's business. Hal may be twelve years older than I am, but there are lots of couples with just as much of an age difference. And anyway, where does anyone get off making a rule about who gets to sleep with whom, especially when it's based on something as stupid as their position in the college hierarchy? You might as well say that seniors shouldn't be allowed to sleep with sophomores—isn't there an unequal power dynamic there, too?"

"Oh, come on, Angelica," said Nora. "There's a big difference between the power of a college senior and the power of a professor. A fellow student can't have any impact on your GPA, for example."

"Neither can Hal," Angelica countered. "It's not like I'm enrolled in one of his classes, you know. If I were, I could see your point about the relationship being unethical—there would always be the question of whether our personal connection affected his ability to grade me fairly, and people might even think I was trading sexual favors for a good grade. That's just prostitution, and whatever you may think about me, there are some things I won't stoop to. But I'm not taking any classes with Hal and I don't intend to in the future—philosophy isn't a subject I'm particularly interested in. So I don't see what the problem is."

"Well," said Nora, "it's not just a question of possible classroom conflicts. The fact remains that in the power structure of this college, Hal Banner is in a much more elevated position than you are. At a small college like CC, there are countless ways that faculty members exert control over students' lives, even outside the classroom. They serve on scholarship and awards committees, they reach judgments in disciplinary or honor council hearings, they advise student organizations, they talk to and socialize with one another—and so there will always be questions about how freely you've entered into this relationship and whether your connection to Prof. Banner is affecting your success at Cromwell."

"That may be true," Angelica admitted, "but that could also be the case with relationships that aren't sexual ones. For example, everyone knows that Prof. Connor's daughter is a sophomore at Cromwell. Isn't it possible that her position as the child of a professor might raise some questions about fairness and objectivity, even if she doesn't take any of her father's classes? And what happens if a professor's husband or wife decides to take a class at Cromwell—do they have to stop having sex with their spouse in order not to violate the policy? It's just not as simple and clear-cut as you make it out to be."

"You're just veering off on irrelevant tangents now. I'm not going to sit here discussing this with you all day," Nora said brusquely. "Whether you agree with the policy or not, the fact of the matter is that it is against Cromwell regulations for professors and students to be sexually involved. If the policy is to have any effect on people's behavior, it has to be enforced. I witnessed enough last night to be able to testify that your relationship with Banner is not a merely platonic one. I'm sorry, but I may have to pay a visit to the provost on Monday morning." With that implied threat, Nora got up and walked out of the dining hall.

Angelica was visibly agitated. She tried to finish drinking her coffee but ended up spilling most of it. Hal Banner could get into a lot of trouble if Nora followed through on her plan to tell the provost about what she had seen on Saturday night. Angelica had heard about a professor at another university who had recently been forced to resign when it was discovered that he had been sexually involved with a student. Could her relationship with Hal—which had only been going on for a couple of weeks—end up jeopardizing his entire career? Had she and Hal really done anything so terrible? She was genuinely fond of him, and she knew he liked her, too. Did Cromwell College have a right to legislate romance? Should she and Hal Banner be prevented from seeing one another socially just because he happened to be a professor at the same college where she happened to be a student?

As these thoughts ran through Angelica's mind, her agitation became more and more apparent. Art and Sondra couldn't help but notice when she unconsciously began to shred her newspaper into little bits. Sondra walked over to ask Angelica if she was okay, while Art discreetly left the dining hall.

When Sondra approached and expressed her concern, Angelica smiled wanly. "I'm okay, but I may have ruined someone else's life," she said. She went on to explain what Nora had seen, and the possibility that she would go to the provost with her information. "What should I do?" asked Angelica.

Sondra did her best during the next half hour to help Angelica think through the issues calmly and carefully. She pointed out that although Angelica could be disciplined for violating the policy, a harsher penalty would probably fall upon the professor involved, who would be presumed to have initiated the relationship. Sondra further noted that Prof. Banner was in a particularly sensitive position as an untenured assistant professor with no job security. Appealing to Angelica's affection for Hal Banner, Sondra suggested that it would be in the professor's best interest to end the relationship as soon as possible.

"The best thing you could do for Hal Banner would be to stay away from him," counseled Sondra. "Don't call, don't drop by to visit. You don't want to make matters any worse than they already are. Maybe if Nora realizes that you're avoiding Prof. Banner, she'll keep her mouth shut."

By the end of her conversation with Sondra, Angelica was convinced that she should steer clear of Hal Banner for his own good. She called him that afternoon and explained the situation to him, filling him in on her confrontation with Nora and on the possibility that their relationship would be exposed to the provost.

"I hate to do this, Hal, but I really think the best thing is for us to stop seeing each other immediately," Angelica concluded.

"No!" protested Prof. Banner. "I like you too much to just call it quits. I don't care what the college policy says. No one is going to tell me what to do with my private life."

Angelica stood firm and hung up in spite of the professor's pleas. For the next few days she devoted herself to preparing for her final exams as best she could, and she screened all incoming telephone calls—including the dozen or so messages from Hal Banner, begging her to call him back so that they could get together. Though it was very hard to resist the temptation, she never returned any of his calls.

Angelica made a point of running into Nora in the dining hall on the Wednesday of finals week. She took her aside and told her that she hadn't seen or spoken to Prof. Banner since the weekend. "You haven't gone to see the provost, have you?" Angelica asked nervously.

"Not yet," replied Nora.

"Now that I'm not seeing Hal anymore, you won't say anything, will you?" she implored.

"I'm not sure. I'm still thinking about it. After all, you did violate the policy," said Nora. With that, she turned her back on Angelica and refused to speak to her any further.

Angelica's last final was on Friday morning, and by Friday afternoon she was on her way to the airport to catch her flight home. She left without knowing for sure whether Nora had ever spoken to the provost—but since Angelica hadn't heard anything from the administration, she assumed that no charges had been made. In any case, Angelica felt that for Hal Banner's sake she had to continue keeping her distance from him, much as she regretted doing so. And so she looked forward to getting away from Cromwell, hoping that the change of scene would take her mind off the difficulties she had encountered this semester.

Angelica was not the only one who looked forward to the winter vacation. Many other members of the Cromwell community were thankful that exams were ending and the semester was winding down. The break was coming none too soon—especially for the once-innocent first-year class, who had been bombarded with more new experiences this term than they had ever imagined possible. Surely the spring semester would be calmer . . . wouldn't it?

Some Questions to Consider

What do you think about Nora's view of the policy concerning faculty-student relationships? Do you think that Nora would be justified in reporting what she saw on Saturday night to the provost? Do you agree with Sondra's advice to Angelica? Should Angelica have given in to Hal Banner's pleas? Was there anything else that Angelica could or should have done to ameliorate the situation?

Thinking Critically

Nora presents a number of reasons leading to her conclusion that a policy preventing sexual relations between students and faculty at Cromwell is necessary. Can you identify each of her reasons? Does her conclusion follow logically from her reasoning? Are there any flaws or fallacies in her reasoning? What about Angelica's reasoning in response to Nora's argument; is it logically sound and convincing?

Reading Closely

Cromwell's policy on faculty-student relationships clearly prohibits "relationships of a sexual nature between faculty members and students," and goes on to define sexual involvement in the second paragraph. Given this definition, was the behavior of Angelica and Prof. Banner on the dance floor a violation of the policy? Was their behavior in Prof. Banner's car a violation of the policy? If Angelica and Prof. Banner had a deep romantic relationship but restrained themselves from expressing it physically, would that be a violation of the policy?

What If

What if, instead of being a professor, Hal Banner was a twenty-two-year-old graduate student teaching assistant who had the responsibility of leading discussion sections and grading the course work of students in his section? Would there be anything wrong with Hal and Angelica becoming sexually involved if Angelica were not enrolled in a class he was instructing? What if Hal Banner was an administrative employee—for example, the assistant to the college registrar—rather than a faculty member? Would that change your perspective on the situation?

Connecting the Cases

In this case, the private relationship between Angelica and Prof. Banner has become a matter of public concern—but this is not the only instance at Cromwell in which personal issues have become public. Who says what to whom, who sleeps with whom and in what circumstances—in such instances, relationships between individuals take on a larger significance. To what extent should such private matters be of public concern? When and why does the personal legitimately become political?

Bringing It Home

Many campuses have policies governing sexual or romantic involvement between faculty and students. Does yours? Should it? Does or should it matter whether or not the student in question is enrolled in the faculty member's class? Do or should such factors as age or rank make any difference?

Suggestions for Writing

1. If Sondra told you everything that had been revealed in her brunch conversation with Angelica, what would your reaction be? Write an entry in your personal journal that expresses your attitude toward the situation between Angelica and Prof. Banner.

2. Do you feel that Cromwell's policy concerning student-faculty relationships is legitimate? Write a memo to the provost indicating your opinion of the policy and making any suggestions you think would be appropriate concerning the policy's wording, enforcement, or penalties. Make sure that you explain the reasoning behind your point of view.

3. Some segments of society may disapprove of Art and Sondra's interracial relationship; some segments of society may also disapprove of Prof. Banner and Angelica's faculty-student relationship. Is there any difference between the two? Are there some cases in which the interests of the community necessitate limits on romantic or sexual involvement? If so, how would you determine when and why such limits should be imposed? Write an essay exploring these questions and arguing for your own position.

Out Loud

Imagine that Nora Quinn is a good friend of yours and that she has just told you that she's about to report Angelica and Prof. Banner's behavior to the college provost. What would you say to her about her intentions? With one of your classmates playing the role of Nora, enact the conversation.

MINI-CASE 1

The Letter
Race and Faculty Hiring

Sondra Johnson trudged across Cromwell College's Academic Quad on her way to the student union for lunch. It was a dreary Friday, the end of a particularly stressful week, and she was ready for a little rest and relaxation. Before heading to the dining hall, Sondra stopped at the campus post office to check her box, hoping some mail from home would cheer her up. What she found was a letter from Benita, her best friend from high school, who had chosen to attend college many miles away at one of the most famous historically black colleges or universities (HBCUs) in the nation.

Of course, at an HBCU Benita didn't have to face the problems Sondra was confronting as an African-American in a predominantly white environment, but it turned out that Benita had some problems of her own. Her letter read, in part, as follows:

> . . . And now let me tell you about my classes, because here's where I really have some serious concerns. You know that one of the reasons I chose to come to an HBCU was that I thought it was important for me to have role models who were successful black men and women. Especially after high school, where it seemed like 95 percent of our teachers were white, I was ready to have some professors who look like me!
>
> But it turns out that of the five classes I'm taking, one is taught by a Pakistani woman, one is taught by a Vietnamese man, and the

other three professors are white! I'm not saying that any of these people are bad teachers—I guess they all get the material across okay—but honestly, do they really have a place at an HBCU? Shouldn't the college be hiring professors who can serve as inspirational examples to the student body?

I'm always hearing people complain that there aren't enough blacks going into higher education. Did they ever stop to think that it might be because we don't have role models showing us the way, even at an HBCU like this one?

I've talked to some of my friends here about it, and they say that any college should hire the best faculty available, regardless of race. I think that's B.S. Aside from the role model issue, teaching isn't just a matter of knowing the subject matter or having some arbitrary set of classroom skills—students need to relate to their instructors, and HBCUs have a special responsibility to hire black professors to create some connection, some rapport between the students and faculty. Frankly, I'm pretty disappointed on this score.

Sondra read Benita's letter slowly as she walked up the student union stairs, so engrossed that she unconsciously bumped into one after another of her Cromwell classmates. Benita had brought up some very interesting points, and Sondra wasn't sure how she felt about the issue.

Sondra remained preoccupied throughout lunch, pondering her own situation as well as Benita's. Although Cromwell had made an effort to diversify its student population, the majority of the faculty still consisted of white males. There weren't many African-American professors at CC, and Sondra wasn't happy about that; however, she hadn't really expected anything different. But was Benita right that things shouldn't be that way at an HBCU? Or were Benita's friends right that race shouldn't be an issue in faculty hiring at any university? How should Sondra respond when she answers Benita's letter later in the day?

MINI-CASE 2

Believe It or Not
Religion in the Classroom

Max Urban was sitting in a corner of the student union lobby studying biology with his classmate Nelson when he noticed his friend Aisha approaching, grumbling under her breath.

"What is it?" asked Max.

Aisha sighed. "It's Professor Peters. I wish I had never signed up for his stupid World Lit. course. There are lots of other classes I could have taken to satisfy the humanities requirement!"

"Was he doing his Bible-thumping routine again?" Max asked sympathetically.

Aisha nodded, but before she could speak, Nelson cut in. "Just because the guy knows the Old and New Testaments backwards and forwards is no reason to get ticked off at him, is it?"

Aisha replied, "That's not what bothers me. I'm willing to admit that the Bible is a significant text in the history of world literature, even though it doesn't have the religious significance for me that it obviously has for Prof. Peters. When he quotes chapter and verse at us, I guess the allusions are relevant to the other literary works we're reading.

"What really gets me," she went on to explain, "is the way he approaches everything from a Christian perspective, assuming that everyone in his class comes from a Christian background. Like today, he was talking about ancient celebrations of the winter solstice and comparing them with modern-day customs. He said, 'When we celebrate Christmas. . . .' *We*? Who is this *we*? Not everyone celebrates Christmas. Since I'm a Muslim, I don't, and I know there are Jewish students in the class who don't celebrate Christmas either.

"And he's so blatant about his religious beliefs—he wears a gold cross on the lapel of his suit jacket, and he's always talking about how this or that thought came to him on his way back from church, and whenever some problem comes up he says he's going to pray about it," said Aisha.

"So?" responded Nelson. "The cross-shaped lapel pin is no big deal, and anyway it's his right to wear it. Would you want to prevent religious Jewish students from wearing skullcaps, or religious Moslem students from wearing headscarves?"

"But it's different with a professor," said Aisha. "He's an authority figure, and when he openly expresses a religious preference it can't help but affect the classroom dynamics."

Nelson snorted. "Nonsense. I certainly don't see how mentioning his religion, like saying he goes to church or prays, is a problem. He's not forcing you to do what he does, is he?"

"No," admitted Aisha, "he's not telling us what to think or how to act, but I can't help wondering if his religious beliefs affect his objectivity in the classroom."

"I know what you mean," agreed Max. "I heard that in his senior seminar last year he gave the highest grades to students whose term papers focused on Christian interpretations of literary texts, even if the papers weren't all that good."

"Unfounded rumors," scoffed Nelson.

Aisha shook her head. "In our class," she said, "there are a couple of students who clearly are devout Christians, and although I haven't done an exact count or anything, it sure seems like he calls on them twice as often as everyone else."

"If that's true, it's not fair," Max commented.

"No, it's not," Aisha said. "It's all getting to the point that my class performance is being affected. I sit there so alienated from Prof. Peters because of his Christian perspective, so angry every time he makes one of those statements assuming that everyone believes in Christ the Savior, that I can't pay proper attention to the subject matter. What should I do?"

MINI-CASE 3

Beg, Borrow, or Steal
Theft and Friendship

Stephanie Ziska searched her room from top to bottom, but it was no use; she couldn't find the gold hoop earrings she had planned to wear. With only five minutes left to make it across campus to her art history class, she couldn't afford to keep searching, so she grabbed her back-pack and left. She couldn't get her mind off her earrings, though; they were a recent gift from her mother and she hadn't had a chance to wear them yet, so their disappearance was especially disturbing. As her art professor showed slides of Picasso's early work, Stephanie kept think-ing about the shiny hoops that had vanished into thin air.

Several of her other possessions had vanished in the last few days, as well: a brand-new CD still in its plastic wrapper, a silver-plated ball-point pen, and a fifty dollar traveler's check she had been saving in case of emergency. Stephanie was baffled; she and her roommate Miriam were careful to keep their door locked at all times, and they hadn't had any visitors lately.

Although she had known Miriam since high school, Stephanie caught herself wondering if her roommate might be behind the disap-pearances. After all, Miriam had been in trouble before. She was al-ready on disciplinary probation for several infractions of college rules. Moreover, Stephanie knew Miriam was short on cash, and desperately needed to come up with two hundred dollars for a plane ticket to get back home for the winter holidays. But yesterday Miriam herself had remarked that she was missing three new pairs of pantyhose and her pocket calculator. Besides, Stephanie couldn't believe that Miriam would stoop to stealing from an old friend.

What was going on? Stephanie wasn't sure, but after her art class was over she decided to skip her usual workout in the weight room and instead go back to the residence hall to search again for her earrings. As she turned her key in the lock, she heard a scurrying sound. Opening the door quickly, she saw Miriam shoving something under her pillow.

"Aren't you supposed to be in chem. lab?" Stephanie asked Miriam.

"What about you?" Miriam responded. "I thought this was your regular workout time."

"I do usually go to the weight room after art, but today I decided to skip it," said Stephanie. "You still haven't told me why you're not in lab—and what did you just put under your pillow?"

"None of your business," retorted Miriam.

"Listen, you know I've been missing a few things lately, and no one's been in this room but you and me. So when I see you hiding something from me, I can't help being suspicious."

"Well," replied Miriam, "I've lost some stuff, too. You're not the only one."

"How do I know that you didn't just hide your pantyhose and calculator somewhere to make it look like you're a victim and not the thief?" Stephanie asked.

"How could you think such a thing, Steph? We've known each other for years!"

"All right, then, what's under your pillow?"

"I already told you it's none of your business."

Stephanie lunged toward Miriam's bed and grabbed her pillow. There, in full view, were the missing gold hoops.

"I can't believe it!" Stephanie shouted. "How could you?"

Miriam sobbed, "I couldn't help myself! I'm in desperate need of money, and it just seemed so easy to take your things. I returned the CD to the store, and I was going to pawn the earrings and the pen—I didn't think you'd miss them. I'll give everything back to you, and the fifty dollars, too. But please don't report me—you know that since I'm on probation for multiple policy violations, if I get caught for one more it means automatic expulsion. You don't want that to happen to me, do you? You won't say anything, will you? Will you?"

MINI-CASE 4

Wrong Place, Wrong Time
Keeping Bad Company

Yvonne Toufaian shook her head. "You're crazy, Wendy. You're out of your mind. Isaac is bad news. How could you lend him your car?"

Wendy gazed at her roommate with a hurt look on her face. "How can you say such hateful things about Isaac?" she implored. "You know I love him, and love means trust. I would trust him with my life—so of course I trust him with my car."

Yvonne shrugged. "All right, I give up. You're so head over heels with that jerk, you can't see what a scumbag he is. Just make sure you don't get caught up in any of his sleazy deals."

"What are you talking about?" Wendy asked.

"You've been going out with Isaac for six weeks now. Haven't you caught on to the fact that he's one of the biggest drug dealers on campus?" Yvonne responded.

"Isaac? Dealing drugs? Now you're the one who's crazy!" exclaimed Wendy. "Just because he looks a little different, you think he's dealing? Okay, he smokes weed, but so do a lot of other people we know. He's not stupid enough to sell it."

"Wake up, girl. This doesn't have a thing to do with Isaac's weird appearance. Everyone on campus knows he deals—and not just weed, either. Who do you think is the major supplier of Ecstasy around here? Why do you think he keeps disappearing on weekends?" asked Yvonne.

"I know why he's gone on the weekends," answered Wendy. "He told me all about it. He has an uncle who's dying of AIDS, and he goes to be with him whenever he can."

"Oh, no," Yvonne groaned, "I can't believe you fell for that line."

"Give it a rest, Yvonne. You're just going to end up making me furious with you."

"Okay, okay. So when did he say he'd bring the car back? Remember, you promised you'd take me to the mall after dinner."

"Actually," Wendy said, "he's due back just about now. I'm going to walk over to the parking lot and have a look." With that, she left the room.

Just as Wendy reached the student lot where she always parked her car, she spotted Isaac pulling into an empty space. She ran over and, as her boyfriend stepped out of the car, she gave him a big hug. Instead of hugging back, he just stood there, staring over Wendy's shoulder. She turned around to see what he was staring at. There were three uniformed police officers pointing their guns straight at her.

The next few minutes were a blur. All Wendy could remember was one of the police officers opening the trunk of her car and finding some mysterious-looking bags that she knew hadn't been there before she loaned the vehicle to Isaac. "You have the right to remain silent," intoned an officer—and Wendy took advantage of that right. Indeed, she was in such a deep state of shock that she couldn't have spoken even if she had wanted to.

On the way to the police station, Wendy began to wake up to the realities of her situation. She was under arrest, but she knew she hadn't committed any crime. All she had done was trust the man she loved. If only she hadn't gone out to the parking lot at just that moment! She had just been in the wrong place at the wrong time. How could she make the police believe she was innocent?

And what about Isaac? Wendy wanted to believe he was innocent too, but the circumstantial evidence certainly didn't point in that direction. Should she try to save him, give him an alibi, somehow attempt to protect him from the police? She loved him, didn't she—and wouldn't she do anything for the man she loved?

MINI-CASE 5

Something in the Air
Conflicting Claims and Culpability

Henry Xavier tried to ignore the laughter of his roommate Samir Nasser, who was sitting on the floor talking on the telephone. But Henry couldn't concentrate on his philosophy reading, and when Samir hung up, he asked what all the hilarity had been about.

"That was my cousin Raffi," Samir explained. "He's coming to visit Cromwell next weekend. I haven't seen him in ages."

"Wait a minute," interjected Henry. "Isn't he the 'bad sheep' cousin you told me about—the troublemaker, the one who messes around with drugs and who knows what else?"

"That was before. From the way he was talking on the phone, he's changed a lot. He says he realizes he was hanging around with the wrong crowd, and he's determined to turn his life around. He's applying to college now, and he and one of his buddies want to check out CC."

Henry shook his head doubtfully. "Better keep an eye on them while they're here."

"Oh, come on, Henry," said Samir. "Don't you believe in rehabilitation?"

The next Saturday Samir met Raffi and his buddy Scott at the bus station. He arranged for them to take a campus tour with his friend Victor, who was a tour guide for the admissions office. Samir then headed back to his room for a nap. As he snored blissfully, the phone rang.

Samir picked up the receiver just as Henry walked into the room. "Victor? What's wrong? What do you mean? Well, they'll have to turn up sometime, probably back at my room."

As Samir hung up, Henry asked, "What is it?"

"Well, it seems that Raffi and Scott somehow slipped away from Victor. He's been hunting around campus for the past hour, but he can't find them anywhere," Samir said.

At that moment the door opened, and Raffi and Scott stumbled in. They reeked of marijuana, and looked happy but disoriented. Raffi fell onto Samir's bed and Scott fell onto Henry's.

"Get up!" shouted Henry. He and Samir tried unsuccessfully to push Raffi and Scott off the beds. Something fell out of Raffi's pocket, but in their concern they didn't take note of it. Suddenly they heard a loud knocking at the door.

"Must be Victor," said Samir, "coming to see if the guys turned up." He flung the door open and saw, not Victor, but the resident assistant of the hall, Baptiste.

"Samir? Henry? What's going on in here? I thought I smelled something—and now I know I do! Who are these guys?" he inquired.

"This is my cousin Raffi and his friend Scott. They came down this weekend to visit Cromwell," Samir answered.

"Looks like they're having a great time," said Baptiste sarcastically. "Whose weed is this?" he continued, picking up a plastic bag from the floor.

"It's not mine, honest. It must have fallen out of Raffi's pocket," replied Samir.

At that moment Raffi sat up.

"Is this yours?" asked Baptiste, holding the bag up in front of him.

"Never seen it before!" exclaimed Raffi in amazement. "I guess it's Samir's—and I'm terribly shocked and disappointed to find my cousin indulging in illegal substances!"

"He's lying!" shouted Samir. "It's his!"

Baptiste looked at the plastic bag he was holding, at Samir and Henry, at Raffi, and at Scott still half-asleep on the bed. He sniffed the heavy smell in the air, and decided that he needed to do something swiftly and decisively to address the situation. But what?

MINI-CASE 6

Food Fight
Eating Disorders and Intervention

Rachel Fromm was having problems with her room key; to open the door, she needed to jiggle the key repeatedly in the lock. Her roommate Lily was secretly grateful, since this gave her ample warning of Rachel's arrival. Tonight Lily was especially glad of the advance notice, as she rushed to hide a bag of marshmallows, a box of cheesy crackers, and half a loaf of cinnamon bread. She had just managed to stow all three under some dirty laundry when Rachel walked in.

"I can't believe I'm finally done with that sociology paper!" exclaimed Rachel as she dropped her backpack on the floor. "Come on, Lily, let's go get a pizza and celebrate."

"I'm thrilled you're finished," Lily said. "You've been no fun to live with lately with all your agonizing! But count me out on the pizza. You know I'm trying to lose weight."

Rachel didn't reply, and pretended to busy herself with some papers. The truth of the matter was that she was worried about Lily, who had gained over twenty pounds in her first months at college but who didn't seem to eat enough to keep a gerbil alive. In fact, Rachel had never seen Lily eat anything but bran cereal, raw vegetables, and an occasional dollop of plain yogurt. Lily attributed her weight gain to a "slow metabolism" and appeared to be dieting strenuously, but Rachel had begun to suspect that her roommate ate on the sly—that when no one was looking, Lily supplemented her meager mealtime intake with additional food.

Rachel's suspicions had been heightened the previous day. Searching for a blank computer diskette, she had found a bag of chocolate bars and a box of doughnuts in one of Lily's desk drawers. She knew that although the two of them often shared school supplies, she shouldn't have been looking in Lily's desk, but she had been in desperate need of a diskette for a project due in an hour. Embarrassed by her discovery of what appeared to be evidence of Lily's hidden binging and doubly embarrassed by the illicit nature of her discovery, Rachel had said nothing.

Now, however, she wondered if she should speak up. Of course, she had no proof that her roommate had a pattern of binging, or that she was doing more than just a little occasional snacking. But why, then, was Lily gaining so much weight in spite of her stringent diet? Why did she spend more and more time alone in the room? Why was she always going off on long walks—walks that generally took her across campus in the direction of State Street, where several grocery stores and take-out shops could be found?

As these thoughts ran through her head, Rachel absent-mindedly moved toward the closet and contemplated the pile of dirty laundry on the floor, to which both she and Lily had contributed. As she bent down to pick up a T-shirt, Lily exclaimed, "No! Leave it there!"

Rachel was stunned. Why should Lily care whether or not she picked up the dirty laundry? She scooped up her shirt and some other clothes—and there, in full view, were the bread, the marshmallows, and the crackers. Rachel turned to Lily and said, "I think you have a problem."

"Nonsense," said Lily. "Those are just some things I got so I could offer snacks to guests."

Rachel shook her head. "Why hide them, then? Lily, you have an eating disorder."

Lily snorted. "Do I look like I'm anorexic or bulimic? If I were, then at least I'd be thin! Anyway, even if I were pigging out on all this stuff, that would just be overeating. It might be gross, but it isn't any kind of disorder—it certainly isn't dangerous or anything."

"You're eating secretly. You're out of control. You're binging, I know you are. I care about you, Lily."

"If you care about me so much, then don't accuse me of problems I don't have, okay?" shouted Lily, as she stalked out of the room and slammed the door behind her.

"I'm only trying to help," said Rachel feebly, but the slamming door drowned out her words. What should she do now? How could she help Lily? Did Lily even need her help?

MINI-CASE 7

On and Off
Inequities in Campus Communications

Claudia Balthazar gazed at the flyer posted on the bulletin board out-side her Introduction to Psychology class. "FINANCIAL OPPORTU-NITY!" was boldly printed at the top of the sheet. Claudia, who in addition to being a full-time student at Cromwell was also a single mother, was always eager to find new ways to supplement her income. And so the flyer's announcement of a $1,000 grant for first-year stu-dents facing "life challenges" was of great interest to her.

Claudia read further, and discovered that the money to fund the grant was coming from a Cromwell alumna who had faced dif-ficult times during her own undergraduate career, and who now wished to make things easier for struggling CC students. After read-ing through the list of requirements for the grant, Claudia con-cluded that it was tailor-made for her. Then she noticed the line of fine print at the bottom of the flyer: the application deadline had been the previous day!

Claudia was crestfallen. How could she have missed such a per-fect opportunity? As she was about to walk away from the bulletin board, her classmate Gina approached her.

"Looking at the flyer advertising that new grant?" Gina asked.

"Yeah, but I missed the deadline," Claudia replied. "I didn't know about it till I saw it posted just now, and the due date for applications was yesterday."

"Didn't you get that letter from the financial aid office in your mailbox a couple of weeks ago, letting us know about the grant? Everyone else did."

"I don't have a campus mailbox, Gina. I live off-campus, remember? No one who lives off-campus gets a box in the CC mailroom," Claudia said.

"But all the on-campus students were notified. Didn't they mail anything to your home?"

Claudia shook her head. "No, they never do. When you have an on-campus mailbox you find out about all sorts of things going on—social events, speakers coming to campus, job openings, grant opportunities. But as for us off-campus students—well, if we don't happen to see the flyers on the bulletin boards, we're in the dark."

"That's not fair!" exclaimed Gina. "I think you should go to the financial aid director and talk to him. Maybe he can give you an extension on the application."

Claudia merely shook her head; then, realizing that her psychology class was about to begin, she walked into the classroom. She couldn't keep her mind on psychology, though, and when the class was over she decided to follow Gina's advice.

Walking across campus to Vanburen Hall, Claudia prepared herself to confront the financial aid director. As luck would have it, the secretary in the outer office was out to lunch, and the director was "unprotected"; she found him playing computer solitaire.

When she told him about missing the grant deadline, he expressed his regret, but insisted that no late applications could be accepted. When she complained about the unequal distribution of information to on- and off-campus students, he shrugged his shoulders and said, "You made the choice to live off campus, knowing it would put you out of the information loop. Now you have to face the consequences."

"But I didn't have a choice!" Claudia exclaimed. "I have an eight-month-old daughter; obviously we can't live in the residence halls! The very reason that I need to live off campus is what makes me such an obvious candidate for this particular grant."

"I'm sorry, but I can't make any exceptions," the director replied. No matter what Claudia said to him, he would not budge. Claudia was becoming increasingly frustrated—and increasingly outraged. She felt that she simply could not let this opportunity slip away because of the college's inequitable treatment of off-campus students, but she was clearly making no headway in the financial aid office. Should she simply resign herself to missing out on the grant, or was there anything more she could do?

MINI-CASE 8

Doorway Dilemma
Campus Security Versus Accessibility

Jamal Porter carefully placed a folded piece of paper between the door and its frame so that the lock would not catch but the door would not be visibly propped open. A quick glance by a passerby would only show the usual locked entrance of the Gilman Annex, where Jamal spent many of his evening hours engaged in mathematical speculation.

Jamal had been selected as part of a research team working on a difficult problem in applied mathematics, and had found himself becoming even more involved in the work than his supervisor, who generally quit around dinner time. The rest of the annex denizens followed suit, and evenings in the building were quiet—which suited Jamal, since he worked well alone.

But he soon discovered that he worked even better with Naomi. A classmate in his Real Variables course, Naomi was not on the research team but was as fascinated by the problem as was Jamal. Their combined speculations were stimulating and productive. Jamal invited her to work with him in the evenings, and she readily accepted. It had taken them awhile, though, to solve the problem of getting Naomi into the Gilman Annex.

The annex, which contained a good deal of expensive equipment, was kept locked after 5:00 P.M. Jamal, as a member of the research team, had been given a key but Naomi had no such privileges. Moreover, she couldn't just come in with Jamal, who liked to return to the annex right after dinner, since she had a sculpture class that met in the evenings.

The annex was equipped with an intercom that enabled anyone wishing to gain entrance to buzz someone working inside, who could then come to the door and let the person in. This was the method Jamal and Naomi had used initially, until one Friday night when—in the time it took Jamal to get from the upstairs study room to the front door—Naomi had been accosted by a pair of drunken biology majors who proposed to teach her everything they knew about anatomy and began with a demonstration of their own body parts. From that time on, Jamal had surreptitiously propped open the annex door so Naomi could come right in without risking molestation.

Tonight, though, someone other than Naomi made use of the open door—someone who had noticed Naomi on previous evenings gaining entry through the door Jamal had propped open; someone who knew about the valuable equipment housed in the Gilman Annex and who had decided to quietly walk off with as much as he could carry. No one was in the vicinity to take note of the dark-clothed, shadowy figure who slipped through the annex door and tiptoed down the first-floor hallway.

As the figure entered, the folded paper fell out and the door shut. A few moments later Naomi arrived, and tried to open the door. When the door wouldn't budge, she buzzed Jamal on the intercom. A puzzled Jamal ran downstairs to see what had happened to his piece of paper. He opened the door for Naomi, who walked in—and then he felt the skin on the back of his neck prickle as he heard indefinable scurrying movements coming from down the hall. He realized someone else must be in the building, a suspicion that was confirmed when he recognized the unmistakable sound of footsteps.

Jamal's heart raced. Who was in the building? What had he done? He had only been trying to protect Naomi from danger when he thought of propping the door open. Now had he caused an even greater problem, an even greater source of danger to both Naomi and himself? Was he to blame for whatever the stranger might be doing—and might be planning to do?

MINI-CASE 9

Cut and Paste
Internet Plagiarism

Irene Oban had only fifteen minutes left until she finished her shift as a peer tutor in Cromwell's Academic Assistance Center. She wasn't expecting anyone else to come by, but suddenly the door to her cubicle opened and Joe Kalidis walked in. Irene had tutored Joe on several previous occasions, helping him to clarify his careless and confusing writing style.

As he walked in, Joe said, "I have a paper due tomorrow in my child psychology class, and I have it all done—I just need you to look it over and tell me whether it's okay to hand in."

"Let me see the assignment first," said Irene. She skimmed the handout Joe gave her and saw that students were asked to provide a brief overview of recent developments in any one area of child or adolescent psychology.

Irene then began reading Joe's essay. It was unlike anything she had seen him produce before: clear and informative, with a sophisticated use of discipline-specific terminology. There was a bit of a choppy feel to it, a lack of connection from one point to the next, but on the whole it was a perfectly acceptable paper—which made Irene wonder if it was Joe's original work. She looked Joe in the eye and asked, "Did you really write this paper yourself?"

"Of course!" Joe exclaimed. "One of my classmates suggested some psychology websites to check out, but I did all the research myself and stuck the information I found into my paper."

"You know, the vocabulary is a lot more elevated than you usually use in your papers, and the style seems more polished and academic than I'd expect from you. . . . "

"Hey," Joe interrupted, "are you saying I can't write a good paper? I know I'm not great at expressing my own ideas, but this time I just have to present what other people have said. It's like those reports we used to do in elementary school, putting together bits and pieces from the encyclopedia. It's a lot easier nowadays, though, when you can just use the Internet to find what you need."

"So you went to an Internet site, found some information, and copied it into your paper?" asked Irene.

"I'm not an idiot," Joe responded huffily. "I know about para-phrasing. I changed a few words here and there so that no one could accuse me of plagiarism. And it isn't all from one source, either—I used four different websites, so I had to do a lot of cutting and pasting to get it all together. The assignment handout doesn't say anything about in-cluding a bibliography, so I didn't bother to cite my sources."

Irene turned to the desktop computer sitting beside her. She called up her favorite search engine and typed in a sentence from Joe's second paragraph. In a matter of seconds, she was staring at an almost identical sentence in an article posted on a child development website, the only difference being that in the posted article the author had used the term "youth," which Joe had replaced with "young people." She checked another of Joe's sentences from later in his paper and found that it too was almost identical to one from an article posted on a dif-ferent psychology-related website; Joe had again made a minor change in wording, rephrasing the expression "mother-infant bonding" as "the bond between a mother and her baby."

"You can't do this, Joe," said Irene. "Changing a couple of words here and there and putting together material from a number of differ-ent sources still doesn't make this your original work. This paper is plagiarized."

Joe grabbed his paper from Irene's hands. "I'm turning this paper in tomorrow, and I don't care what you say!" he shouted.

As Joe stormed out of the tutoring center, Irene wondered what she should do. Was Joe's paper a violation of Cromwell's Honor Code, which prohibited plagiarism? Should she try to contact him and dis-cuss the matter further? Was it her responsibility to report what she had seen to anyone else, or should she wait and see if Joe's psychology professor noticed any problems?

MINI-CASE 10

Here, There, and Everywhere
Pulled in Different Directions

As she walked into her room, Jennifer Reyes noticed that the light on her telephone answering machine was blinking. She took a closer look: three new messages. She knew she ought to press the playback button and find out who had called, but she couldn't summon up the energy.

It had been a difficult semester for Jennifer. She had transferred into Cromwell as a sophomore, after having spent a very successful year at Crosstown Community College—so successful that she was not only admitted to Cromwell, but was awarded a lucrative scholarship that made it possible for her to attend. Jennifer had known that Cromwell would be academically challenging, but she looked forward to the greater intellectual stimulation and she was excited about experiencing on-campus residential life. She had lived at home with her parents and two younger brothers while attending Crosstown, and although she loved her family she had felt socially stifled. The relative freedom that Cromwell offered was especially appealing to her, as was the opportunity to meet people totally different from her neighborhood friends.

Her parents weren't happy about Jennifer's insistence that she move into the residence halls, since they lived only half an hour away from Cromwell and it would be an easy commute, but they gave in when she said that she would pay the housing costs herself out of the money she earned from her part-time job at a biotechnology firm. However, they still called her almost every day, and assumed that she would come home most weekends.

Jennifer was finding Cromwell to be even more academically difficult than she had anticipated, and she needed to use her weekends for studying—but studying at home was next to impossible, given the boisterous nature of her brothers as well as her parents' expectations that she participate in family activities. She struggled to keep her part-time job, maintain acceptable grades, and meet her family's demands, but it wasn't easy. In the meantime, Jennifer was having problems making friends at Cromwell. Several students had invited her to join them for weekend activities, but she felt that it was her duty to go home instead. Her Cromwell classmates didn't seem to understand, and were beginning to resent her repeated excuses.

The blinking message light couldn't be ignored. Sighing, Jennifer pressed the play button.

"Jenny," the first message began, "it's Mom, calling to remind you that Araceli's baby shower is Sunday afternoon. You'll want to get her something special—we can go shopping together on Saturday. Anyway, I guess I'll see you home for dinner Friday night, so we can talk about it then."

Actually, Jennifer had forgotten about the baby shower, even though Araceli was her favorite cousin. She had an organic chemistry exam on Monday and this was one weekend she had hoped to spend at Cromwell doing some intensive studying, but missing Araceli's shower would be viewed by her family as a sign of disrespect and disregard. Jennifer's head began to throb as she listened to the second message on her machine.

"Jennifer, this is Nelson Odo from your organic chemistry class. I wanted to let you know that a group of us are going to be having an exam study session on Sunday afternoon. We'll be meeting at 2:00 in Study Room C at the student union. See you."

Nelson was one of the few students who really seemed to understand what was going on in organic chemistry. Jennifer knew that studying with him would help her get a much stronger grasp of the course material. As she grabbed a piece of paper to write down the time and place of the study session, the third message began.

"Jenn, it's Rachel Fromm, with an offer you can't refuse: free tickets to the Midtown Music Fest on Sunday afternoon. Turn me down this time and I won't ask again! Get back to me, okay?"

Jennifer had really been hoping to become better friends with Rachel, and the Sunday afternoon lineup of the Midtown Music Fest featured some of her favorite bands. But Araceli's baby shower was on Sunday afternoon, and the organic chemistry study session was on Sunday afternoon. Jennifer couldn't be in three places at once—what should she do?

APPENDIX

Cromwell College Regulations and Responsibilities

DISCRIMINATORY HARASSMENT

It is the policy of Cromwell College that employees and students be able to work, study, and live in a campus community free of discriminatory harassment. Such harassment directed against an individual or group that is based on race, religious belief, color, sexual orientation, national origin, physical disability, age, or gender is prohibited. Any student or employee who violates this policy may be subject to disciplinary action up to and including dismissal from the college. Student organizations in violation of this policy may be subject to the loss of official recognition.

Discriminatory harassment includes conduct (oral, written, graphic, or physical) directed against any person or group of persons because of their race, religious belief, color, sexual orientation, national origin, physical disability, age, or gender and that has the purpose or reasonably foreseeable effect of creating an offensive, demeaning, intimidating, or hostile environment for that person or group of persons. Such conduct includes, but is not limited to, objectionable epithets, demeaning depictions or treatment, and threatened or actual abuse or harm.

Complaints relating to misconduct involving discriminatory harassment should be reported to the dean of students. Complaints will be carefully investigated, and cases that may require disciplinary action will be handled according to the established procedures of the college.

SEXUAL MISCONDUCT

Cromwell College prohibits any student from engaging in sexual conduct with another person without the consent of that person. Sexual conduct is defined as including vaginal intercourse; anal intercourse; fellatio; cunnilingus; touching of the genitals, buttocks, or inner thighs; or any other physical conduct or touching of a sexual nature.

Students are subject to this policy whether misconduct occurs on college premises, at college-sponsored activities, or at any off-campus location when such conduct is brought to the attention of college officials.

Complaints relating to sexual misconduct should be reported to the dean of students. Complaints will be carefully investigated, and cases that may require disciplinary action will be handled according to the established procedures of the college.

FACULTY-STUDENT RELATIONSHIPS

To guard against abuses of power, relationships of a sexual nature between faculty members and students are absolutely forbidden at Cromwell College, whether or not the student in question is currently enrolled in one of the faculty member's classes. The policy covers full-time, part-time, and temporary faculty, as well as full-time and part-time students.

This prohibition applies to vaginal intercourse; anal intercourse; fellatio; cunnilingus; touching of the genitals, buttocks, or inner thighs; or any other physical conduct or touching of a sexual nature. Consent of the parties involved is not a relevant factor; the prohibition applies regardless of consent.

Complaints relating to sexual relationships between faculty members and students should be reported to the provost. Complaints will be carefully investigated, and cases that may require disciplinary action will be handled according to the established procedures of the college.

HAZING

Cromwell College prohibits the hazing of students as a requirement for membership in any student organization, club, fraternity, or sorority. Hazing is defined as: (1) any act involving physical mistreatment of a student, causing undue discomfort or bodily injury; (2) any act involving psychological mistreatment of a student, including acts of personal servitude or humiliation; (3) any act that endangers the life and health of the student; or (4) any act that interferes with regularly scheduled classes or academic pursuits of a student.

Complaints or information concerning an alleged violation of the hazing policy should be reported to the dean of students. Complaints will be carefully investigated, and cases that may require disciplinary action will be handled according to the established procedures of the college.

STUDENT PUBLICATIONS

Cromwell College supports the publication of a student newspaper, *The Cromwell Clarion;* a campus yearbook, *Kaleidoscope;* and a literary magazine, *Chiaroscuro.* Since these publications are funded by revenues collected by the college, the ultimate responsibility for the publications lies with the college.

Cromwell College values freedom of expression, and expects campus publications to function responsibly as autonomous student organizations. However, should a publication funded by the college present material detrimental to the college's educational mission, or should staff members of a publication violate existing Cromwell policies or use their positions irresponsibly, the college administration reserves the right to intervene.

THE HONOR CODE

To promote the value of intellectual honesty, all academic work at Cromwell College is done under the provisions of an Honor Code. Violations of the code are: (1) cheating—using unauthorized assistance (materials, resources, etc.) during or in preparation for an examination, and (2) plagiarism—representing someone else's words, ideas, data, or original research as one's own and failing to acknowledge the source of such work.

Both students and faculty have the responsibility of reporting suspected violations; failure to report a violation is in itself a violation of the Honor Code. Reports should be made to the dean of academic affairs, whose responsibility it is to determine whether there is sufficient evidence of a violation. If the evidence appears to be adequate, an honor council of three faculty members appointed by the dean of academic affairs and three students elected yearly by the student body will be convened to conduct a hearing, decide guilt or innocence, and in the event of guilt levy one of two penalties: a one-year suspension, or permanent expulsion from the university.

Upon deciding to matriculate at Cromwell College, all students will sign a statement indicating that they have read and understood the provisions of the Honor Code, and that they agree to abide by its stipulations. Ignorance of the code can thus be no excuse for its violation.